Violent Night

Violent Night

Urban Leisure and Contemporary Culture

Simon Winlow and Steve Hall

BERG

Oxford • New York

First published in 2006 by
Berg
Editorial offices:
1st Floor, Angel Court, 81 St Clements Street, Oxford, OX4 1AW, UK
175 Fifth Avenue, New York, NY 10010, USA

Paperback edition reprinted in 2006

Berg is the imprint of Oxford International Publishers Ltd.

Library of Congress Cataloging-in-Publication Data
Winlow, Simon.
    Violent night : urban leisure and contemporary culture / Simon Winlow and Steve Hall.
        p. cm.
    Includes bibliographical references and index.
    ISBN-13: 978-1-84520-164-7 (pbk.)
    ISBN-10: 1-84520-164-7 (pbk.)
    ISBN-13: 978-1-84520-163-0 (hardback)
    ISBN-10: 1-84520-163-9 (hardback)
    1. Youth and violence—England, North East. 2. Urban violence—England, North East.
3. Urban youth—Recreation—England, North East. 4. Youth—England, North East—
Social conditions. 5. Youth—England, North East—Social life and customs. 6. Youth—
England, North East—Attitudes. 7. Counterculture—England, North East. 8.
Subculture—England, North East. 9. England, North East—Moral conditions. I. Hall,
Steve, 1955- II. Title.

HN398.E54W55 2006
303.60835'0942—dc22   2006007278

British Library Cataloguing-in-Publication Data
A catalogue record for this book is available from the British Library.

ISBN-13 978 1 84520 163 0 (Cloth)
ISBN-10 1 84520 163 9 (Cloth)

ISBN-13 978 1 84520 164 7 (Paper)
ISBN-10 1 84520 164 7 (Paper)

Typeset by Avocet Typeset, Chilton, Aylesbury, Bucks
Printed in the United Kingdom by Biddles Ltd, King's Lynn

www.bergpublishers.com

Contents

Acknowledgments

Over the two years it's taken us to actually research and write this book we've accumulated many debts; most of them are of course financial, but we also owe numerous debts of gratitude. Most importantly, we'd both like to thank the young people who gave up their precious time to talk to us, especially those who tolerated our repeated requests for additional information and those who suffered the indignity of having to introduce their friends to an aging academic. Ray, Phil and Donna in particular contributed enormously to this book, and somewhat at odds with our central thesis, they appeared to do so with no practical benefit to themselves. We owe you a pint and a favour.

Simon Winlow would also like to thank the students of the University of Teesside's School of Social Sciences and Law for helping to cultivate some of this book's central themes, and colleagues at the Universities of Teesside and York for their encouragement and thoughts. Simon Winlow's initial preoccupation with the night-time economy had nothing to do with sociology or criminology, but with the help of Dick Hobbs, Phil Hadfield and Stuart Lister (his co-authors on the book *Bouncers,* Oxford University Press, 2003), it became increasingly clear that the surface pleasures of drunkenness needed to be explored with the requisite theoretical depth. Simon would also like to thank his family, especially Sara, and his co-author, Steve Hall.

Steve Hall would firstly like to thank co-author Simon Winlow for seeking his mainly analytical and theoretical input throughout the ongoing research project that spawned this book and many other publications. Also, he would like to thank a number of fellow academics, who, despite initial hostility from some representatives of prevailing schools of thought, encouraged him to develop and persevere with his theoretical ideas, especially Colin Sumner, Kevin Stenson, Betsy Stanko, the late Ian Taylor, Tim Newburn, Tony Jefferson, Mark Little, Peter Francis, Mike Randall, Steve Taylor, Rob Horne, Graeme Kirkpatrick, Ronnie Lippens, Craig Ancrum and Chris Greer. Special thanks to Jeff Ferrell, Mike Presdee and Wayne Morrison for supporting the publication of some of our central themes despite, we suspect, disagreeing with most of what we say. They represent the true spirit of the dialectic, the key to honest and fruitful debate. Very special thanks to staff at Northumbria University and, more than anyone, his family – Chrissie, Chris and Alex – for tolerating his increasing grumpiness and solitude during the final stages of the book.

–1–

Introduction –
Contemporary Youth Identities in Context

This study of youth identities, consumerism and violence developed from our earlier work on masculinities, the night-time economy and the fragmenting nature of Britain's working class (Hall, 1997, 1999, 2002; Winlow, 2001; Winlow et al., 2003; Hall and Winlow, 2003, 2004, 2005). Although our backgrounds are in criminology, our primary aim has always been to investigate the fortunes of the fragments of the former industrial working class as they attempt to cope with the shifting demands of the advanced capitalist economy. As our research progressed from the mid-1990s, we became rather dissatisfied with the celebratory nature of some of the more popular sociological theories that were attempting to chart the fate of young people in the epochal shift from industrial capitalism to consumer capitalism. Some of this work tended to retreat into romanticism, positing young people's destructive acts as reactions to oppression or indications of an underlying tendency for resistance to dominant political authorities. The compulsion to avoid moral judgments and appreciate diverse meanings appeared to pressure many researchers to gloss over the serious problems that are besetting young people – anxiety, drugs, violence, suicide, loss of traditional forms of identity, consumer pressure and so on – or explain them away as temporary phenomena that would melt away as young people settled into the new order. The reactionary discontent of conservative declinism seemed even less satisfactory, so we began this project with the vague aim of taking an empirical 'look for ourselves', producing some penetrative ethnographic data and using this work to assess some of the prevailing theories that attempt to illuminate current ways in which young people are constructing their identities, locating themselves in the changing economy and social structure, and generally making sense of their lives.

Much has been written recently about the changing nature of youth transitions (Coles, 1995; Furlong and Cartmel, 1997) and the influence of consumerism upon youth identities (Miles, 1996, 1998; Mackay, 1997), but we found that since the early 1980s the economic processes in which identity is constituted and reproduced have, at best, been taken for granted or, at worst, neglected. From the inception of our research the incoming data about young people's experiences and perceptions seemed to suggest a tight, direct connection between the consumer economy and the individual, virtually demanding that a challenge should be made to the currently fashionable notion that identity is potentially free to construct itself individually or inter-subjectively in personal spaces within – or in opposition to – prevailing economic processes, ideological power and cultural hegemony. Cultural theory after Horkheimer and Adorno's (1972) classic essay denouncing the culture industry as 'mass deception', and the rejection of the influential Althusserian (1971) depiction of Western individuals 'interpellated' by capitalism's ideological apparatuses, seemed to take a distinctly optimistic turn in the 1980s, oddly enough at a time when the left was reeling under its heaviest political defeats. As we perused the literature we gained the distinct impression that, as the left saw its social democratic institutions breaking apart under the unrelenting hammer blows of neo-liberal ideology and monetarist economics, it was forced to take libertarian and culturalist turns, attenuate traditional critique and redirect its energies to the maintenance of its deepest Utopian undercurrents. Perhaps to convince itself that a reservoir of autonomous oppositional energies will always exist in the interstices of the prevailing social order – scattered nooks and crannies that advanced capitalism's hegemony has somehow failed to penetrate – some leftist theory from the 1980s onwards became increasingly beholden to the developing paradigm of defensive optimism, detecting signs of resistance in any slightly unusual stylistic development of youth culture.

It is unfair to single out individuals in a body of work that produced so much spangling rhetoric, but perhaps Michel de Certeau (1984) deserves a mention as he eloquently described the ordinary individual as a Utopian agent dreaming against the 'legislative order' of the bourgeois city. However, despite our obvious suspicions about this modified leftist paradigm, we do not intend to dispute the phenomenological proposition that crime and criminals, rather than being objective phenomena to be 'measured' and 'controlled', are subjective and cultural phenomena that can be experienced and defined in ways that are different to those of the current state administration and its reactionary supporters. Nor do we wish to dispute what has become the orthodox left-liberal convention that indeed some of the minor hostile acts defined and punished as 'crime' by the state might be a product of the 'righteous anger' of marginalized and oppressed groups (for example, Cohen, 1955; Hebdige, 1979; Brake, 1980). We have no quibble with the accompanying convention that the gravity of the crimes committed by the powerful elites who dominate Western societies outweighs that of the crimes committed by street-criminals who inhabit economically impoverished regions (Chambliss, 1975; Clinard and Yeager, 1980; Box, 1983, 1987; Pearce and Tombs, 1989, 1993; Croall, 1992). The problem our data compelled us to address is the *politicization* of street-crime: the rather romantic notion that it often signifies the stirring of the 'political imaginary', the eternal wellspring of cultural dissent and resistance – albeit possibly misdirected – to the power that dominates it. Much of the violence we encountered, like much of the general street crime we have encountered elsewhere (Hall, 1997; Winlow, 2001; Hall et al., 2005; see also Hallsworth, 2005) seemed to us to be strikingly apolitical, extremely reactionary and conformist in a complex way that we will attempt to explain later.

This hastily redecorated leftist ideology has heavily influenced the theoretical direction of youth studies, but, in some instances, it seemed to be a victim of its own compulsory optimism, compelled to search for signs of cultural dissent in the interstices of a fragmenting social world during a bleak period when its organized political opposition had been dealt shattering blows by a rampant neo-liberalism. In an effort to present itself as the most feasible opposition by distancing itself from the wreckage of the ostensibly vanquished traditional left, it made gestures indicating a locking of horns with neo-liberalism, which had convinced large numbers of the Anglo-American populations that all the freedom, justice, equality and opportunity promised by the left 'after the revolution' had already arrived, courtesy of advanced capitalism's consumer society. However, the reader will quite quickly become aware that although our data reveal excessive romanticism amongst this new left-liberal opposition, it also points out even greater flaws in the neo-liberal nostrum, which claims that burgeoning opportunities for self-advancement and liberation are now opening up for most young people (see for example Fukuyama, 1999) who are compelled to tread individual paths of survival away from the fragmenting hulk of the industrial working class. Despite the uneasy homology between a popular rhetoric and a sociological establishment, which both tend to support the claim that old rigid and repressive structures of modernity are 'melting into air', allowing individuals to construct their own identities and determine their own biographies in either the consumer mainstream or the shadowy interstices of transgression, our data suggests a less optimistic view. Behind the façade of low unemployment, the growth of higher and further education and the expansion of opportunities for personal prosperity and happiness, we found copious evidence of novel forms of social division, atomization, anxiety and hostile interpersonal competition that threaten to erode the very principle of sociability, the portent of which is yet to be fully understood by social sciences.

Put simply, from the very beginning our data suggested that we cannot simply assume that resistance, in the form of Utopian dreams of a better world, continues to exist as a proto-political energy in the psyches or cultural meanings of young people. At a time when dangerously subversive political and intellectual discourses, which were generated in older forms of class struggle and inspired so much resolute opposition (see Rose, 2002), have been severely attenuated, the possibility exists that each generation of young people is becoming ever more deeply immersed in the consumer economy's seductive semiological life (see Baudrillard, 1983; Bauman, 2004). Perhaps, in an effort to protect ourselves from a bleak reality, we have underestimated the power of a megalithic system whose principal politico-economic strategy is to infiltrate the dreams and desires of the individual and promise their easy fulfilment in the shape of exotic and seductive lifestyles (Hall and Winlow, 2005). To base social scientific analyses on something that appears to be little more than an optimistic belief hastily constructed in adversity would be intellectually irresponsible and, in the long term, politically irresponsible if false hope promotes the neglect of the deeper ethical principle of ensuring that social science serves social justice and progressive social change.

In an effort to sail beyond the towering straits of Utopian neo-liberalism and left-liberalism, whilst avoiding the Siren calls of conservative declinism, this book attempts to take a fresh empirical look at what it means to be an everyday young person in a Western world whose traditional structures and practices appear to be 'falling apart at the seams', to be replaced by a nascent and uncertain new order (Hobsbawm, 1994). By exploring young people's feelings about work, education, relationships, consumption and leisure, we seek to describe in detail and explain some of the values, meanings and practices emerging in advanced capitalism's consumer economy and its radically reconfiguring social milieu. The findings are the product of a year-long ethnographic study, in which we interviewed and observed in detail about forty young people who work in the insecure non-tenured sector of the north-east of England's labour market, and play in its burgeoning night-time economy of pubs and night-clubs. Here we did not find a surfeit of liberation or fulfilment, nor the tell-tale signs of cultural dissent and resistance, but rather a tight connection between anxiety, competitive individualism and rising rates of violence, which, eventually, will become the book's main topic.

To be more specific, the data raised questions about the relative security of a number of aspects of young people's lives. Has, for instance, the end of traditional industrialism in the West allowed employees to improve working practices, redefine power relations with corporate employers and live more fulfilling and time-flexible lives (see Angell, 2000)? Has the information economy's demand for technical knowledge and skills created more opportunities for employment and the proliferation of small businesses, and has it created a powerful incentive for the workforce to educate itself (Brint, 2001; Michaels et al., 2001; Brown and Hesketh, 2004)? Has the establishment of consumerism at the centre of everyday life allowed the consumer to use the symbolism attached to consumer items to construct new forms of emancipated, playful and flexible identity, or freely choose membership of symbolic micro-communities that are no longer restricted by the structural position, cultural conventions and geographical locations of traditional communities (see Ewan and Ewan, 1982)? Have the end of Keynesian economics and the decline of Fordist working arrangements, organized labour and the welfare state enabled all individuals to choose their own path to prosperity and fulfilment? Are there any signs of active resistance (de Certeau, 1984; Ferrell and Sanders, 1995) or 'alternative narratives of dissensus' (Stanley, 1996) in the cultural practices of young people in consumerism's urban environments (see Hayward, 2004), or are there signs of increasing absorption and conformity (see Calcutt, 1998)? And, most importantly for us, has capitalism's consumer phase encouraged the continuation – or even the improvement – of the essential civilized interpersonal relations that constitute the basic bedrock on which a more convivial future world might be built, or can its disruptive tendencies be associated directly with increases in competitive instrumentalism, hostility and violence amongst young people (Elias, 1994; Hall, 2000; Hall and Winlow, 2004)? This book will attempt to mobilize its ethnographic data and analysis to exert further critical pressure on these assumptions and others, moving towards the construction of a more rigorous and perhaps less euphoric theoretical approach to the relationship between culture and economy.

Throughout the history of industrial modernity young people have been at the forefront of all periods of socio-economic and cultural change, simply because they tend to be much more energetic, adaptable and flexible than the often more weary, cynical and ossified older generations. Unkind cynics might say more impressionable and gullible too, especially to the seasoned rhetoric and hegemonic semiology of what is by now a veteran capitalist social power. As we shall see, Britain's recent and rapid entry into the mercurial world of consumer capitalism has been no different. In fact, the category 'youth' itself is an invention of the post-war consumer market-place, replacing the categories 'young woman' and 'young man', a development that impacted powerfully on the transition from child to adult in the sense that it placed a whole new lifestyle phase in between the two, primarily because young adults' newly acquired disposable income was a lucrative target for the advertising industry (see Jencks, 1996; Furlong and Cartmel, 1997). Thus, because of the tight genetic connection between youth and post-war consumerism, the attitudes, feelings and cultural practices of young people combine to provide us with a particularly high-resolution lens through which to analyse critically Anglo-American consumer society as it is – and where it might be going – in the opening decades of the twenty-first century.

As we shall see in Chapter 2, forms of transition from youth to adulthood have been forced to evolve rapidly to keep pace with an economy characterized by uncertainty, perpetual flux and the vagaries of the global commodity market (Beck, 1992; Bauman, 1998, 2001), so here we will see how young people make sense of these changes and cope with the anxieties and practical problems that flourish in this climate of general instability. The traditional class-based relationship between social structure and education has loosened as more young people from working-class backgrounds have been channelled into further and higher education (Brown and Hesketh, 2004). However, at the same time a widening and hardening polarity between socially excluded groups and the rest also means that many more young people simply remain stranded on the bottom rung of the educational ladder, and often leave education with no qualifications and minimum social skills (Bedell, 2005; Hutton, 2005; Toynbee 2005). Rather than being solely the province of youth, education is now regarded as a continual process because all those seeking employment now need perpetual training in order to keep pace with the rapid and constant mutation of a 'knowledge-based economy' (Brown and Hesketh, 2004), perhaps more accurately described as a *symbol-processing* economy in which even menial functional positions fall under the authoritative code of educational accreditation (Amin, 1994; Rifkin, 1995; Taylor, 1999). University education has become a means of making it to the starting gate rather than winning the race or even qualifying in pole position and, as university education expands, so young people are forced to postpone the traditional trappings of adulthood, such as marriage, a mortgage and a career. Many young people are sold the dream of education as a portal to success, but the harsh realities can be very different (Brown and Hesketh, 2004). If we consider lost wages, the accumulation of debt and the mundane hardships of the low-paid service work that actually constitutes the vast majority of opportunities in the expanding employment sectors (Hutton, 1995; Toynbee, 2003), we can begin to understand the perilous terrain that a growing number of young people now confront. Rather than the alleged self-enabled upward mobility facilitated by further education, the decline of traditional youth transitions and the increasingly unpredictable nature of labour markets generate a riptide of downward mobility and concomitant feelings of insecurity.

It is worth noting here that, throughout the book, our main focus is on socially and economically incorporated young people, those who still possess a stake in civil society, no matter how small and fragile, and not the growing ranks of the long-term excluded languishing in areas of permanent recession. The end of industrialism meant the demise of a range of manual occupations that, although exploitative and alienating (Roberts, 1993; Winlow, 2001), provided the consolation of financial reliability and social stability in the lower strata of the rigid 'geological' class structure of the time. Since the mid 1980s, however, permanent contracts for tenured jobs have become increasingly rare (Amin, 1994; Angell, 2000) and employees are expected, either by choice or by necessity, to change occupation, employer and place of residence numerous times throughout their working lives (Beck, 1992; Furlong and Cartmel, 1997). As union power and union membership has declined over the last decade, so has the ability of workers to exert pressure through collective bargaining to advance their working conditions and pay levels. In other words, not only has a permanently excluded underclass emerged in specific geographic locales across the post-industrial West (Wilson, 1987, 1996; Gans, 1995), but the everyday lives of many of the young people who inhabit the lower echelons of the mainstream economy have also become increasingly unstable in a number of ways that our data will hopefully illuminate.

In Chapter 3 we will argue that traditional social bonds, which connected many young people in communities, at work and in cohesive friendship networks during industrial modernity, are being eroded, and that forms of instrumentality and self-interest now dominate young people's engagement with society, culture, economy and, to some extent, each other. In this chapter we include interview data that seem to indicate that forms of instrumentalism – even in apparently close friendships and relationships – are becoming unavoidable as neo-capitalism's consumer economy tightens its grip on the means of identity, the valuation of cultural capital and the emotional constitution of the *habitus*, moulding youth culture to suit its needs.

Chapter 4 addresses the changing nature of working-class leisure – more specifically the practical and ideological construction of night-time leisure in relation to the evolving demands of the neo-capitalist economy. The idealized world of leisure is not only a powerfully seductive respite from the monotony and exploitation of labour (see for example, Clark and Critcher, 1985), and not only a hedonistic pleasure we allow ourselves as a reward and to prepare us for what lies ahead (see for example, Presdee, 2000), but also a key sphere of economic activity as the weekend leisure industry makes a significant contribution to Britain's GDP and becomes an important aspect of market expansion and capital investment (Hobbs et al., 2003, 2005). Simultaneously – and, we will argue, probably not coincidentally – night-time leisure is no longer simply a break from the tedium of the working week but a growing daily need and vital cultural ritual as symbolic significance is transferred from the world of work, politics and community to the world of leisure. In this chapter we also make the central suggestion that the contemporary night-time economy is not characterized by playful identity construction, resistance and cultural innovation but rather by powerful cultural and economic *pressure* that renders the consumer-driven night-time leisure scene fraught with anxiety, insecurity and hostility. This pressure must be seen in the macro-context of a troubled British capitalist economy where the leisure and service industries are displacing traditional industry as the main generator of profit in many urban areas. It has expanded with remarkable rapidity from the early 1990s to the present day, now generating an annual turnover in excess of £25 billion and continuing to grow at a rate of 10% per year. The currents of neo-liberal political economy and ideology sweeping through Britain since the 1980s continue to force municipal authorities into partnerships with the business community in an effort to rescue the flagging prosperity of old urban areas that have lost much of their traditional manufacturing base. The night-time economy of night-clubs, pubs and restaurants is a major target for investment and a major hope for the maintenance of prosperity in large urban areas otherwise faced with the daunting prospect of economic decay and all the serious social problems that follow in its wake. Today's politically and financially hamstrung local authorities, operating in a system of brutal inter-city competition for inward investment and consumer populations with disposable income, have no choice but to administer as best they can all means of generating profit in the new consumer economy, even though some of these means float on or beyond the boundaries of legality and codes of civility, presenting risks in many dimensions ranging from health to consumer debt and interpersonal violence. National government is also bound by the inescapable economic fact that the nocturnal leisure industry now makes such a significant contribution to the British GDP, attracting investment and generating profit and tax revenue, and neo-liberal economic logic and ideology insist that the myriad risks that participation in this economic zone presents to the population are worth taking.

Chapter 5 charts the emergence of a similar process that seems to be occurring in the dimension of peer groups and friendships. Here we shall see in detail how young people, who spend their most meaningful free time seeking their promised reward of hedonistic fun and entertainment in the consumer economy's night-time leisure scene, have moved on from what were once often very durable and deep relationships to relationships that are relatively fluid, rather superficial and often deeply instrumental. The burgeoning night-time economy now has a magnetic attraction to millions of young people throughout Britain (Malbon, 1998; Chatterton and Hollands, 2001; Winlow et al., 2003), but it is also the permanent site of an array of social and health problems, connected mainly to violence and excessive alcohol consumption (Shepherd, 1990; Nelson et al., 2001; Hadfield et al., 2001, 2004). These problems are beginning to attract so much public attention that they cannot simply be ignored in favour of Utopian analyses of post-modern leisure culture, and they seem to epitomize the potential pitfalls of the 'work-hard-play-hard' ethic of intensive and purely instrumental work, rewarded by instant and excessive gratification, which is now the normality in the deregulated 'risk society'. Here our data will allow us to examine in detail the attraction of the night-time economy to those young people who ascribe huge significance to it and use it to replace politics, the community, the school and the workplace as the principal location for the establishment and maintenance of group identities and self-identities.

Chapter 5 is also the point at which we will introduce and discuss in some detail what we will suggest is the under-reported and burgeoning problem of alcohol-related violence, without doubt the most spectacular and disturbing feature of the night-time economy (see, for example, Shepherd, 1990; Homel et al., 1992; Tomsen, 1997; Lister et al., 2001). We sincerely hope that we will not stretch the reader's patience by spending four-and-a-half chapters laying out the context before introducing the book's pivotal subject, but, in our estimation, this context of generalized disruption, pressure and anxiety is far too important to be glossed over briefly. We will argue here that the night-time economy promotes a rather impoverished and paradoxically conformist form of transgression that results in inebriation, disappointment, disorder and a rather dismal background static of petty violence rather than liberation and satisfaction. The 'edge' that permeates the atmosphere of this 'liminal zone' (Turner, 1969), in stark contrast to the regimented world of daylight comportment, is of course what many youthful consumers find so appealing about night-time leisure, and is therefore a central dynamic force in the successful growth of this important sector of the consumer economy. However, our findings indicate that this specific form of transgression is not in the main 'carnivalesque', and it most definitely has no connection with 'narratives of dissent' or the potentially subversive symbolism that made the Saturnalian rituals of the past a window in the wall of the oppressive norm, through which we could see the dangerous politics that until quite recently bubbled through the popular culture of the lower orders (see Bakhtin, 1984; Presdee, 2000).

Chapters 6, 7 and 8 offer samples of interview data with the perpetrators of violence, the victims of violence, and the policemen expected to deal with it. We present these data with the hope that they will help the reader to construct a picture of the rather grim reality of life in the post-industrial pleasure-dome, and perhaps reveal an important aspect of the fallout from the incumbent form of neo-liberal politics that, as we have seen in Chapter 4, quite slavishly serves a business community that appears to place the maximization of profit above public safety (see Hobbs et al., 2005). Britain's night-time economy has proven itself to be extremely difficult to regulate by the traditional means of policing and licensing control (see Budd, 2003). Many venues are now policed by private door-minders, with a minimal police presence providing unreliable back up, and this rather tense and historically regressive partnership is forced to deal with a level of aggravation that is considerably higher than that of the daytime consumer environment. Our data will reveal how young people and police officers are coping with a rapidly normalizing climate of aggression and violence in the night-time economy, and we will ask the question of how constant exposure to violence and aggression in a sparsely regulated zone might be impacting upon the psychological and cultural micro-processes of identity-construction and *habitus* formation discussed more generally in Chapter 5.

The concluding chapter essentially offers a critical reading of the current condition of youth culture in the specific areas in which the ethnographic studies were carried out. Throughout the book a fundamental theoretical question will be asked and, hopefully, partially answered by the data and analysis in each chapter. Put very crudely for the sake of brevity, the principal partition in the sociology of culture is that which divides the notion that cultural values, norms and practices can always be autonomous, creative and transformative – no matter what the underlying material conditions, practical imperatives and cultural reinforcement thrust upon individuals by the prevailing politico-economic system might be – from the opposing notion that they are established and reproduced quite stringently by enforced participation in that prevailing economic form, and that most individuals conform to them with little dissent or practical resistance. This keys into the fundamental agency/structure debate in sociological theory, but it also digs beneath a *social* structure that is now too fluid and fragmented to be a feasible determinant to raise the ghost of economic determinism, albeit in an economy now driven by the manufactured 'culture' of consumerism. We have already pointed out that philosophical liberalism and its principles of autonomous agency and dissent tend to dominate this debate in the Anglo-American academe, although post-structuralist and postmodernist thought that draws upon the instability and playfulness of meaning has posited the existence of unpredictably subversive and transgressive cultural forces, which allegedly override both Cartesian/Kantian subjectivity and structured social relations based upon politico-economic power. At a time when the dust caused by the explosion of post-structuralism and post-modernism onto the scene is settling somewhat – after some of their theoretical excesses have been exposed as perhaps a little hasty and over-enthusiastic (see Eagleton, 1996, 2000) – we will attempt to bring the economy itself back into play. Since the mid-1970s the West's advanced capitalist economy has undergone spectacular and radical mutation, and it is now driven by the imperative of expanding consumption in an era of over-production and out-sourcing of manufacturing. Our data, combined with our suspicion of incumbent theoretical paradigms, prompted us to ask a very old question in a new context; that is, in our specific geographical areas of study, has the consumer economy combined manufactured culture and economic activity into a totalizing bloc that shapes everyday life to the extent that it even creates the forms of dissent and emancipation that it prefers? If this looks likely, and if we also find that the core value promoted as a logical necessity by the consumer economy and largely accepted by a significant majority of young people is indeed atomized competitive instrumentalism in the virtual absence of committed dissent and dreams of egalitarian communality, this will be of vital importance to the analysis of not just the pressing issue of youth culture and violence but to social science in general. If we can be permitted to pre-empt the debate ever so slightly, we are aware that our standpoint will elicit inevitable criticisms of economic reductionism and over-simplification, perhaps even that we are conveniently avoiding the complexities of primary socialization, micro-power, negotiated meaning, morality, transgressive desire, shifting social relations and so on. However, we acknowledge the many perspectives and contributory factors at play in the study of human violence, and we are not attempting to construct a 'unified theory'. Rather, we are simply pointing out that, from the outset, our data suggested that the pressures of the consumer economy loomed very large indeed in young people's lives, and this provides an explanatory context for specific types of violence. Thus, the recent tendency to marginalize it or take it for granted might well have encouraged esoteric analyses that are in danger of drifting just a little too far from the pressing restraints of everyday life. There are signs of a shift from constructivism to a revised materialism as the bedrock of contemporary sociological and criminological work, which is beginning to reintegrate symbolic and existential concerns with neo-capitalism's ineluctable economic logic (see for example Miles, 1998; Hayward, 2004; Hallsworth, 2005). If most intellectual changes are indeed based on renaissance rather than pure neologism, we are happy to contribute to a change already in motion by providing a modest and concise reminder of the economy's power to influence one specific aspect of human behaviour.

Methodological Note

We cannot deny that we began our fieldwork amongst young people with the expectation of uncovering signs of social inequality and considerable pressure to conform to the logical needs of the consumer economy. Our previous research made this expectation unavoidable, but because it grew out of empirical work we have conducted in the past (see Horne and Hall, 1995; Winlow, 2001) and informed the development of our theoretical approach, we were able to avoid the 'chronological lie', which of course entails the construction of a hypothesis that, lo and behold, upon testing is found to be correct (Cohen and Taylor, 1976). Commitment to a theoretical perspective that has grown out of previous empirical testing conforms to all the rules of a grounded theoretical approach, and in this case our data have constantly suggested to us that many of the principles of popular liberal theories, from symbolic interactionism and humanist Marxism to post-structuralism and post-modernism, should be questioned at the fundamental ontological level (Hall, 1997). As we shall see, it has also suggested that the time might be ripe for re-opening the casebook on some of the less fashionable theoretical approaches that draw upon Marx, Durkheim, Freud, Elias, Bourdieu and others, some of which have been criticized as overly deterministic, or even downright bleak.

However, we did not wish to be entirely reliant on classical ideas, and as our data began to filter back, the words of our respondents created new, synthetic ways of understanding youth culture and identities, and enabled more nuanced observations and conclusions, even though they must be set against a backdrop of what presented itself from the outset to be the neo-capitalism's relentless economic logic operating on an increasingly fragmented social landscape. Our initial batch of interview data suggested straight away that negotiating the phase of the life course that in post-war Western societies came to be known as 'youth' now appears fraught with risks, anxieties and cultural pressures that are notably more intense than their traditional equivalents, and also more intense than many contemporary theorists suggest. It also seemed that the traditional inequalities of wealth, power and opportunity in an interconnected socio-economic structure are now even deeper and wider chasms separating successful entrepreneurs and technical workers from insecure service workers and excised 'problem populations'. As our research data began to accumulate, we became increasingly convinced that taking anything other than a highly critical theoretical stance towards neo-liberal consumer capitalism and the cultures it creates would not do justice to those young people who were kind enough to give up their time and talk so honestly to us about the pressures they face.

This short book by no means claims to be a definitive or comprehensive critique of consumer capitalism and its complex processes of social fragmentation and ethico-cultural mutation (see Bauman, 1999, 2004), but we hope that it contributes in its own way to the case for re-orientating the sociology of youth towards the reconnection of micro-analyses of subjectivity to the extreme pressures placed on individuals by a rampant consumer marketplace and its attendant neo-liberal politics and culture. From the very beginning of our project, the data demonstrated quite clearly that the demands of the consumer-service economy and the meanings and values promoted by its attendant cultures were at the forefront of the minds of young people in their consequentialist rationalizations of action, and also active at the deep emotional level as both anxiety and seductive opportunism. The stark presence of the mores of advanced capitalism in their symbolic and communicative lives occasioned us to consider the possibility that the autonomous inter-subjective group and the free negotiation of meaning and identity amongst individuals might not be the bedrock of life.

Given the unavoidable presence of theoretical templates, with all the potential they have to corrupt research data, combined with the additional problem that our previous research had already furnished us with very suggestive data that had cultivated quite strong theoretical preferences, we decided that the methodological approach should be open and non-directive, with as little dialogue between the researcher and the interviewee as possible. Despite our past experiences, things could always be different this time, in this place, with these individuals. So, rather than conducting structured interviews replete with questions about personal and inter-subjective sentiments and meanings – which might have risked leading questions and the researcher and interviewee becoming entwined in long dialogic spirals that might have encouraged the immediate creative construction of unusual thoughts that do not really belong to the interviewees and do not influence their everyday practices – we decided to allow the young people to speak naturally, with minimal prompting, about the feelings and thoughts that pervade their everyday working and leisure lives. Deeper questions about anxieties, friendships and other relationships were asked in very minimalist ways during quiet times when they could perhaps become a little more reflective, but it must be said at this point that the lack of depth in many of the answers, and the continued presence of personal ambitions and instrumentalism even in their deeper personal reflections about themselves and life in general, were quite surprising and influential in the analysis and theorization that follows later in the book.

Our research was carried out in the north-east of England, although we have attempted to disguise specific locations in this region. The vast majority of our forty-three interviewees (this figure does not include policemen interviewed for Chapter 8) were between the ages of eighteen and twenty-five, and all were under twenty-eight. The names of all our respondents have been randomly fabricated. As the reader will hopefully become aware, the majority of the data we offer come directly from interviews, but we incorporated broader elements of ethnographic method to inform our descriptions and theoretical critique of the night-time economy. Drawing upon our sympathies for ethnographic method in depicting social and cultural life in all its richness, we set out to develop a range of key contacts, whom we hoped would become portals to contemporary youth culture. Our aim was to observe and engage with young people in a natural everyday setting, and, to the researchers' eternal gratitude, this occasionally involved going out drinking. Our primary method of data collection was however semi-structured and unstructured interviews, the majority of which we recorded. We also conducted quite lengthy observational work, primarily to add depth and insight into how young people's night-life tends to be organized and performed.

As we take great pains to emphasize (see Chapters 2 and 3), our respondents came overwhelmingly from what we might call the dispersed former working class, and this links crucially to the rather tenuous forms of biographical development and vague social positions that characterized our young respondents. Their exact position in the social hierarchy was very difficult to determine and, given the huge growth in further and higher education, the breakdown of class-based industries and the advent of unstable forms of labour for this social group in particular, guessing at social class was fraught with pitfalls. Where they stood in terms of status, opportunities and prospects perhaps increasingly now seemed to be influenced not by traditional structural location but by the ability of individuals to acquire various forms of symbolic and cultural capital (Bourdieu, 1977, 1984) in the forms of educational/vocational qualifications and transferable skills, and to present a 'marketable' self-image to the fluid and unpredictable labour market, and also to the harsh judgements of others who characterize consumerism's lifestyle and leisure scenes. Very few subscribed to class-based cultural signifiers, or demonstrated any awareness of the history of the class from which they came, yet all were acutely aware of the symbolism of consumer culture and competent in manipulating it as individuals for their own benefit. There were no references to flat caps or whippets, unless it was a conspicuous display of post-modern irony and parody. Rather, the majority were painfully conformist in their displays of identity, yet they seemed well adapted to the fluidity of culture and the instability of employment and labour markets. This gave the impression of both comfort and creativity but, as we shall see later, it is quite probable that this is an illusion that masks profound anxiety about the constant threat of rapid downward mobility from their increasingly precarious positions in the emergent social hierarchy, which for most appears far more likely than an ascent to the realms of the elite.

Our initial contacts were made largely using personal connections. Joe, for example, is the cousin of a previous research contact, Donna is the sister of a family friend and Ray was a sometime co-worker of one of the researchers' family members. The strategy was to persuade our gatekeepers to then ease the access of our researchers into extended friendship networks, allowing us to develop further contacts and interview friendship cohorts in order to cross reference data and aid our assessment of the nature of youth friendships and relationships. This worked for the most part, but we were also opportunistic in the sense that we also attempted to interview individuals whenever the chance arose, and even interviewed a small number of students recruited from our respective universities. We carried out interviews in a diversity of settings; in our offices at work, in respondents' flats, in the parental home, in pubs and cafes, even in a car, and wherever possible we'd try to organize follow-up interviews to clarify issues that developed from the initial transcripts or to record their opinions on issues raised by other interviewees although, we must emphasize again, we were very careful not to press issues that we considered to be important. Our intention was to record a true and accurate reflection of how our respondents felt about issues that were important to them, and allow them to enunciate the various pressures and strains that we learned were such a central part of their everyday lives.

Our work with young call-centre workers developed rapidly, greatly aided by a key research contact who arranged access to an extended and loosely connected group of employees of a local mobile-phone call centre in the north of England. Initially, immediate work contacts who fitted our general youthful profile were approached by our contact and asked if they would mind being interviewed. Gradually, our first batch of interviewees opened the door to other call-centre workers, and in a small number of instances we were granted access to their friendship networks, which helped to facilitate our analysis of the night-time economy and the shifting significance of leisure in relation to labour. We were able to tape most interviews. Some respondents objected, but all of the quotations attributed to respondents throughout this book are direct transcriptions from taped interviews.

Some of our interviews were gloriously easy as our respondents were given full rein to complain about social and cultural pressure. Others were slightly trickier. As we were keen to consider the nature of biographical development in some depth, we asked a lot of respondents in the broadest possible terms how they felt about the future and where they saw themselves in ten, twenty and thirty years' time. While some were instantly optimistic or pessimistic about careers, relationships and so on, the majority had no idea, and voiced the stereotypical youthful response, 'dunno'. This prompted us to change our tack a little, occasionally breaking our own 'minimal prompt' rule in order to get some kind of response, until we ultimately gave up this line of questioning. The fact of the matter was that the fluidity of post-industrial life had rendered any attempt to guess at the future rather redundant, at least in the minds of many of our respondents, a point that has been noted and analysed by other researchers and theorists (Furlong and Cartmel, 1997; Ball et al., 2000; Miles, 2000). Generally, they seemed to think that dealing with the present was sufficiently difficult without trying to plan some semblance of future success and stability.

There were also a number of rather awkward moments during interviews with the perpetrators and victims of violence. The perpetrators talked at length about their involvement in violence, and in many cases were keen to accentuate their fighting skills, their willingness to fight and the 'tough but fair' credentials that fitted in with their mythological image of the 'reluctant hero' standing guard over a moral order threatened with extinction (see Slotkin, 2000). Persuading them to discuss the esoteric role of violence in their lives, and the meanings and attractions of violence within both the individual *habitus* and the milieu of night-time leisure was relatively easy, yet they tended to lapse into scripts of justification (Matza, 1964, 1969) that were entirely understandable but revealed little about the complex relationship between perpetrator and victim, or between equally committed protagonists in violent conflicts. We developed a tactic of simply allowing the justificatory rhetoric to burn itself out, waiting patiently for some deeper revelations to be forthcoming later in the interviews.

The victims of violence were keenly aware of the cultural fallout of violent incidents, and the impact of victimhood upon their reputations and their masculine identities. All the respondents who offered narratives of victimhood were men and we felt that, in what essentially amounted to a conversation between two men, much was left unsaid. Some appeared keen to amplify the myth of the manly struggle against insurmountable odds – a typical victim romance in which the victim can emerge as a potential hero – whereas others gave the impression that they might be underplaying the extent of their victimhood and its impact upon their social status and psychic security. Others analysed the context of the assault in detail, seemingly searching for ways to brush off the incident as unimportant. None of our respondents were keen to undertake the stereotypical role of the victim (see Newburn and Stanko, 1994), and a great deal of care and patience was required to negotiate the emotions that unavoidably accompany violent assaults. Whilst our analysis of violent incidents and victimhood focuses on the cultural context of the night-time economy, and others have focused on the crucial importance of control and policing (see Hobbs et al., 2003), in our opinion there remains much to be said about men as victims of violence in this particular cultural milieu.

Our data tended to reveal that the distinction between victims on the one hand and perpetrators on the other is far from clear cut. Those we define as perpetrators of violence, as a convenient heuristic for the purely practical organization of data, had also been the victims of violence and tended to define assaults of sometimes staggering intensity as virtual rights of passage; extreme beatings, to generalize, helped to make them into the men they were, and directly reflected a mythology in which the visceral pleasures of violence – of which they tended to talk at length – seemed to represent a seductive terror and a vital initiation into the identity they desired. Some of these interviews lapsed into one-sided dialogues that took the form of a lecture in which these men – so well-schooled in the intricacies of violence – taught us what it all meant; the punches, the wounds, the slights and insults, and the thrilling intensity of combat (see Katz, 1988). Violence was a vital part of life, and, as we shall see later, the enthusiastic Homeric tales about victory in the jaws of defeat, about literally rolling with the blows and getting up again suggested to us that the victor's status is enhanced to its ultimate where the line between victory and defeat is at its thinnest (see also Jackson-Jacobs, 2005). These dialogues often tended to detract from the central concerns about night-time leisure but they were nonetheless particularly illuminating and they added a further layer of thick descriptive detail that both confirmed much of what has already been written about the mythological status of violence in traditional male culture whilst simultaneously revealing further complications. It also confirmed the well-known but currently neglected notion that status-anxiety, now being experienced in intensified forms in the unstable, culturally driven consumer economy, continues to be a principal factor in the psychogenesis and sociogenesis of young people's identities and *habitus*.

This project continues apace. Thus far our findings have opened up a range of new avenues for analysis and we hope to pursue these with vigour in the coming years, as the pressures bearing down upon contemporary young people certainly do not appear to weakening. It's perhaps worth noting that our current research has begun to look at how the macro-level social and economic pressures we address in these pages impacts upon young people in decidedly less supportive and secure social settings (Hall et al., 2005). Rather than the socially connected and economically aware young people we focus on in these pages, we have begun to look at socially excluded micro-communities, where forms of instrumentalism and extreme competitiveness manifest themselves in far more problematic ways, such as long-term involvement with criminal markets and the more nakedly instrumental and brutal forms of violence that often seem to be associated with them. For the moment, however, this analysis will reveal how some socially and economically *included* young people on the lower rungs of the ladder react to the pressures and anxieties that the consumer economy foists upon them.

–2–

Working to Live: Contemporary Youth Identities and Labour Markets

In this chapter we want to explore how changes to the global economy and local labour markets have impacted upon the working lives, identities and intricate cultural practices of young adults in contemporary Britain. Drawing upon qualitative data, our core suggestion is that the replacement of traditional industrially based social life by an unstable and divisive phase of capitalist development has rendered working-class life inherently perilous. For many young people, what was for millennia a very simple and routine task of connecting themselves to the social and economic mainstream has now become fraught with difficulty and anxiety. The communities that developed around traditional forms of industry have now all but gone, and contemporary social relations are now orientated towards *compulsory* self-interest and atomization in a cultural climate where it is becoming increasingly difficult to make moral decisions (see Bauman, 2001). As we shall see, most aspects of young people's lives appear to be driven by the twin ethics of egoism and competition, and these characteristics are clearly exhibited in their engagement with today's labour markets.

From Exploitative Stability to Anxious Instability

The decline of industrial employment during the 1980s and 1990s was perhaps the most profound effect of the foundational transformation experienced by British society in the final third of the twentieth century. Although industrial capitalism's quasi-meritocracy did allow for some mobility, the social world organized around heavy industry was structured by a fairly rigid class system. However, the experience of generations of working-class people trying to enrich their lives – or at least make them tolerable – in the dormitories that grew around industries added a cultural context to the class structure. This was explored by a number of British sociologists, perhaps most notably Raymond Williams (1961) and the Birmingham School (Cohen, 1972; Cohen and Robins, 1978). During the war-torn first third of the twentieth century and the 'golden age' that followed (Hobsbawm, 1994), the social world appeared grounded in 'universality, homogeneity, monotony and clarity' (Bauman 1992: 188). This was a social structure that, although shot through with tensions and injustice (Cohen, 1972; Walby, 1986), was relatively stable and above all *comprehensible* by the majority of individuals, especially in terms of functional roles, identities and transitions into adulthood. Generally speaking, most people knew who they were supposed to be and what was expected of them. Although the social mobility of individuals made possible by the early bourgeois revolutions was much in evidence (Bendix and Lipset, 1967; Goldthorpe et al., 1970; Goldthorpe, 1980), it did not seem to affect the rigidity of the overall structure, which held firm despite many people passing up, down and across its transoms and ledgers. Individual biographies within clearly defined social groups were clearly laid out and rendered perceptually unproblematic by a range of ideological and cultural processes that served to legitimize and reproduce the prevailing system of social organization. Being born male or female into a clearly delineated class culture provided the practical context for biographies guided by relatively clear values, meanings and practices that constituted a stable identity and helped individuals make sense of who they were and where they were going (see Dennis et al., 1969; Willis, 1977; Corrigan, 1979). Even the upwardly mobile who abandoned their parent class cultures had comprehensible class-cultural destinations to move into.

A complex set of working-class cultures evolved around the simple principle that capital needed the whole population to be active in specific functional forms of labour. The demands of the industrial capitalist economy shaped a gender order that valorized hard, physical work and the 'breadwinning' role for men, and the subservience and exploitation of women in the private sphere. Even the Christian religion supported the hegemony of the ruling bourgeois class and promoted the interests of the industrial economy (Weber, 1930, 1948), affirming the repression, hard physical labour and controlled militaristic aggression of working men in its ethic of 'muscular Christianity' (Beynon, 2002). Work was – and in a different way still is (see Chapter 3) – the core rationale of working-class life. In most industrial settings, practical economic requirements, converted into human energy by the threat of poverty and exclusion on one hand and the internalized reproductive forces of culture and *habitus* on the other, propelled most young working-class males towards adulthood to obtain the dubious advantage of a life grounded in exploitative work settings (Willis, 1977; Bourke, 1994). Even though 'different masculinities' undoubtedly existed as private and sub-cultural forms (Beynon, 2002; Whitehead, 2002), their ability to alter the individual's life course in this stringently demanding era has perhaps been over-stated (see MacInnes, 1998). Historical accounts indicate that many sons followed their fathers into the workplace, adopting similar occupational roles and biographies (Bourke, 1994; Hobbs, 1994; Winlow, 2001). Most women were also compelled by a powerful combination of practical economic imperatives and cultural pressure to marry and adopt the same familial roles as their mothers (Bourdieu and Passeron, 1977). A key aspect of this motherhood role was the unwitting fostering in children of the desire and the expectation to enter class-specific gender roles, thus replicating the class system and sustaining the industrial capitalist economy. In this way, the class structure and its attendant cultures reproduced themselves not simply by means of culturally transmitted meanings and learning processes, but also by the continuation of the industrial economy's needs for specific forms of labour and the subsequent continuation of the same practical pressures and hardships that had been experienced by prior generations (ibid).

The relatively stable social structure provided rigid models for class-specific forms of social engagement and 'social being'. For instance, in most working-class cultures, transgressing the established gender order was in most cases very difficult, and the few transgressors who overcame these difficulties were met by a range of severe social sanctions and cultural pressures to return to the norm. Working-class cultures thus tended to be largely homogenous, as individual biographies were reproduced generation after generation by the largely homologous economic and cultural imperatives of working-class life. Instances of real transgression tended to be limited to bohemian middle-class individuals who, by taking advantage of inherited wealth or systems of patronage, secured the financial means required to pursue their personal identity projects (Rose, 2002), or to the emerging 'underclass' whose members tended to reject bourgeois normative practices, if not the core values. Indeed, to describe the industrial capitalist order as one of the historical eras where class-specific social being appeared in some of its most durable forms would not be overstating the case.

As well as conforming to structurally coherent values, meanings and practices, class-specific biographies tended to parallel those of the broader peer group as young people of the same age experienced similar alienating and exploitative experiences, buying into, or in some cases politically and collectively resisting, hegemonic systems of meaning. For much of the industrial period, a great deal of emphasis was placed upon young males 'getting a trade' (Winlow, 2001), and, although clear hierarchies of trades (Roberts, 1993) and political differences between individuals did exist, work cultures still tended to be relatively homogenous in nature as the workplace provided a setting in which most workers could find mutual support in opposition to their exploitation, even though that 'opposition' could range from espousing communism through collective industrial action to constantly muttering complaints in a fatalistic and often comically grumpy manner. The communities that developed around specific industries also tended to exhibit cultural characteristics based upon their mutual reliance upon and experience of work. Work influenced virtually every facet of their lives, and it remained a certainty, an objective and seemingly timeless fact of life; just *there,* like Ayre's Rock, at the centre of their world. Industrial work was an exploitative certainty, and before today's norm of geographical and sector mobility most workers tended to stay in the same job – or at least the same type of job – in the same geographical region for their entire working lives (see Dennis et al., 1969). Movement tended to be between employers in the same sector, so a miner might work at a number of mines situated close to his birthplace, or a steel worker might work in a number of steel mills, but in general most working lives were fairly stable and static.

The parallel biographies that developed in working-class cultures during this highly structured historical period tended to establish and reproduce personal and communal relationships that were more intimate and durable than those of today. Bonded together much more tightly in community, culture and economy, individuals lived with more of a feeling of biographical certainty, which, although often highly restrictive, provided a degree of stability and predictability, which might well be primary needs for the innately insecure human being. As each unique individual experienced similar biographical trajectories in which mutual interests to some degree became cognitively and emotionally internalized, transitions from one stage of the life course to another were relatively unproblematic, even though they could often be psychologically traumatic for a minority of individuals unsuited to the specific functional and cultural demands of this way of life. Individuals who grew up in the same locale would probably be subject to similar socialization experiences, become competent in the valuation and manipulation of the same cultural capital and internalize similar meanings and practices at the emotional level to constitute a similar *habitus,* none of which precludes the existence in either public or private life of the quirky differences that make individuals unique. Most inhabitants of a working-class community would attend the same school and often feel the same way about schooling (Willis, 1977; Corrigan, 1979); many would progress to the same workplace, and some would even work side-by-side on the same production line for the entirety of their working lives (see Lockwood, 1975; Bulmer, 1975, 1978b). They would marry, have kids and progress through all the various social, cultural and economic tribulations that typify the quintessential working class social experience. We can also add a basic cultural perspective to this picture by including the workers' sense of self and gender, their leisure preferences, their attitudes, political views and general beliefs, which would all be closely related to the class-based culture they inhabited, the economic relations that underpinned it, and the close, affective bonds that existed within it. In the vast majority of cases every aspect of being was unavoidably connected to work and the industrial capitalist economy (Benney, 1978).

It is obvious that work, especially during Britain's productive phase of industrial capitalism, was not simply a shallow form of exchange or a means of acquiring money, but the practical and organizational centre of life (Dennis et al., 1969; Roberts, 1993). It was also rich with meaning, and located the individual at some point in a clearly demarcated and rigid structural hierarchy (Bourdieu, 1977,

1984). The class system in Britain during the nineteenth and much of the twentieth century provided a ready-made biographical template for the whole population. At stark variance with the supposed 'do-it-yourself' biographies and lifestyles currently sold to the population by the mass-mediated rhetoric of liberty and enterprise, the industrial capitalist class system structured virtually every aspect of social life and, by means of an array of symbolic and cultural capital that was difficult to acquire and reproduce (Bourdieu, 1984), constructed boundaries and barricades over which only the unusually determined or fortunate could pass. Aside from the requirement to graduate from the correct formal education and become competent in the public display of the correct forms of cultural capital, the desire to take on the battle for upward mobility was comparatively rare. This remained the case until the basic needs of the economy shifted from production to consumption, and marketable forms of socially and economically valuable identity were disseminated through the burgeoning mass-media, which now act as a sort of open-access finishing school for consumerism's new debutantes, making graduation less demanding and desire more diverse.

As the data tend to confirm throughout this book, this new social and economic life also generated a new cultural game. It demanded a new 'feel' and new forms of *habitus* that could act as the unconscious guide for the acquisition, display and exchange of the specific forms of revised cultural capital required for social advancement (see Bourdieu, 1990) and prosperous forms of participation in the work and leisure environments of the consumer economy. Both the prevailing neo-liberal ideology and what to some has latterly become its rather domesticated opposition (Baudrillard, 1983; Žižek, 2000) tend to portray this new cultural game as the product of a liberating current that has swept through advanced capitalist society in the West since the Second World War, while at the same time portraying all past ways of life – especially those inclined towards collectivism – as onerous, repressive and restraining (see for example Levin, 1996). Some forms of industrial labour were dangerous and exploitative (Williamson, 1982; Douglass and Krieger, 1983; Patterson, 1988) and their attendant communal cultures were often insular and repressive, but the collective solidarity often found within them helped individuals to cope with the everyday exploitation, alienation and subservience that were inevitable aspects of the industrial capitalist project, and have certainly not disappeared in today's call centres and fast-food outlets (Ritzer, 1998; Newman, 1999). Mutual resistance, such a key dynamic of sociological and cultural studies during the twentieth century (and a topic that we will explore in some detail later), offered a powerful consolation (see Evans et al., 1985); pilfering from work offered a means of gaining one's true worth from the employer (Mars, 1982); close relations with work colleagues offered solace and support both in and out of work (see Bulmer, 1975; Benney, 1978); mass trade unionism worked to advance the rights of workers (Beaumont, 1987); male workers constantly campaigned for a 'family wage' and improved working conditions (see Dennis et al., 1969); the shop floor often provided adequate opportunity to construct and maintain meaningful personal friendships, and the everyday mutual experience of the work environment tended to reinforce communal bonds (Willis, 1979). These concessions may have been handed over by the captains of the capitalist economy in order to legitimize its practices and neutralize political opposition, but they were still *valuable* to the members of industrial communities. The closure of the British coal mines during the 1980s, for instance, was bemoaned not simply as the loss of a livelihood, but rather the loss of a *way of life* (see Callinicos and Simons, 1985; Adeney and Lloyd, 1988) that impacted negatively on the wider community on a number of levels. Despite the threat of political collectivism, capitalist administrators tolerated cultural communalism in the productivist era because it performed a very useful stabilizing function and did not interfere directly with the basic logical needs of the capitalist economy. This situation, as we shall see, changed dramatically in the 1980s.

There's been a slight tendency to overstate the stability of work in Britain during capitalism's industrial period – typified as it was by a perpetual cycle of boom and bust, occasional outbursts of hostility in class relations and the existence of a large, disenfranchised casual labour market (Stedman-Jones, 1971). Nevertheless, for the most part men were able to sell both basic and highly sophisticated skills to employers with a reasonable degree of continuity. Indeed, it was the relation between capital and labour that was relatively stable rather than the commodity cycle itself, and this was a continuation of the fundamental relation between labour and the satisfaction of basic needs that had existed as a transcultural norm throughout human history. However, it has often been noted that although the pre-modern compulsion for hard physical labour alongside mental skills was ubiquitous and unavoidable, people with any degree of autonomy did not work all the time. The technique of compelling certain classes to work longer than was necessary to fulfil basic needs was unique to slave and capitalist economies (de St Croix, 1989), both of which generated logics of human obsolescence and dispensability that did not exist in other economic systems. Because of the nature of lower-class men's allocated tasks in capitalist economies, compounded by the male's underlying biological dispensability, periods of unemployment, which threaten the physical security of the family unit, impacted disproportionately on the fragile psychic security of the male breadwinner (McClelland, 1991; Kimmel, 1996).

Even if this fragility and its associated feelings of insecurity and paranoia are not hard-wired ontological properties of the male psyche (see Ehrenreich, 1997, for a discussion), or psychic 'archetypes' in the Jungian sense, they are certainly much in evidence in any masculine culture that emerges in conditions of instability and risk. The importance of male employment and the accompanying terror of unemployment in a wage-labour economy were reflected in the make-up of many working-class cultures throughout the nineteenth and twentieth centuries, especially those that grew around heavy industries. As Britain emerged battered but victorious from the horrors of the Second World War, a short age of economic prosperity and stability in the 1950s and 1960s – which might not have been 'golden' but could be described as slightly scratched silver – advanced the fortunes of the nation's working classes, generating feelings of security and hope that coincided with the lowest crime and interpersonal violence rates in British history (see Gurr et al., 1977; Gurr, 1981). Full employment, the growth of trade union power, the establishment of a welfare state and capitalism's shift into a consumerist phase where a measured increase in the spending power of the masses became a vital economic fuel, together created a combination of affluence and security previously unseen in working-class communities (Goldthorpe et al., 1970; Goldthorpe, 1980). This did little to challenge structured forms of social inequality, and cultural 'lifestyle' divisions began to emerge within a proletarian class once characterized by deep understandings of mutual interests and distinct practices of solidarity. Some working-class individuals retained the traditional proletarian hostility to the owning classes but others willing to knuckle down and work hard in established industrial firms could secure a family wage that allowed them to buy their own houses and swim deeper into the waters of consumer markets (Beynon, 1984). Most sections of the working classes – even those employed in the semi-skilled and unskilled sectors – could expect to remain in paid work for the entire period of their working lives, and in many cases continued to work for the company that employed them as youths until their eventual retirement (see Blackwell and Seabrook, 1985). Although many workers expressed dissatisfaction with the grinding routine and lack of autonomy and opportunity, in many other cases those who worked for companies initiated by philanthropic industrialists such as Salt, Rowntree, Parsons or Armstrong developed genuine affection and gratitude towards their employers, and retirement was experienced as a rather gloomy occasion, the end of a period of their lives where work had become a comfortable, rewarding and status-enhancing routine. They could relax in the knowledge that they would remain employed, pay the mortgage and satisfy the needs and expanding desires of their increasingly consumer-orientated families, often living with the hope that their kids would make it to the next rung when their time came to enter the labour market (see Hyman and Price, 1983).

To those commentators who value the principles of personal ambition, unrestricted freedom, entrepreneurship and meritocracy, the comfortable niches that had established themselves in the labour market are often depicted as restrictive and parochial, constraining workers to sectors from which they could otherwise escape if they acquired new skills and increased the performative competencies and 'personal capital' that were valued in entrepreneurial circles (see Hall and Jacques, 1983; MacInnes, 1987; Evans, 2004). This view fails to appreciate the fact that consumer capitalism is far more culturally driven than industrial capitalism, which has radically altered the climate in which working-class values and aspirations grow. Engagement with the world of personal enterprise, flexibility and mobility is now *compulsory* for those who desire even moderate success; every bit as compulsory as traditional work once was. During the 1950s consumer markets did not dominate life to the extent they do now, and consequently, although motivations for social advancement did exist and were beginning to grow, as Robert Merton (1938) famously observed, they were far less extreme and not at all ubiquitous. Although status aspirations and anxieties that permeated the writings of the Classical Greeks have always been part of human societies (Phillipps, 1984; De Botton, 2005), the majority could live very meaningful and satisfied lives without the ostentatious exhibitions of desire and status that now suffuses consumerism, where, in both work and leisure sectors, the new 'ornamental society' provokes individuals into the frenetic, narcissistic and often extreme transformation of their personal identities, images and self-presentational skills (Lasch, 1979; Faludi, 1999).

As the organized industrial economy began to decline during the 1970s and 1980s, job stability and communal stability also declined, and this trend spiked upwards during the 1990s as service-sector and leisure-sector employment began to rise (Hutton, 1995). The traditional norm of spending an entire working life with one employer became at once unappealing and highly unlikely as the job market became increasingly unstable and fluid. During this period, industrial capitalism's primary dynamic force of manufacturing and selling innovative products to fulfil basic needs in ever more efficient and convenient ways was displaced by the circulation of the cultural signifiers that are now attached to commodities, which, logically, is the only way that human beings can still be convinced that the project of continually improving their 'quality of life' is still up and running (Horkheimer and Adorno, 1972; Baudrillard, 1983). In the West, artificially stimulated desire displaced the efficient production and circulation of necessities as the primary human aspect of the capitalist economy's dynamic (Lasch, 1979). The stimulation and subsequent satisfaction of desire in a consumer economy is a much more complex, manipulative, intrusive and disruptive psycho-cultural process than that which accompanied the production and distribution of basic necessities in a productive economy.

It could – and probably will – be considered banal to remind the reader that consumer capitalism is indeed based on a powerful mass-mediated illusion of the continual 'improvement' of the quality of life. However, we have reached the conclusion that some of the most profound, fundamental and quite obvious ramifications of the epochal shift that has occurred since the 1980s (see for example, Lash and Urry, 1987) are being glossed over in much of today's social theory. Not only did the installation of consumerism's mass culture – and, as we have stated clearly elsewhere, it is indeed 'mass' despite its superficial lifestyle differences and ethnic histories (see also Eagleton, 2000) – at the heart of capitalism's economic engine demand a new set of performative skills and a rather novel redefinition of the term 'experience' (see Wilson, 1987), but it also eroded the stability and pre-dictability of the traditional working-class life course in ways that need to be reported with more honesty and explored with more clarity. The personal benefits of this process have been glorified with a powerful popular neo-liberal rhetoric about freedom, opportunity, innovation and progress, or criticized with gelatinous caution by left-liberal analysts who are keen to emphasize the progressive aspects of post-industrial societies (see for example Ray and Sayer, 1999), but the social costs have been largely downplayed or exempted from criticism. As past and current imperatives for 'orderly disorder' demonstrate, both the modernist and post-modernist phases of capitalism contain the apparently oppositional forces of order and chaos (Rojek, 1989) and as these forces are harnessed by late modern capitalism, a rhetoric of diversity and freedom has developed that masks the under-lying marketization of contemporary emotional life and the comprehensive manip-ulation of social being. As Žižek (2000) has noted, the more we believe in self-determination, the more we exhibit the ubiquity of the market and the power of its ideological apparatus.

The intellectual politics accompanying late modernity have also undergone con-fusing changes. Criticism and resistance have declined amongst the left, diluted by a sort of sheepish enforced optimism based on an overwhelming feeling of *fait accompli* about the historical triumph of consumer capitalism, the seductive images of which, we are told, helped to bring down the Soviet Union. Conversely, because they offer standpoints that oppose the rampant, solipsistic individualism that both right- and left-liberals seem to think is a general 'good thing', the com-munitarian discourses that were once considered rather conservative (see, for example, Etzioni, 1994) are now beginning to appear oddly radical. We intend to defer engagement with this important new political configuration until we have presented some evidence and analysis, but at this point we can state quite clearly that the edict of compulsory optimism that emanates from a rather hazy and elusive liberal-capitalist authority was cast into doubt very early in our research project. Indeed, as we shall see, it did not take too long to scratch below the shining surface of optimism and hedonistic excess to reveal that the instability, risk, melancholy, instrumentalism and violence that characterize everyday life in advanced capitalism have engendered palpable degrees of discomfort and insecu-rity in the emotional lives of its inhabitants.

Nevertheless, even a very brief account of the shift to a novel phase of capi-talism would be incomplete without an initial mention of the political hands that were on the tiller. Even though from the 1970s onwards the ship was being swept along in an economic storm of change so powerful that it probably would have fractured the wings of Klee's *Angel of History*, it cannot be assumed that some minimal control over direction could not have been exercised, and that a course less traumatic for some of the former working-classes could not have been plotted and steered. As industrial society entered its twilight years and the strange metaphysical 'logic' of the market began to seep into every sphere of social life (Hall and Jacques, 1983; Evans, 2004), trade unions began to lose the influence they had wielded over British economic policy throughout the 'golden years' of the twentieth century when capital, despite continuing innovation in manufacturing technology, still needed labour (Crouch, 1986; Grant, 1992; Galenson, 1994). However, by the mid 1980s the labour-intensive Fordist manufacturing processes and organizational systems that had permeated industry throughout the twentieth century had been largely phased out. These practices belonged to the era of the productive worker, and throughout the post-war period both Labour and Conservative parties remained committed to the principle of full employment and the maintenance of the welfare state (Bogdanor and Skidelsky, 1970; Hutton, 2001; Skidelsky, 2004) as the twin bases of social stability. This era had ended.

In the late 1970s and 1980s the shift to a global consumerist economy was lubricated by a powerful and deliberately engineered ideological shift. In Britain, the ideology that depicted the 'free market' as the only feasible economic organizing mechanism and the ambitious atomized individual as the fundamental socio-political entity was embodied in Britain by Margaret Thatcher, and this neo-liberal political orientation demanded the Conservative party's rapid disassociation from the goals of both organized labour and traditional 'one-nation' Toryism. The commitment to manufacturing, full employment and welfare provision gave way to consumerism, entrepreneurship, unregulated free markets and economic 'rationalization'. Under this new regime, ailing British industry was no longer to be subsidized by the taxpayer (Campbell, 2004; Evans, 2004), and what had been traditionally regarded as public utilities, such as British Gas and British Rail, were to be sold off in order to save the taxpayer money, in the belief that the market's 'invisible hand' would naturally produce lower costs and greater efficiency. The 1980s became a period of tax cuts and the cultural glorification of individual choice and lifestyle, and this type of political ideology found great currency with the increasingly affluent middle classes and the more entrepreneurial individuals among the fragmenting working classes (see also Mills, 1991; Sewall, 1997; Thompson, 2003; Troy, 2005). However, there was, of course, far less enthusiasm shown by those who were committed to collectivist solutions to economic and social issues, or those lower down the social scale who had become accustomed to the security and benefits that stable manufacturing industry, welfare and public services could provide (see Hall and Jacques, 1983; Rentoul, 1987).

The myriad complexities of this epochal shift have been discussed in detail elsewhere (see for example, Lash and Urry, 1987; Bauman, 1992; Amin, 1994;

Hobsbawm, 1994), but the upshot for us is that underneath the heavily publicized material prosperity, hedonism and consumer choice, the 1980s became a period of profound social instability and division (Wilson, 1987; Hutton, 1995). Despite significant economic growth and increasing affluence for those who found a niche in the new economy, and despite Thatcher's infamous claim that society itself did not really exist, traditional social divisions remained. Not only that but they appeared to be deepening and widening (Rentoul, 1987; Westergaard, 1995), despite the two-tone camouflage of conspicuous consumption and urban regeneration (see Turner, 1993). The miner's strike of 1984 became a key social drama that portrayed the seismic divisions appearing at the end of the modern industrial project (see Turner, 2000). After a bitter struggle that also revealed deepening divisions in what was once the most politically solid of all the working-class occupational groups (Callinicos and Simons, 1985; Richards, 1996) and the underlying weakness of the support offered by other trade unions, Thatcher eventually broke union power and extinguished the mining industry, the powerful and hostile working class Behemoth that had shaped the British economy and provided the model for working-class community and political solidarity for generations (Lockwood, 1975; Richards, 1996; Thomsen, 1996). For some, this became an issue greater than supporting an ailing industry against rationalization and foreign competition. This was, in fact, the death throes of industrialism and an organized and homogeneous working class (Deller, 2002; see also Milne, 2004). From this point onwards the term 'class' lost most of its traditional connotations (see Pakulski and Waters, 1996; Marshall, 1997) as Britain moved into the present era of the atomized competitive individual struggling for advantage and some form of temporary security in the consumer economy.

From the 1980s onwards trade union membership has declined steadily (Beaumont, 1987; Grant, 1992; Thomsen, 1996) along with the unions' formidable economic power, which peaked during the early 1970s (Hutton, 2001). The basic goal of unionism – defending workers' interests against those of employers primarily motivated by the accumulation of profit – appears increasingly lost on most of today's young workers. Many young people see little benefit in joining a union and are also, perhaps understandably, deterred by the practical costs of union membership, which have to be extracted from an already meagre pay packet. The brutal logic of interpersonal competition, rationalization, and individual 'market performance' is at the epicentre of a significant change in the values, meanings and practices of today's young workers, which, as we shall see shortly, our data have revealed in their attitudes and feelings about each other, their work and the purposes of life in the new consumer economy.

Youth Employment Markets in Late Modernity

The decline of traditional forms of employment has impacted upon young people's first experiences of paid labour at a number of levels. The vast majority of those interviewed worked in low-paid service sector work. Only two interviewees were members of a union (although both felt membership to be a waste of money), and while some juggled employment with continued educational commitments (see Chapter 3), all appeared to acknowledge the fragility of their employment status. The vast majority expressed the firm belief – rather than the mere hope – that they would not remain in their present employ for too long. Most actively disliked their work, but the attitudes of some others tended to be more changeable, and the fact that around a third of all respondents were juggling full or part-time work with a variety of educational studies is indicative of the diversity of pressures now bearing down on young people (see Taylor, 1998; Taylor, et al., 2002, 2003, for a discussion of call-centre work).

In many cases these young people tended to see their employment as both transitory and isolating (see Deery et al., 2002). The friendships, group identities and mutual experiences that were important cohesive and reproductive forces in traditional working-class cultures (Willis, 1977; Belcham, 1990; Donaldson, 1991; Charlesworth, 2000) were often grounded in industrial working environments, such as factory floors (Willis, 1979; Roberts, 1993), production lines (Beynon, 1984) or coal faces (Dennis et al., 1969). As numerous studies have indicated, a unique camaraderie often existed within traditional industrial settings, grounded in mutual interests and experiences and enabling forms of collective resistance against the exploitation that has always characterized the relation between capital and labour (Willis, 1979; Roberts, 1993). However, many of the young people interviewed here experience work very differently (see for example Taylor and Bain, 1999). Rather than camaraderie, many expressed feelings of isolation (see also Deery et al., 2002), and were firmly convinced that they shared little in common with their colleagues, quite often speaking about them in an unguardedly derogatory manner that lacked the underlying affection of traditional banter. The sense of mutual interests and common fate that permeated traditional work cultures was palpably absent. Very few invested work identities with any particular significance (see Capelli, 1997), regarding work as something to be done and forgotten, or in some cases blocked from the mind. For many, relationships forged at work were regarded as unavoidable but totally unimportant. As Joanne, a 23-year-old call-centre employee in the north east, pointed out:

> I don't want to stay there forever, but I need to have a job like that 'til I finish at Uni ... Some of the people there are all right, but I haven't really got to know many people that

well. You go off on breaks and you see different people so it's difficult to get to know many people. At the end of the night, everyone just gets out of there as soon as possible ... I work nights and weekends mainly, but there's thousands of others who you never get to see cos they work different shifts. Plus, when it's busy, the calls are coming in all the time, it's just one after another, so you can't really talk to each other ... They do have staff nights out but I wouldn't go ... I don't really want to, we just haven't got that much in common really. I'd rather go out with my own friends.

For young people such as Joanne, their working personas appeared to be grounded in a kind of hard-edged instrumentality, perhaps indicating the hyper-individualized and competitive nature of contemporary culture, the transitory nature of work and the extreme alienation that has estranged them from labour processes, the products or services they produce, and their workmates. Both economic relationships and culture appear to be working with a good deal of synchronicity to impose the ethos of instrumentality and personal ambition upon individuals, simultaneously discouraging the mutual recognition of economic and political interests that some marginalized groups might continue to possess (see Beck and Beck-Gernsheim, 2002) or, possibly more precisely, might be able to generate in a different overall politico-cultural climate. In fact, it became apparent as our data was returned in greater bulk that almost everything appeared to be appraised on the criterion of instrumental utility to the individual's desires and ambitions, as young workers attempted to steer a course through the choppy seas of advanced capitalism's consumer culture and service economy. For example Judith, another call-centre worker, appears to regard work in a purely instrumental fashion, devoid of any wider significance whatsoever:

I don't care about it really [work]. It's just to get the money so I can buy stuff I want really ... The people there are just people, they're not really my friends. It's only the managers that care about it, with targets and monitoring calls and that. They're the only ones who care, who maybes see it as a career or something. The other people there, some are trying to get a bit of extra cash for the family or whatever, some are students getting a bit extra cash, some are older people. We talk and get on OK, but I just think everyone there just hates the place.

(See Bain et al., 2002; Belt et al., 2002, for related discussion.)

Here Judith appears to be indicating that, to her, life can be clearly compartmentalized and judged according to the instrumental utility and potential benefits and pleasures of each sphere. Work is unimportant aside from the fact that it provides the funds for other, more pleasurable, spheres of personal activity (see also Cappelli, 1997). Her work identity is a product of her daily determination to get through each shift as an isolated individual as quickly and with as little difficulty as possible, without forming close personal ties:

I'm polite to everyone, I smile at people, but underneath I'm just thinking about other things. What's on TV that I'm missing, anything apart from work. Some people are obviously more chatty than me and you can tell some of them are friends, but I think a lot of the people there just use work to get money, and couldn't care less about it. Now, people just talk to me if they need to or to pass the time.

Moe, 21, who works in a supermarket, expressed similar sentiments:

I feel sorry for some of the people there ... they're older and have to work in a super-market. The money and everything, I don't know why they put up with it. I know I'm not going to be there for long, so really it's just a way to get some money. For me, it's just the money, it's not like it's my career. I just go in, do it, get it done and then that's it.

Paul, who works in a call centre in the north-east, describes his feelings in more direct and impolite tone:

Paul: I hate work ... I get this feeling, before I go in, like feeling sick. I just hate every-thing about it. Most of the people there are just arseholes, petty, and pushing you about tiny things. They just want to wear you down. I've been there seven months and loads of people have left. The pressure they put on you for targets, they just can't take it ...

Q: So why don't you pack in?

Paul: I need the money. It's only just over six quid an hour but I couldn't do without it. If I could find another job with more money I'd do it. I'll try anything, I don't really care ... It's got to the stage where I just go into autopilot, just blank out and take calls without really thinking about it. I need my wages for, just stuff really: fags, clothes, rent a video, whatever, and you're weekend money...the money to go out on a weekend ... I can spend around seventy quid on a Saturday ... It's the only reason I keep going to work ... I just love going out I suppose. After a week's work, it's good to go out and have some fun.

Malcolm, another call centre worker:

You've just got to get used to the idea that it's work. If you want the money you've got to go and do it. Everyone I work with hates it, everyone ... The single most common thing we talk about, at work, is how shit it is. Everyone just goes on about all the bad stuff they have to deal with from callers, about how the team manager won't let you have holidays, how they keep putting targets up, how they shout and scream when you do something wrong ... If I'm out, down the town, and I bump into someone I work with, the thing we end up talking about is how shit work is. It's like a competition to see who's got the worse thing to say about the place ... I've been on the work nights out. It's crap cos people just talk about work ... I wouldn't go out with people from work. It's not very nice, but to be honest, a lot of them, I just wouldn't want to be seen with them ...

The manner in which many of these young people situated employment within their lives seemed to indicate a desire to remove the negative feelings about their employment from their idea of self. Thus one of the important reasons why they don't recognize their mutual interests as workers is because they refuse to label themselves as workers. They tend to see themselves in the quasi-romantic position of 'just passing through', at a brief staging post on their path towards personal success and prosperity in the future, possibly in some professional or entrepreneurial role that carries high status and rewards, a higher position from which they can look down on the 'mugs' who are stranded in the low-status service sector. There is a strange, premature quality to this, as though many of them are counting their chickens before they are hatched and acting as if they already occupy that higher position simply because they perceive themselves to be on the road to it. The possibility of personal failure is purposefully erased from the agenda. As work biographies become unstable products of constant adaptation (Beck, 1992; Bauman, 1995), most interviewees appear reluctant to attempt to improve work conditions at all. The preferred option is to constantly move on and convince the self that each move will be an incremental improvement, thus staging no collective resistance to the exploitative and alienating work that is the general condition of the lowest echelons of the service sector (see also Newman, 1999; Toynbee, 2003).

The Sociogenesis of Insecurity in Youth Transitions: Work, Family, Housing and 'Capitalization'

The gradual departure of traditional employment structures has created not only a highly unpredictable labour market but also an increasingly perilous social and economic terrain that British youth must traverse. As instability and anxiety have become the defining characteristics of contemporary labour markets (Beck, 1992; Angell, 2000), and the service and leisure industries become mass employers, many young people face the prospect of being swept into a riptide that drags them downwards into unemployment, under-employment and marginal social and cultural positions, rather than a slipstream that propels them upwards towards a material nirvana.

The post-war 'golden area' of British capitalism exhibited a range of exploitative and alienating work practices but it succeeded in raising the standard of living of most working-class families. From the early 1950s onwards, stable industrial employment, mediated by powerful trade unions, allowed working-class families to sample the delights of consumerism and relax into the relative safety of a socially incorporated lifestyle. Successive generations could also rest easy in the knowledge that their children would in all probability maintain or better their family's social position as full employment, formal education and an improving standard of living allowed successive generations of the working classes a better chance at upward social mobility (Bendix and Lipset, 1967; Goldthorpe et al., 1970). The late 1960s and 1970s became an era at least partly characterized by embourgeoisment and the gradual evolution of traditional aspects of working-class culture, but it was followed by the rapid social fragmentation of the 1980s, which further divided the traditional core proletariat along economic and cultural lines in a much more abrupt and chaotic manner. During the former period an apparatus of upward social mobility was subtly constructed by the capitalist economy and its attendant culture industry, and a steady flow of working-class youths were admitted into the expanding lower middle-class sectors of the economy, concomitantly achieving the status positions of 'respectability' signified by mildly conspicuous consumption. Although these developments were in no way a magnanimous gesture on the part of industry's captains, nor a reflection of the declining relevance of social inequality, new spheres of non-manual labour became conceivable goals for generations of young men no longer expected to follow their fathers into the travails of heavy industrial labour. Many families could also secure their own homes, which represented a kind of Holy Grail for some sections of the industrial working classes (Young and Willmott, 1961). Although social housing continued to predominate until the mid-1980s, 'affluent workers' could now obtain mortgages based on their stable, steady industrial income and have a home of their own in which to raise their families (Goldthorpe, 1980). The expansion of working-class suburbanism has been taken as a key feature of the gradual break up of the traditional working class and the increased opportunities created by progressive capitalism as manual workers secured mortgages, bought cars and started to go on foreign holidays. Whilst most individuals retained many of the dispositions and mannerisms of the traditional working-class habitus, distinct 'lifestyle' differences began to emerge amongst the working classes.

At first sight, the rapid expansion of further and higher education and the increasingly diverse and fluid nature of capital would seem to indicate the continuation of this trend of working-class dissolution, gradual upward mobility and equality of opportunity. In fact the opposite appears to be occurring. Rather than the gradual erosion of class boundaries and social inequalities, evidence seems to indicate that social inequalities are in fact increasing, and that the gap between the rich and poor is growing (Westergaard, 1995). In the current 'winner-takes-all-society' (Frank and Cook, 1996) not only can those born into the bottom third of the social hierarchy expect to stay there, but those previously operating on the solid ground of middle-class work and culture face the hazardous task of maintaining their social position and avoiding the pitfalls that could result in their rapid social and economic descent (see Beck, 1992; Bauman, 1999, 2001). This instability of course becomes all the more grave for those working hard to remain employed and avoid the abrupt drop over the precipice into socially excluded locales (Hall, 1997), as escape from these abandoned groups appears all but impossible (Wilson, 1987, 1996; Byrne, 1999).

Many of our interviewees appeared to be juggling the parental expectation of social advancement with an awareness of the instability of contemporary youth labour markets and the stark reality of a fragmented social order. As Donna explains:

My Dad really wanted me to go back to school and he really wanted me to just, like, make something of myself ... just move on and do something with my life ... and not be one of those people who just sits about all day ... He tells his mates and everybody about me about to be getting a degree, and I think everybody's really proud.

Peter also appeared to be struggling under burden of parental expectation:

They think once you've got a degree that everything's sorted, that you'll get a job no bother. I don't know what's going to happen and neither do they. I'm glad they're proud, but to be honest there's no guarantees is there?

As there is now evidence to suggest that large numbers of graduates are frustrated in their attempts to gain the types of employment that traditional degrees used to bestow, disappointment may be in store for the parents of Donna and Peter and many in a similar situation. More and more graduates are struggling to find employment that realistically matches their skills (Brown and Hesketh, 2004), and consequently they are falling into the low paid and often highly exploitative service and leisure sector (see Toynbee, 2003 for a compelling description) as a means of getting by until things change. Of course, many things never change, only get worse, and an increasing number of graduates are now finding themselves trapped in employment sectors that they entered higher education to avoid.

The majority of our respondents across the whole sample continued to live with their parents, and the vast majority of our student sample lived with parents, seeing this continuing for the foreseeable future (see Coles, 1995). Traditional transitions between 'youth' and 'adulthood' have, of course, changed enormously in a relatively short amount of time (Coles, 1995; Ball et al., 2000), and these processes are closely related to changes in the economy and the growth of highly unstable labour markets. Unable to experience the joys and the sorrows of full participation in mainstream, adult society, many young people may now be experiencing some of the infantilizing aspects of late modern capitalism (Lasch, 1979). Indeed, as young people enter the quasi-adult world of lifestyle consumption earlier and never really leave it, the whole idea of distinct 'youth' and 'adult' social categories appears to be increasingly meaningless. As consumerism's sign-value system and practical imperatives colonize all phases of the life-course, the disturbing thought crystallizing in our minds is that ensuing generations will no longer encounter the experiences of either childhood *or* adulthood in any traditional sense of the terms.

For young men and women such as Donna and Peter, actual downward mobility remains a distinct possibility despite being the first in their families to receive a university degree. Unless they can join the fortunate few who manage to obtain one of the sought-after professional or managerial jobs that form the bedrock of the fabled 'knowledge economy', they must find work in those labour markets that remain, and those that remain are fraught with anxiety-inducing difficulties and dangers. Apart from the decline of wages in real terms (see Rentoul, 1987; Westergaard, 1995), many young people have a range of other factors working against them, and perhaps the most pressing is the rapidly changing nature of the housing market. The last seven years has witnessed huge rises in property prices, massively disadvantaging first time buyers. Donna, for example, who would ideally prefer to be earning £20,000 per annum upon graduation, faces a serious problem in finding a mortgage to buy her first house. She comes from a working-class background and lives in a rather leafy middle-income estate on the edge of one of the north-east's major conurbations, where house prices currently range between £160,000 and £230,000. With a degree in the social sciences and a fictional job paying £20,000 a year, Donna faces the prospect of significant downward mobility even if she does manage to land her dream job and leave the parental home. Even if she marries someone earning roughly the same income in the near future, she will still struggle to match the lifestyle of her parents – her father a plumber and her mother a part-time secretary. In the short term she faces a move to a much less expensive part of the city, but even in the long term, Donna's future social and economic position may well be radically different to the grand ideals being disseminated by government and the post-industrial 'knowledge' economy. For a number of interviewees who have grown up in a similarly tranquil and salubrious social setting, the future looks even bleaker. Michael, for instance, is twenty-five and works in a call centre. His father owns a small building firm and his mother a sun-bed shop. He lives in a large semi-detached house on a pleasant middle-income estate on the edge of Northville:

I've been close to moving out loads of times ... Just arguments with my parents mostly ... They'd get on at me for daft things and when you get to be my age it just gets ridiculous because they still think you're a kid ... You know, coming in late, tidy up, get a job, all that ... I've stayed over at me mates and things like that but how can you move out? You've got to move away to get out ... You've just got to stay out of their way ... It's the money. I'm working full-time now and it's killing me, but the money you get, there's no chance of having enough to move out ... [I spend my wages on] going out mostly, some clothes, I don't keep track of it … on my money I'd have to move into, like the worst flat in Northville there is, and even then, I'd be completely skint. You've got rent and then bills and all the rest of it, just to live in some shithole … You'd have to do your own washing, everything … I mean, why bother? At least I get food and washing and everything done for me, so even if you do get the constant nagging it's better isn't it? … [At least this way] I can use my wages for actual stuff I like, without having to worry about all the serious stuff …

There's no sense in trying to work it out [when he'll be able to move out]. I can't afford anything on the money I've got. I think my Mam and Dad will let me stay as long as I want really. I can't see the point in trying to plan it or save up or any of that stuff … I'd rather just leave it till I'm going to get married or something … It's just one more thing to worry about.

There's no way I could earn enough money to buy my own house. It'll be ages. How can you afford it? I can't even afford going out and things on the wages I get now. It's just not even a possibility.

Without the benefits of higher education or vocational qualifications, Michael is left to scramble for work on the lower reaches of the service sector, earning around £11,500 per year doing a job he hates. Skating across the slippery terrain of an unstable and unpredictable post-industrial economy has not liberated Michael from the restrictive working-class culture from which he hails, nor has it enabled him to reach the material heights that are usually associated with intrinsic personal worth. For Michael and many like him, left clinging on to low paid service work and his parent's coat-tails to remain socially incorporated, the neo-liberal market offers a choice between stagnation and downward mobility.

For Emma, Michael's girlfriend, things appear very much the same. After dropping out of a degree in law in her first year at Eastville University, Emma now works in a city-centre clothing store. Whilst she quite likes the work, the money it provides will not allow her to advance from – or even come close to replicating – the social and economic position of her now retired parents. Emma's father was a low-level civil servant and her mother a housewife.

I think the most important think is to enjoy the work you do, that way it's not a pain going in everyday … The money is pretty bad … just over a fiver a hour … but I get a good discount on clothes which is what I spend most of my money on anyway … The wages is just for pocket money really until I get a proper job. I haven't really thought it through … You can't tell what's going to happen in the future and I try not to make money that important, where, you know, it's like the only thing you think about … My Mam and Dad do a lot for me and I'm very lucky … I'll stay with them as long as I can, I'd be daft not to really … I don't want to leave my Mam and I just don't think I could handle it, being on my own. When I'm older, yeah, but not now … Well, you've got all the money side of things to sort out and I don't think there's any way I could afford it. I don't know what's going to happen.

Ray comes from a decidedly less privileged background. Although he describes his childhood as relatively happy, his home life during adolescence was rather unstable and he rarely attended school after his fourteenth birthday. Ray, however, has a strong dislike of the sedentary lifestyle welfare dependency brings, and has actively sought work, primarily in the construction industry, which, in a similar way to the service industry where the vast majority of our respondents work, is now plagued by job insecurity. Unlike Donna, Michael and Emma, staying in the parental home was not an option for Ray, and he moved between the homes of relatives and friends for some time before obtaining a small welfare-funded flat on a run-down estate in Northville. Ray's flat represents the antithesis of Donna's leafy suburban home.

Personal contacts allowed Ray to enter the building trade and work cash in hand while claiming benefits, waiting for the occasional legitimate work contract, which usually means travelling outside of his home town. Ray's lifestyle thus represents a microcosm of a 'boom-and-bust' economic cycle. A short-term building contract means a high life of drinking, drugs and designer clothes. The end of the contract means return to his hometown, signing on the dole, trying to find fiddle work and staying a step ahead of the benefits agency:

> When I get older, I'm after a proper flash house somewhere, a nice car, holidays and the rest of it. If you can get kept on permanent by a building firm you can be coming out with twenty, twenty five grand a year no problem, and if you're working away they put you in digs so you don't really need owt to live. Get out of this fucking shit pit.

Of course, even landing a permanent contract with a building firm, that rarest of things, doesn't guarantee the material pipe dreams which make up Ray's hopes for the future: £25,000 a year, he ponders, would mean regular money landing in his bank account every month, which in turn would make it much easier to secure a mortgage despite his self-employed status. But Ray's dreams are unrestricted by reality, and the mortgage and house that a regular wage of this size would secure does not come close to living up to the expectations he places on this mythical full-time contract that he may well never receive.

Ray is seduced by consumerism and readily admits his inability to save and plan for the future. After a month or two of 'working away' Ray can return to Northville with quite a tidy sum of money in his pocket, but:

> It just goes. You start going out every night. That's costing you, what, seventy, eighty quid, then you chipping in for coke and you get a few Es and maybe you get a half-ounce [of dope] in. Just getting stuff in for the fridge and that, it mounts up so you think

you're loaded, a week later you're skint, sitting in the dole [office] ... Clothes is obviously a big thing because you've got to go out. A pair of jeans, a shirt, that's maybe two hundred quid.

While Ray's hopes for the future were not orientated to following the 'rules of the game' (Merton, 1938), which are now based upon entering higher education and applying for high-paid knowledge jobs or joining the youthful enterprise culture by setting up in business, he had clearly hoped to be somewhere very different to his current situation. Coming from an unstable and problematic lower class background has not prevented Ray from internalizing the signifying power of consumerism and material success. Ray instead has tried to achieve success in a way that is trapped in the traditional form of working-class gender identity. However, the affluent working classes are being squeezed from all angles, and using traditional working-class skills in one of the few remaining traditional working-class industries has left Ray generally frustrated, despite his periodic and relative affluence. Rather than getting the '... proper flash house somewhere, a nice car, holidays and the rest of it' Ray faces the worrying prospect of descending into the benefit culture that he so despises. Any form of contractual employment, full-time or otherwise, has become harder to obtain as traditional labour markets shift and competition grows, and a full-time permanent job-contract is as much a part of a mythical past as Camelot. Working cash in hand at very low wage rates has become more risky as the net tightens on benefit fraudsters. Losing his benefits would mean losing his flat, which would rapidly propel Ray into genuine social exclusion and, as he wryly notes, possible criminality:

Why not? I'd rather do time than sit on me arse like a lot of the lads round here. They've got fuck all, and they're never going to have fuck all either. If the worst came to the worst, get a big bag or coke laid on [on credit], try and make some money.

For Ray, traditional working-class transitions to adulthood are irrelevant to his everyday life. Despite occasional spells of relative wealth and a deep attachment to consumer culture, Ray is clinging on to the mainstream by his fingertips. If circumstance conspires to weaken his grip, his slide down the social and economic scale could be a rapid one. Mortgages seem out of the question for the time being, and marriage is a distant consideration, not only because of prohibitive economic problems but also because he is keen to play the field and prolong the pleasure of promiscuity that is constantly on offer in the night-time economy. Kids are an impossibility, because his self-perception is based on the observation that he 'can't even sort out [his] own life'.

The passing of the massed, homogenous working class does not herald the end of serious structural inequalities, and its fragmentation has been hastened not by opportunity or choice but by the increasingly unpredictable and fractious nature of employment. The consolations of community and mutuality that were possible in the traditional economy and the work cultures it created have been replaced by competitive individualism and an often brutal scramble for safety and status. There seems to be good reason why so many of our respondents talk of purposely avoiding plans for the future as there is little to contemporary youth transitions that can be accurately predicted and mapped. The supposed liberties and choices championed by neo-liberals and affirmative post-modernists, which are so much a part of contemporary popular culture and that so many of our respondents presumed to be true, are being rapidly unmasked as a myth, very useful as an ideological instrument that can disguise the gradual increase in social inequality and the decline of the political ambitions of achieving social justice that once inspired the labour movement. Rather than rapid leaps forward in real incomes, rather than the flowering and economic utilization of diverse 'talents', and rather than rising standards of living, advanced capitalism's consumer economy has transformed the sociopsychological lives of the bulk of Britain's youth into a maelstrom of instability, disorientation, disappointment and anxiety.

While the triumph of technology over traditional forms of human labour might nudge increasing numbers into 'multi-activity' work, indicated by the current annual decline of the number of people receiving a full-time wage from a specific employer (see Beck, 2000), the endless competition for jobs and the expensive forms of cultural engagement they make possible continues to create a range of emotional and practical problems for many young people. It might be true to suggest that '… to our counterparts at the end of the 21st century today's struggles over jobs will seem like a fight over deckchairs on the *Titanic*' (Bridges, 1995), but portentous intellectual prophecies such as that do not ease the daily anxieties of contemporary workers or make the inability to find adequate work any less significant; a nervous, atomizing and preoccupying way of life that is not likely to encourage the sort of culture or politics required to recognize icebergs or do anything about avoiding them. For now, even socially engaged and culturally advantaged young people are fighting a battle to stand still that many of them will lose, and those who enter this battle from lower economic and cultural positions face a stern test to remain part of the mainstream at all. Rather than fulfilling its traditional role of providing a platform for reasonably smooth transitions into adulthood, advanced capitalism's labour market is an unstable milieu wreaked by anxiety, and as such we can reasonably assume that the identities and *habitus* that are being forged within it are very different from their traditional counterparts.

–3–

Instrumentalism in Relationships, Culture and Education

The data in the previous chapter seem to suggest that the core liberal-capitalist value of competitive individualism permeates the sentiments and interpersonal relations of our respondents in the service-work sector. However, at this stage of our research it would be far too speculative to suggest that this value has installed itself at the heart of a complex social system consisting of numerous 'fields of power' (Bourdieu, 1990), or as a durable drive at the emotional cores of individuals. Indeed, because attitudes to work have never been entirely collectivist and competitive individualism has indeed exerted a powerful force on the West's economy and culture since the Reformation, any claims about it becoming a totalizing and emotionally driven value must be further supported by explorations of young people's attitudes in other dimensions of their lives. All we can do in one short book is to explore the elements that were revealed in the data from the interviews, and here we focus on the fields of personal relationships and education.

Relationships and Culture: Courting Disaster

Many traditional social scientists regarded the entry of young people into a 'serious relationship', such as marriage or long-term cohabitation, as a vital point in the maturation process. Indeed, David Matza (1964) argued that, in the immediate post-war period, the acceptance of the responsibilities that inevitably accompany committed relationships – breadwinning, childcare, jobs, mortgages and so on – was the major factor in the 'drift' of many young males out of petty adolescent crime and delinquency. Left-feminist commentators such as Bea Campbell (1993) enter into an unlikely alliance with essentially conservative commentators such as Norman Dennis (1993) to agree that women have for a long time had a civilizing effect on young men, although of course there is intense disagreement between these two authors about the role of fathers and the social position of women. However, research suggests that since the 1980s there has been a decline in the number of young people entering into long-term committed relationships in their early twenties (Ball et al., 2000; ONS, 2000, 2001; see also Furlong and Cartmel, 1997). The first step in this part of the analysis is to construct a more nuanced picture of the attitudes behind this shift and look for evidence of firm connections between the way young people feel about commitment and the economic, cultural and social forces that constitute the context in which their attitudes have developed.

Ray

Ray, whom we met in the previous chapter, proved to be a key research contact and one of our most vocal respondents on the topic of personal relationships. Here he offers some insight into his attitudes towards women and entry into a long-term, committed relationship:

> I don't think I'll ever get married or anything like that. It just doesn't suit me, and I've never been one of them that always thought they'd get married or anything … I just can't see the point. You just get bored and when it gets like that with a bird, I can't see the point … I've had girlfriends before and all that but it's always got to the stage where they just get on my nerves, just daft things, and I just can't be bothered with all that. I've got mates who get courting and they just disappear, just sit in the house and watch the box with their lass. That's just like the most boring thing in the world to me … Me, I think, you're dead a long time, why bother putting up with it? If you get bored of a lass, why bother keeping it up?

> I mean, the big thing, you can just go down the town and you've got women all over the shop, some of it real top class and all. There's all these different kinds of birds and I can't see really why you'd want of just stick with one, especially cos you know she's going to start to get on your nerves and you're going to get sick of her … The lasses I've been with, you start out think they're amazing right, and then after about a couple of months they just turn into boring old women who want to nag you about daft stuff, sit and watch TV, go to the pictures, stuff like that.

Rather than a convergence of formerly polarized forms in the gender order, allegedly ushering in an era of egalitarian androgyny, Ray still seems to adhere to rather traditional and stereotypical conceptions of gender roles and identities. He is quite clear that he has very little in common with young women, and is quite comfortable with it. If that labels him a 'Neanderthal' in the eyes of those young people who consider themselves to be progressive, then our research, which reveals that these attitudes to women and relationships are extremely common, demonstrates quite clearly that he is by no means the last of the Neanderthals. The young person whose identity is constructed around 'not being the marrying kind' was once the member of a minority but our research confirms that of others, mentioned just above, who have found that more and more young people are delaying their entry into committed relationships and, even when they do enter into them, try to remain childless and free of the more weighty commitments for as long as possible. Ray's cynicism seems to have erased any romantic notions of relationships that a young person in his social position might once have harboured, and indeed his attitudes seem to be driven by utilitarian-hedonistic values of self-interest and pleasure maximization in the form of thrills and excitement. To him, women lack interesting individual characteristics and threaten to become a drain on personal finances, but it is quite telling that he supports the principle of sexual equality and does not demonstrate any apprehension about the possibility that instrumental hedonism can be reciprocated and 'birds' are quite entitled to go out and get what they can from 'blokes'. He is quite supportive of their entitlement to partake in all the pleasures available in consumer capitalism's leisure culture:

I think you've got to pack in this kind of stuff while you're young so there's no time to be messing about with some bird you're getting sick of ... At first it's all exciting, then it just gets knackered and you have to start all over again.

I can see why some of the lads are starting to settle down – it's to do with the type of person you are really ... I mean, getting to know a lass and all that, it might happen but I just can't see it. Apart from the obvious, they're all the same I think. If you want to be with a lass then you can pick any one you want because the crack and that's just the same. All that stuff about love is just complete shite isn't it? I've seen people in love, next thing they're going mental and they fucking hate each other ... I get the bit about having kids but all the rest of it is just made up. I was on at my mate, and he said you just get used to them. It's got nothing to do with love, you just get used to them being around, and that made me think, well why bother with all the shite if that's all it is? As soon as it gets boring, get rid of her and get someone else in ...

I don't think it's sexist, I'm not a sexist person. Women are like that, or at least some of them. They should be doing the same.

I'd like to have kids one day, but not yet. Years away ... I can picture being a Dad, going to the match and Christmas and all that, but I can't really see all that being with a wife or even a regular bird. It just seems impossible to me ... Some of my mates have got kids and to me it would be a nightmare cos I've haven't got the patience, I just couldn't handle it ... It turns you into an old man, they've never got any money or anything ... When you're older maybes it would be a good thing and then you'd say you'd have more time and stuff to do a better job ... No one wants to be an old bloke all by themselves, but they can do whatever they want really can't they? Their money's their own, they can go off whenever they want, work away whatever they want because they're not tied down to anything ... I don't know, we'll just see what happens... You can't say what's going to happen so we'll see what happens, but I know I'm not getting married, I don't even want to get settled with a bird at the moment ...

My mate got married last year. Hell of a lad right, married at twenty odd years old. Got a good job working on the roads or something. He used to be out all the time, now you never see him. Had a pint with him last week and he's saying, all he does is go to work, sit in front of the box then go to sleep. He's saving for a house or something, this that and the other, but their lass doesn't work, just sits about. No kids or anything right, just doesn't want to work. Amazing to me. He's doing all this, and she's doing nothing. He paid like, I don't know how much for the wedding, thousands right? Honeymoon in Mexico all the rest of it. It just seems unfair because he's said, right, I'm not going out, I'll work me arse off, I'll pay the rent, I'll pay bills, I'll do all this, no other birds, and she's said, I'll do what? Nothing right? So now he comes out once in a while and he gets paralytic drunk, because he's trying to get ten nights out into one. He's looking at all the birds and I can see he must be thinking he's fucked up proper, and I feel a bit sorry for him ... He says they're arguing, this and that. Made me think, she's going to take the lot and you're going to be back at your Ma's mate ... You do all this and then you end up with nothing. You see all these blokes not even allowed to see their kids, she gets the house, it's just amazing to me. Why bother? You give all this up, you get nothing back, and you're still risking however much money.

Most of the lads I turn out with are the same, they just want to be going out enjoying themselves and not get tied down ... I mean down the town, there's women everywhere, and to be honest right, a lot of them, they're out for the same thing ... It's not really all of that going out on dates and things as much these days, and that's just the way things are.

Whilst the post-modernist suggestion that we have witnessed the 'death of love' might be somewhat portentous and premature at the moment, Ray appears to be suggesting that his relationships with women, at this specific stage of his life course, will never possess the selfless commitment we might usually associate with supposedly close and supportive relationships. Anything other than unbridled self-interest appears anathema to Ray; why bother to be 'tied down' or give up the hard-earned freedom that everyone else enjoys for the restrictions inherent in long-term commitments to another human being? Once the initial spark of attraction has faded, why not simply replace your girlfriend with a new version, reproducing the pleasure of novelty indefinitely? As Ray is quick to point out, the night-time economy is dripping with sexual opportunity and experimentation, so it is not difficult to carry on experiencing the thrill of the new, the same feeling that a stereotypically preoccupied neophile might crave when absorbed in the symbolism of manufactured commodities. Just as the market is driven by the need to discover, purchase and then discard (Bauman, 1998) some forms of human relationship appear to be drifting towards a perpetual cycle of momentary absorption, followed quickly by disappointment, loss of interest and then the inevitable regeneration of excitement, whereupon the cycle begins again with another night of seemingly limitless opportunity and excitement 'down the town'.

Appearing to be highly constrained by committed relationships, Ray's friends act as the characters in a cautionary tale, and he feels certain that he has exercised a keen critical intelligence to see through the facade of love and discover the trap that it camouflages. The pleasures of mutuality have yet to register with Ray as attractive and valuable, and he seems to be aware only of the inhibiting aspects of commitment. He also seems acutely aware that commitment brings with it a number of difficult utilitarian considerations that are fraught with the likelihood of personal costs and risks. For Ray, any young male who fails to ensure that his investment in a relationship is at least matched, if not bettered, by the partner, and that the relationship will produce various economic, social and cultural 'profits' to balance and hopefully exceed the investment, is courting disaster. After all, why bother to remain with a partner who might contribute nothing to Ray's personal inventory of preferred benefits other than companionship and regular sex? To presume anything other than the same extreme self-interest on the part of a female partner would be a remarkable oversight that is not likely to be made by a 'realist' like Ray.

Phil

For Phil, the pleasures of the leisure economy appear closely related to the procurement of sex and, although he still recognizes that social attitudes towards promiscuity are different across the gender order, he concurs with Ray in his moral affirmation of sexual equality. Although he does not dismiss the possibility of entering a long-term relationship after he has milked his roaring twenties for as much personal pleasure as possible, his cynicism and fatalism about the potential durability of relationships 'these days' is quite telling. However, he still expresses a wish to father children, and, if that is combined with his fatalism, it seems that his attitude conforms to the growing cultural norm of regarding heterosexual relationships as a temporary means of breeding and performing the essential child-rearing in early years, before the inevitable boredom sets in and the couple split. Life-long dedication to anything apart from personal pleasure and gain seems to be receding into the past in our 'finger-buffet' lifestyle. Phil is quite clear about the 'problems' of divorce, which indicates a lack of willingness to share property equitably with a partner or compromise with her preferred lifestyle. The level of trust about women's sexual fidelity also appears to be low:

> I think a lot of the reason we all go out is because of women really. We all go out to enjoy ourselves, and it's good to be out with the lads, but really in the back of your mind is meeting girls ... I think you can see it when you stand back and watch what goes on. I mean there's all of this acting up, and really you can tell they're just showing off trying to get attention ... Or with clothes and things, everything right, dancing, it's

all just a way of getting girls' attention ... I mean, we do talk about blokey type stuff, the standard stuff, but a lot of the time, to be honest, we're just eyeing up women ... we talk about sex a lot ... Sometimes you'll go weeks and you want to talk to her and you'll see her in the same bars at the same times and its one of the main reasons you go out.

Some of the lads are really promiscuous and there's a lot of showing off. A lot of it might be shite, but ... it just seems to me that whoever's the cockiest does the best because if you're shy you just get blanked ... It must be the same for them [women] as well because, they're not having sex by themselves are they? ... There's probably a lot of lying and all the rest of it, but girls must be more willing to have sex than they were. It's just equality now. For men it's still like a badge of honour isn't it?

It's supposed to be the best bit of being young isn't it, that you can go out and meet all different kinds of people and go out with different girls and just having sex without worrying about commitment and all the rest of it? ... It's up to the person whether it's a good thing, because I still think there's a lot of people out there who want to have long-term relationships but it's difficult because there's other things to think about. You've got all sorts of other things going on ... Then you've got people who think it's great because there's no commitment and you don't have to get tied down ...

[I think] ultimately, I'll end up married, because most people do don't they? They might get divorced more, but it doesn't stop people getting married ... [I think] the chances of staying married these days are getting less ... It's just the way it is these days. People think everything is going to be perfect, that they're going to be the ones who stay married, but when it comes to the crunch I think it is harder to stay married than it used to be ... It's just, I don't know, it's just, like both parents going out to work, and just the stress of it all. You see it all over. It's easy to just say, that's it, and get divorced ... It's still the idea that it'll be perfect, that you'll always get on all right and that, but really, I think, more and more, people just think that once you get married, it's boring and it stops you doing what you want to do. It's just, I don't know, just impossible really ... People still want to have kids because it's a natural thing, and because of that they still think they have to get married.

[If you ask them] most of my mates will probably say they don't want to get married, but that's just because they're young, they're just saying it. I think a lot of them will settle down with girlfriends, but I think they're getting scared that marriage isn't a good thing in case they get divorced ... I think it's in everyone's mind now, it's not talked about, you might get divorced, so it's like you're trying to protect yourself just in case ... I think more and more you'll see couples getting together and then splitting up, and moving on to someone new and just keep going like that because I think this idea of getting married and staying together is hard ... I think people still want to do it, but it's just harder ... Maybe people are more selfish and so you get more people being unfaithful and so you can never settle down because it's always in the back of your mind. You can see it happening down the town [meaning in the night-time economy], and after you've been out with someone for a few months you're thinking, maybe I should try and look for something better? Because there's all these women, every-where, down the town, so you're thinking, she's better looking or she'd be easier to get on with or I don't know, because you always have to be looking for the best of what you can get.

I'd like to have kids one day. You want to get married and have kids and all the rest of it, it's not like a lot of people are saying that they can't be bothered with all that. It's just things have changed, people are just different than like our parents were.

Now you've got all these one-parent families and people are still really judgemental about it, but when you think about it that's got to change because more and more people are going to find themselves in that kind of situation … You watch the news and there's all that stuff about dads not being able to see their kids and it makes you think a bit, but really all that kind of thing's a million miles away and there's no sense in worrying about it … That, I want to be married by the time I'm thirty, kids at thirty-five or whatever is just ridiculous because you can't tell what's going to happen. I've really just got to be trying to sort out a job and that and hopefully the rest will just fall into place.

In a similar vein to Ray, Phil appears aware that long-term relationships are challenged by the general fluidity of contemporary culture and the risk inherent in everyday forms of social and economic engagement (see Beck, 1992; Bauman, 2001, 2003). The idea of marriage and active involvement in the idealized nuclear family still seems appealing in a rather novel consumerized manner, but the enthusiasm for a pre-packaged wedding experience and the taking of the next step along life's long road is tempered by the realization that marriages are largely expected to fail (see Giddens, 1992; Beck and Beck-Gernsheim, 2002; Bauman, 2003). Phil and his friends appear to be aware that once the novelty of wedlock has faded, and each partner becomes increasingly conscious of the restrictive nature of the institution they have entered, the image of the unobstructed freedom that lies outside the marital home becomes all the more appealing. At any moment, if a partner fails to live up to his or her side of the unwritten deal struck between them, commitment can be rapidly abandoned. As Beck and Beck-Gernsheim (2002) have aptly noted, a keen awareness of individualism on the part of both partners is now the foundation upon which contemporary marriages are constructed and maintained, rather than the rapidly receding principles of selflessness, altruism and empathy. After securing 'the best [partner] you can get', one has to ensure that this partner's individual needs do not encroach on one's own, and continue to defend resolutely the personal interests that have been constructed in response to the instability of everyday life and the symbolic and practical demands of consumer capitalism. As anxiety about the future increasingly affects young people's values and practices, the desire to defend oneself against the potential disaster of a broken relationship appears to be influencing some young people to construct defensive boundaries between themselves and their partners rather than leaving themselves 'open' to the emotional heartache and damaging economic ramifications of relationship breakdown.

Joe

For Joe and Fred, the very idea of a long-term relationship in the immediate future is simply rejected out of hand. The terror of boredom, the array of hedonistic opportunities and the possibility of an increasing number of sexual encounters in an era of sexual equality in which the old 'promiscuity gap' appears to have been virtually eliminated, are for these two paramount in their life-plans; or perhaps non-plans, to be more precise. Their attitudes towards relationships with the opposite sex appear to be grounded upon the assumption that everyone within their immediate social sphere approaches each new day with a renewed commitment to self-interest:

No, I can't see ez getting married. Just, I don't know, I can't see it, I'm not the type. I can't be having with a women tell me what to do, saying when you can go out and stuff … If you're single, you can go out whenever you want, come in whenever you want. I mean, if you want to get laid then fair enough, but you can go out and there's women all over the place. You get a proper girlfriend, then it's just you and her. Me, I'd just get bored … Why bother getting tied down? … It might be different when you get older … just, I don't know, maybe you can't score down the town, then you settle down, because otherwise it's just daft … you see these women, the way they go on, and you know they've got boyfriends, and you can't trust them the same way they can't trust us [men].

Everyone I know my age who's married, you can tell, they're either sick of it or it's just a matter of time 'til it goes tits up … I don't know, I just think, these days, getting married, there's just too many down sides. When you're my age [early twenties] you'd just be mad. Even thirty, forty, you want to have kids, that doesn't mean you have to be married. There's not a lot of people round here who's married, or at least been married for years is there? You still see loads of kids running about though.

Money wise, women still expect you to pay for everything, so what's that about? If you're married, I just can't even picture it … [I know] everyone says you'll all get married one day but that's just shite. I won't be by myself, I'm not bothered about kids. If I want to have kids then you have kids, but you don't get married …

Fred

There's no way, just no way [I'd get married]. I can't see the point these days. You don't need to get married like you used to … People still want to have kids, but the marriage stuff is just pointless to me … The money and everything, and then if you have to get divorced … If you want to just be stuck with one lass, then fair enough, but you don't have to get married to do that. You get divorced, you lose everything … [I don't] really need a full-time bird anyway. You can get tied down when you're young, then it all goes tits up and your stuck, middle aged, thinking, what happened there? You've missed out on all the going out and meeting different women and that and going on holiday … I

mean, women, really, they're just the same. They're out for what they can get. They're
not bothered. They want a man who's got the cash, and if you're just a normal bloke
then tough luck, because that's all some of them's bothered about. You see it all the time
... It's not just men [being unfaithful], it's just the way it is nowadays and there's no
sense in worrying about it. Just get yourself out there and enjoy it while you're young.

Donna

The general norm of an extended and pleasure-filled adolescence in private life
and a quasi-mature but highly instrumental attitude to work in public life also
seems to govern many of our female respondents' attitudes. Independence and the
ubiquitous 'terror of boredom' – where boredom is equated with the enduring
familiarity of landscapes, people, practices and other aspects of everyday life that
once could often foster great commitment and affection – seems to indicate that
the desire for constant novel experience has indeed turned many young women
into 'cultural tourists' (Bauman, 1996). However, this is heavily qualified and
perhaps tempered by unavoidable biological facts and the continuity of traditional
cultural norms about the inherent goodness of reproduction, the essential mother-
child relationship and childcare responsibilities. Alongside her own wish for independence and constant amusement, Donna accepts the possibility of having
children while acknowledging the unreliability of today's males, so her delay in
committing herself to one person is driven more by foresight of the future need to
have some semblance of security in her life, by either finding the right person or
securing adequate financial means. However, although this understandable caution
is nothing new, she no longer directs harsh moral judgements at unreliable men to
the extent of previous generations of working-class women, who tended to insist
that men should 'settle down' and rehabilitate themselves in preparation for their
full participation in a female-dominated world of 'family values' and an economy
that was in part geared to the reproduction of the workforce (Bourdieu and
Passeron, 1977; Willis, 1977). Instead, she tends to see the problem in her own
rather instrumental terms, based on the relative inability of women to enter the
world of consumer values and join the men in the quest for individual pleasure,
material gain and lifestyle symbolism. Such conflict between traditional pressures
and proliferating opportunities has instilled in Donna some rather ambivalent and
uncertain feelings that are very difficult for her or any commentator to define
simply as expressions of 'disadvantage' or 'advantage' for women, because to
come down on either side would be to make a huge value judgement about tradi-
tional-interdependent or innovative-independent lifestyles in general. However, it
is quite noteworthy that, for Donna, both lifestyles still exert palpable pressure,
and she considers a key generator of pressure in the new lifestyle to be interpersonal competition amongst young women themselves:

There's no way I'd get married at the moment ... There's girls I went to school with who ended up having kids or getting married when they were still dead young, and it's just not the kind of thing I'd do because you miss out on so much ... Like going out and having fun, going on holiday ... getting a career and having your own money ... I see myself getting married about thirtyish, then you've kind of got some experience and you've done the stuff you're supposed to do when you're young ...

[Marriage] is just something, I think, that people think they have to do eventually, but there's so much to get in before you settle down and have kids ... The big thing is what you do once you are married: do you keep working? Do you just give everything up and look after your kids? It seems strange to me because at the moment, it's such a huge commitment, to do that ... I think people more and more just don't care about it [marriage]. They want to get married but they don't want all the pressure and stuff of raising kids and going to work, and you know, being stuck with the same person.

All of my friends [want to get married eventually]. A few are kind of career-orientated and there's a few who want to get married and settle down ... I don't want to sound critical, cos I'm not, but some I think want to just marry someone rich so they don't have to worry about money or going out to work ... There's a lot of that, you know, trying to pull someone rich when we're out and a lot of talk of getting married because it's like the easy life and that's what people want ...

[There's still] a lot of pressure to be in a couple even though it's easier to go out and have fun and do whatever you want to do. You should really be taking your time to find someone you know is right for you ... because the last thing you want to be married and then end up by yourself, divorced, bringing up a kid by yourself ...

I don't think there's as much stigma attached to sex these days, but obviously there's a pressure not to be seen as a slag or something, and it's weird because it's mostly women who are bothered about that kind of thing ... I'd say there is [more promiscuity today]. You can see it happening every weekend, people are getting off with each other all over the place ... There a lot of pressure, because there's the competition to pull, then there's who can pull the best looking and all of that, and then you've got the pressure not to be seen as being slutty, so it can be tricky ... There's a lot of gossiping and complaining and criticizing even amongst us [Donna's friendship group] ... It can get really competitive ...

Annette

Annette displays many of the same concerns as Donna and finds negotiating the seemingly competing pressures of marriage and career quite tricky:

You just can't tell what the future's going to bring so I can't really say [if I'd like to get married] ... You've got to have a job and I think in the back of my mind I'd probably like to get married at some point ... You've got to find someone you can trust and someone you can rely on ... I think ideally you'd want to give up work. I mean ideally he's [the imaginary husband] bringing in enough money so you don't have to ... I honestly don't know. You can't tell. Some of me wants to say, you know, I'd keep on working and all that, but then obviously, why work if you don't have to? And then what if you get divorced because then you've given up your career to have kids and just be married and then you've got to start all again, so it's impossible really, to tell what's going to happen.

Annette also voices the common belief that the actual wedding experience itself continues to be rather alluring to many young women:

> I think a lot of people just see it as the be all and end all. It's like all the kiddy stuff is over and they can just be adults because they're married. There's all that stuff about the big day and everything, and I think a lot of women get sucked into all that, without thinking about what it's actually going to be like [being married] … It's probably not like it used to be because, you know, you talk to friends and they'll say, I don't want to get married. But maybe underneath it they still want to, I don't know.

The subtle seductions of 'wedding consumerism' continue to influence many young women who are enmeshed in serious relationships (Otnes and Pleck, 2003). The image comprising the dress, the cake, the photographs, the ceremony, the reception and all the associated regalia appears to have eclipsed the other ideal of long-term commitment and contentment, which of course involves a good deal more personal sacrifice and effort. The growth of the wedding industry in recent years has been considerable, and the obsession with displaying the signifiers of the 'right' type of marriage indicates that the tradition itself has been drawn more firmly into consumerism's 'fashionable lifestyle' hierarchy (see Wallace, 2004). Many of our respondents alluded to the cost of getting married as a reason not to, but underneath there may well be a strong desire to become immersed in the signifying theatrics of this very public ceremony (see Freeman, 2002). As this data suggests, the attraction of the consumerized 'wedding experience' is often seen as something others have been duped into and the rational, calculating self has avoided. Underlying all of these allegedly rational calculations appears to be a nagging feeling of anxiety about the future, which seems to propelling some young men and women rather hastily towards potentially fractious relationships whilst simultaneously breeding apprehension and the desire to postpone commitment in others. In a way of life where selflessness and altruism are usually interpreted as signs of a façade, a trick or a weakness, the need to protect oneself against the risks that permeate this rather unforgiving environment can make the solutions of either rugged and cynical individualism or a hasty plunge into a suffocating and short-lived form of closeness all the more compelling. The bleak conclusion to this appears to be that the long-term closeness and emotional security many still seek might have moved permanently out of reach.

Michael

Michael's attitude to relationships is shot through with uncertainty and confusion. He displays the same cynicism and fatalism as the other males about the durability of relationships in a culture grounded in proliferating opportunities for individual pleasure. However, the presence of a mild romantic streak, a realistic assessment of his own material desires and an underlying feeling of insecurity that is difficult to specify seem to have influenced Michael to engage in the sort of uneasy, surrogate 'steady relationship' that is becoming quite common amongst young people. Sometimes these pseudo-relationships – not to be confused with the traditional 'long courtship' – can exist from late teens right up to the early thirties, when decisions are made either way, and in the meantime they allow the individuals to indulge in the required hedonistic and acquisitive excesses while retaining a semblance of security and companionship and, at the same time, sometimes setting the stage for a long-running drama of splits and reconciliation that adds a little spice to the mundanity of working life and a theatrical form of depth to the froth of leisure culture:

There's obvious pluses to being single, isn't there? It gives you the freedom to go off and do whatever you want to do, go out, get off with people, it's up to you … Having a girlfriend kind of limits the time you can spend with your friends because you've got to spend more and more time as a couple. It's just part of growing up and a lot of my friends are in a couple now … [the benefits of being in a couple are] hard to explain. I'm not really comfortable talking about it to be honest … I suppose I do love her [Emma, his girlfriend]. It's just that when you start getting in to your twenties it becomes less important to be out all the time with your friends and more important to be with someone really. I still go out with my mates every week and she still goes out with her mates, so it's not like we're married or anything.

I know plenty of people who are unfaithful. It's all over the place and it's just so easy if you want to be like that I suppose. It's women as well …

I wouldn't want to be married until I'm thirty … it just doesn't make any sense to do it before … you've got to get the important things sorted out, get a career and get some money behind you before you can go into something like that … We both know that it's not going to happen any time soon, and she's the same, it's not like she's desperate to get married or anything … I know she wants to have kids eventually but there's no point at our age even thinking about it because everything could change … you might have to move away for work, you might split up, you just never know what can happen or what's around the corner …

I think I want kids eventually but I really haven't thought about it. You don't want to be stuck by yourself when you're old … It's just a million miles away for me. I couldn't cope with the responsibility, I'm too young to even think about it yet.

The material pressures upon young people, and their vague place within labour markets and our changing social hierarchy, cropped up in virtually every topic we discussed in interviews. Rather than marrying for love and having kids to satisfy both social and biological imperatives, our young respondents seemed compelled to approach these issue in a rather pragmatic and calculative manner. There seems to be an historical discontinuity here, in that even the bourgeois and upper-class pairings of the past were based on social climbing and long-term dynastic ambitions, whereas now the extension of hedonistic rights and lifestyle experiences seem to be exerting the heavier influence. Forward planning was acknowledged as an increasingly difficult practice across our sample; most of the data indicate that young people are now forced to evaluate the costs and benefits of many aspects of social life that in previous generations were seen as biographical certainties. Calculations based on projections of the benefits of favourable outcomes and the costs of worst-case scenarios, evaluated with the yardstick of individual pleasure, are now informing young people's attitudes towards social, cultural and economic engagement. This might not characterize British youth as a whole, given the very different problems faced by the socially excluded or the very rich, but in the mainstream we can tentatively speculate that the insecurity and anxiety that is a principal effect of the shift to a consumer capitalist economy and a competitive individualist culture seems to be radically altering many young people's perceptions, feelings and practices.

Losing the Traditional: the End of Parallel Lives and Mutual Experience

As the calculative instrumentalism demonstrated by the vast majority of our respondents in their heterosexual relationships begins to dominate other aspects of social life, the wider consequences of the breakdown of homogeneous cultures grounded in social class, and the subsequent abandonment of the struggle to attain its various forms of cultural capital, are only now starting to be addressed (Bourdieu, 1984; Wacquant, 2002). In this section we want to shift the focus briefly to friendships and friendship groups.

Many of the interviewees would once have been categorized automatically as working class, but in this current climate of transient employment and dispersed cultural capital their affiliation to a particular social class was unclear. Most appeared to have a vague inkling of their lower class status, but none at all could locate themselves in what Westergaard (1995) and Hutton (1995) have described as neo-capitalism's new 'deepening and widening' structures of social inequality. The fragmentation of traditional-working class communities can be seen as socially corrosive at a number of levels (see, for example, Lasch, 1979; Taylor, 1999). The loss of a sense of local obligation and mutual interests, which have given way to the ascent of individualism, has combined with public perceptions of real rises in violent crime to create a general climate in which the right-wing media's traditional attempt to convince us that danger lurks at every turn becomes significantly easier. Rather than mutual support and consolation, rather than camaraderie and the brief pleasures of mutual resistance (for example Young and Willmott, 1961; Dennis et al, 1969; Deller, 2002), we have become eager to keep the world out, avoiding neighbours, padlocking doors and retreating into an ever-more privatized world. What we might be witnessing is a quantum leap towards a society based primarily on self-interest: city life becomes increasingly isolating (Davis, 1990, 1998), work becomes totally alienating, consumerism and status attainment exercise an unforgiving autocratic rule over self-identity and self-esteem, and community, mutuality, empathy and altruism become deviations from the norm. Some social theorists now acknowledge that individualization should not be read as 'the unfettered logic of action' (Beck and Beck-Gernsheim 2002: 3), a return to classical liberalism or celebrated as the beginning of some period of unprecedented emancipation, but instead stress that individuals are forced to conceive of their lives as a precarious and anxiety-inducing process of self-definition and adaptation (see also Giddens, 1992; Bauman, 1995, 2003). Here, attention is drawn to the difficulties that individuals confront in their struggle to retain a sense of identity and moral being, but perhaps less attention is focused on the fate of basic cohesion in the economic and social dimensions, as politics and human relations within them are reduced to a number of increasingly fragile, contingent and peripheral functions, potentially fragmenting the dense web of interdependencies on which the social contract and the civilizing process can be built and maintained (see Mestrovic, 1997).

One specific result of the determining forces of neo-capitalist culture – namely the inculcation of instrumentality as a common value and practice in youth identities and relationships – is of wider significance. During the industrial capitalist era most working-class individuals were bonded together in the cultural forms and habitus that established and reproduced themselves in mutual experiences, such as exploitative employment, schooling, poverty and family life (Dennis et al., 1969), which anchored a whole range of personal relationships (Young and Willmott, 1961; Whyte, 1993) in communities characterized by a significant degree of solidarity and continuity (Callinicos and Simons, 1985; Adeney and Lloyd, 1988). During this period, friendships appeared to be more durable (see Giddens, 1992). In terms of *social being*, lives lived within a grounded working-class community tended to flow along relatively predictable channels of biographical development (Willis, 1977; Robins and Cohen, 1978; Corrigan, 1979). Put simply, those who were born in the same age group in the same neighbourhood, attended the same school, experienced similar family lives, left school at the same time to perform the same alienating and exploitative work in industry, experiencing the same demands and pressures. Friends who grew up together in this manner might also have experienced a range of other life events which further bonded them together, including marriage, child-rearing, military service, periods of unemployment, family bereavements, ageing and retirement.

However, our research shows that the close and enduring personal attachments that often grew alongside these shared experiences now appear less common. Although we accept that close personal relationships continue to exist amongst many young people, we are suggesting that it is a different, highly selective, competitive, fragile and often hasty form of 'closeness'. Bonds are no longer rooted in anything more profound than the instrumental display of lifestyle symbolism and cultural competence in the circuits of consumer signification, and at the moment this seems to be having a corrosive effect on the more enduring friendships upon which the communal, social and political solidarities of the past were built. To reinforce this point, our research suggests that instrumental attitudes are beginning to be displayed in the construction and maintenance of friendship as well as work and heterosexual relations. For some respondents, friendships provided an essential platform for making a personal 'impact' and achieving a sense of significance and distinction in night-time leisure cultures. As 'going out' is the most important activity in the lives of most respondents, friends were often seen primarily as a *means* of facilitating the 'right' type of cultural engagement.

Dan

My friends now are really a lot of the lads I went to school with. I don't see as much of my other friends as I used to ... just because things have changed, not just for me, it's just the way it goes. My mates now, really, we all go out on a Saturday, and sometimes maybe a Thursday or Friday ... The lads who've got courting go out a lot less now and you can see what's happening, people are drifting off a bit because we're just getting older I suppose ... I only really see them in pubs ... I don't know why, it's just the way it is with men, you go out for a pint. I've been in some of their houses, but really it just going out I see them ... we just talk about general stuff, this and that, just normal ... There's a lot of taking the piss and just crack about what's going on and stuff. No one really talks about anything serious ... [no] work or family stuff. It's just, when you go out, you're all geared up for a good night and a good laugh and it's just not part of the crack, having meaningful discussions or anything.

I used to go clubbing a lot with this mixed group, some girls, and we'd go all over the place [clubbing], and I can remember I'd always offer to drive, or book trains or whatever, because I really wanted to go and you're trying to get all your friends to go ... If they didn't go I couldn't go. It was just part of being young, drugs and music and that. I had some of my best nights ever, just, we were all right into the music ... We sort of stayed together because we all wanted to go clubbing together ... [when I think about it] I didn't know a lot of them that well, it was weird ... if I bumped into some of them know I think it would be a bit awkward, it was just so different with them ... just the drugs and that, just weird I suppose because we didn't talk that much apart from drugs and house music … Slowly but surely we started to drift apart.

Colin

[A night out] is just a good way of enjoying yourself after a week's work. You just get into a rhythm of going out all the time and you just go out for a laugh … you're getting pissed, there's lots of women all over, and you're just having a laugh. It's just all part of being out, being out with the lads. There's times where, honest, well, we've just had a right laugh, just comical really … [I've got loads of] memories about the nights out we've had … They're just a good bunch of lads really, they all like a laugh, and that's what you want really. They're just a good set of lads to be around … mostly we just meet up on a Saturday and sometimes I see some of them for a pint on Friday afternoon … some of them go out during the week but I can't afford it … We used to play five-a-side a while back but all that's just stopped really … I don't know it's just people have got other things to do, got girlfriends and that … For me it's just a Saturday because that's the best night to go out, so most of the lads turn out on a Saturday. I can't afford to be going out every night of the week, so now I just really turn out on Saturdays …

There's all sorts really [in our friendship group]. There's lads who do all sorts, just everything … Well, there's a couple of contractors, some do stuff with telecommunications or something, some do just building work I think, I'm not sure exactly. Pete works in a shop down the town, John works in a call centre up in Northville. They just do all sorts … Most of the lads still live with parents and that, I think there's maybe one or two who've moved out. Ray's got his own flat … it's just because we just don't have that type of crack really, all work and families and stuff. I think I know them well, but when you get to thinking there's a lot I don't know … There's maybe ten of us who go out regularly, but really, there's only really Paul who I'd call a good mate, because the others, I mean they're still mates, still good lads. But, apart from going out I don't really see them. I don't even think most of them know what I do. See, it's not really talked about. You go out to have a laugh, and that's it.

The actual knowledge of practical and emotional aspects of friends' lives, in some cases, appeared to have undergone a shift in emphasis. The 'going out' personas of friends were often at the forefront of assessments of friendship, and they were the main source of personal knowledge about the lives of friends. Joe takes up the story:

My mates are really just there for you to go out and just enjoy yourself really. You've got your family, you've got people at work, and then you've got the lads, and, really, we just have a laugh, so that's what we all think about it … If you want to go out, you ring around and see if anyone's up for it and you know most likely you're going to have a good night because we're all the same really, we all like to have a laugh and just enjoy ourselves really … you know you can rely on them, just to cheer you up I suppose … when we turn out that's what we're bothered about … I think we make a conscious effort not to talk about certain stuff. If one of the lads comes out and starts talking about work, complaining about this or that, he's just going to get the piss taken out of him and everybody knows that. We get enough of that ourselves, during the day. We don't want to hear about depressing stuff cos it's going to spoil the night.

Andy offers this glimpse into contemporary male friendships:

There's bit of daft gossiping and slagging people off but mostly it's a good group of lads. You know, we just have a laugh, and that's what's it's all about at the end of the day. … I mean, we all do hard jobs, and you want to go out just to relax and take a bit pressure off. There's all the rest of it as well, but mostly we just go out to enjoy ourselves and have a laugh … there's women, you've just got all the excitement of a night out as well … I don't know really, music and stuff like that. You want to go out just to keep up with the crack, and just be involved really … we all get on good and we're just regular lads. There's not all that living in each others pocket but then that's not what you want. You don't want to get into all that stuff, and know everything about each other. I know I can rely on them if I need to, or at least some of them … I've been dropped in it before by a couple of them, but really you just want your mates to have a laugh with because, just because really.

Others appear to have a profoundly practical approach to friendship. As Emma comments:

[Apart from Paula, my best friend] The others, to be honest, I just see when we go out. They're nice and that, don't get me wrong, but, I don't know, I don't like to get drawn into all that kind of stuff, where, you know, you see each other all the time … We usually get on all right, but I know, if anything happened, or if I stopped going out, I just probably wouldn't see any of them … There's a time and place for friends, and I suppose we all like to meet up now and then, and we text each other and stuff, but really apart from Paula, I'm not that close to any of them.

I used to be when we were younger, but there's just so much gone on that everything's just changed. I mean, we've all had daft arguments and stuff, just petty things and it just changes your attitude. Now, I'll go out with them and everything on the surface can be quite friendly but you know some of them can be quite bitchy and there's all this, you know, like breaking off into different groups, and things like that. Now I just think they can get on with it, it doesn't bother me … Sometimes we'll go out together and you'll be talking and getting on OK, but underneath it all you're not that close at all … it doesn't stop me going out, it's not so bad you've got to stop going out together because people are always going to have rows and there's nothing you can do. You just make the best of it.

Fred

I'm lucky in a lot of ways because I've got some close mates that I know will stand up with ez if anything happens. That's just the way it is with us and we don't even really talk about it ... We're not like birds, on the phone all the time, because it's not necessary. It's just the way it is. You go out and have a bit crack and see the lads, and if you don't turn out then really there's something away, because you shouldn't lose tough with the lads, no matter what ... I don't need to be seeing them all the time, we only really see each other when we turn out ... the work stuff, it doesn't matter because we know that no one likes it, you're not supposed to like it are you? It's just work. For me, I don't want to be talking about all that stuff or anything private that happens to me because I don't want to get on people's nerves or take the piss because it's just not the way it is ... you get your private stuff, and you only get the lads involved if it's something that can't be helped and you've got to tell them.

Once, analyses of working class youth often uncovered a profound sense of kinship, belonging, mutual knowledge, hopes and ambitions (see for example Patrick, 1973; Parker, 1974). Now, the same types of youth groups often reveal growing divisions, fragmentation, alienation and isolation. As the battle for prosperity and distinction enters its consumer phase, it is rapidly becoming both prudent and fashionable to fight unencumbered by enduring affective and social bonds. Attachments, and the obligations and restrictions that inevitably accompany them, appear to be unwanted complications as individuals streamline their lives to deal with the demands and grasp the opportunities of the ornamental consumer society. Whilst reciprocity remains important in intimate human relations, the need to maximize benefit for the self seems inescapable (Beck and Beck-Gernsheim, 1995), and some of the friendships described by our respondents appeared to be entered into entirely for their cultural 'use value'. Some of our respondents talked about maintaining friendships with phone calls, text messages, and the occasional solicitation for information about 'how they're doing', but ultimately their motivations seemed to revolve around personal benefits rather than the virtue of emotional reciprocity. What these young people put into friendships is driven by what they might get out of them in terms of a functional identity:

Now I'm working I've got shifts and stuff and I just can't go out like I used to. You get in from work and sometimes you're just shattered and can't be bothered. It's hard to keep in touch and keep friendships going if you're working and you've got a life of your own. My friends and me used to be really close when we were younger because you spent more time together. It's just the way it is when you're young, you're dead excited and everything. Now, everyone's got jobs ... [and] stuff going on. I keep in touch with maybe a couple, like talk to them on a weekly basis, and I know I can call them if I fancy going out or something. The others, really, haven't got anything to do with me anymore. It's like they're strangers, even though we might go out for a pint and have a laugh together. It sounds harsh, because I still like them and I still enjoy seeing them. I maybe see them once a month or something and we have a chat, but when I think of what we all used to be like it just shows how much you change as you get older ... I think as I get older, I'm more and more happy just to spend time in my own company, just watching the telly or going down my Mam's. Once you get in a couple things just change because you don't have to go out anymore looking for a boyfriend.

The night-time economy is now not only the primary arena for consumption and 'identity work', but also the primary arena for the construction and maintenance of friendships. Seeing friends means going out, and going out means seeing friends. It must be emphasized that some respondents talked in impassioned terms about closeness and mutual support, of standing by friends during the hard times of rapid culturo-economic change. But the actual ephemerality and instrumentalism that they also spoke of suggests that a general shift in emphasis lies underneath these comments, which is not without wider theoretical significance. Whilst the current mode of individualization has become accepted – or in some cases celebrated – by many sociologists and cultural theorists as a development with a good deal of emancipatory potential, most of this data seems to suggest the need for much more circumspection and critique.

Education, Education, Education

To those who uncritically subscribe to neo-liberal ideology, the rapid expansion of university education during the 1990s is construed as a key indicator of the declining significance of social class and the emergence of a fluid and meritocratic social order around advanced capitalism's 'information economy'. This new centre-right consensus posits that, regardless of social or cultural background, anyone who displays the requisite talent and determination can acquire important positions within consumer capitalism's mutating status-hierarchy. To facilitate this ideal, secondary education was reorganized and the higher and further education sectors were rapidly expanded and filled by a range of young people from 'non-traditional' university backgrounds. Education became the swipe card to consumer success, the conduit to upward social and economic mobility. However, those who weren't willing to play the game, or whose performance was judged unsatisfactory, fell by the wayside. The publicity afforded to this dark, Darwinian dimension of liberalism's jaunty meritocratic ideology (see Currie, 1997) is usually couched in the terminology of right-wing 'underclass' theory, which posits a sub-class that exists purely because of its own self-reproducing deficiencies, which are generated by the bad – that is, lazy, feckless and dependent – attitudes, cultural practices and choices of the individuals who inhabit it (Murray, 1996; for critiques see MacDonald, 1997; Hallsworth, 2005).

Apart from these right-wing jeremiads – which are often quite correct at the observational level but hopelessly inadequate at the phenomenological and aetiological levels (see Horne and Hall, 1995; Lea, 2002) – it is now becoming less common to posit the existence of a new and profoundly excluded class as the product of structural change in the latter part of the twentieth century. It will probably not strike the reader as too surprising that government party lines, popular culture and many academic discourses from across the political spectrum prefer to focus on the sunny side of advanced capitalism's street, although we must be fair here and point out that some academics who once enthused about free-market capitalism's emancipatory potential have since the late 1990s reverted back to critique (see for example Gray, 1998). Nevertheless, we are constantly reminded that working-class kids can now ascend the class system in leaps and bounds, leaving the parochial and restrictive world of their parents in their wake. Study, hard work and the cultivation of a range of 'marketable skills' and vague 'corporate characteristics' in their personal images (see Parton et al., 2002; Brown and Hesketh, 2004) will allegedly allow young people of any gender, ethnicity or class to achieve; to 'be who they want to be', to 'live life on their own terms' and reverse the traditional employee's subservience to the employer (see Angell, 2000). This new rhetoric claimed that individual workers can now sell their knowledge and skills to the highest bidder, which places the best of them in a position of bargaining strength that they could only have dreamed of in the old world. No need for compulsory loyalty to employers because labour markets now serve the 'global competition' of market capitalism in which, of course, firms no longer display much loyalty to employees, so there is no longer any requirement to reciprocate what is not received. Despite the well-known fact that many firms outside of the Anglo-American sphere – especially in Japan and parts of Europe – still attempt to retain the principle of reciprocal loyalty, the rhetoric is laid on with a trowel. 'Employability' has replaced real employment as the new watchword of government, and the fundamental prerequisite for economic success has been reduced to the ability of the nation to attract inward investment from transnational companies by arming its workforces with the skills demanded by the global information economy.

In the eye of this neo-liberal storm, the entire economic, social and cultural health of Britain came to depend not upon manufacturing industry but the ability of the nation to produce the flexible commercial skills required by the increasingly mercurial post-industrial economy and global marketplace (Bauman, 1998; Brown and Hesketh, 2004). However, to be sold more effectively to the public, this economic necessity was adorned with high idealism. If the education system could churn out successive generations of young people with the requisite skills and personal characteristics that key employers in expanding sectors now demand, not only would we be liberated from the curse of the boom-and-bust economy, but the great liberal meritocratic principle of freedom through education, hard work and fair competition would be realized. This was no mere adaptation to a changing economy, it was the long-awaited realization of an enlightenment ideal, a potential millenarian moment, the 'second coming' for the more devout classical liberals.

However, from the very beginning of our project the data we began to collect supported a much more pessimistic view. A façade of liberty, equality and meritocracy has been painted on the harsh economic reality behind the rapid development of higher education by promoting the largely discredited belief that high-paid, fast-track jobs will produce a 'trickle down' type of prosperity, which in turn will eventually suffuse the population as more individuals acquire the skills and the nebulous 'personal qualities' required by global commerce. However, the economic reality is that many of today's graduates – especially those from the new universities – are ending up in the low-grade service sector employment that they were attempting to flee in the first place (Brown and Hesketh, 2004). In fact, the social mobility in the Anglo-American societies driven by the minimally regulated free market consumer/service economy and the *laissez-faire* politics of the 'Washington consensus' appears to be significantly more moribund than the social mobility in state-centred social democracies and regulated manufacturing/service economies of Canada and Sweden (Blanden et al., 2005). Rather than loosening up and providing more opportunities, current labour markets continue to be segregated along traditional lines as the cultural and symbolic capital accrued by so many of the graduate job seekers hoping to join the fast track falls short of the mysterious 'personal qualities' preferred by employers. Despite the proclamations of meritocracy and pseudo-scientific testing (Brown and Hesketh, 2004), selection is still determined by individuals who arbitrarily judge other individuals by the rather arcane criterion of 'talent' (ibid). As Brown and Hesketh (2004: 25–6) have noted:

> [e]mployers ... operate with explicit and implicit assumptions about the management and leadership qualities of 'different types' of people. The embodiment of 'talent' is a social construction that will reflect the cultural values of organizations and the wider society.

Despite the daily propagation of the 'rags-to-riches' myth by the Anglo-American media, in real life most graduates from lower social class and ethnic minority backgrounds also tend to restrict themselves to jobs they actually believe they might get, thus failing to apply for a range of attractive jobs for which they might be fully qualified and suited (ibid). The advanced capitalist labour market continues to be a primary site for the reproduction of subtle structuring processes that operate under the smooth veneer of governmental, popular cultural, and in some cases academic, platitudes about liberty and equality. When it's held up to the light, this looks remarkably like yet another mutative phase in the reproduction of what used to be referred to, without embarrassment, as 'class relations' (see Brown, 1995, for a discussion).

Neo-liberal culture not only avoids questioning the fundamental unethical principle of meritocracy – that the 'talented' are worth more than the 'untalented', which turns life into an ugly struggle over 'performances in the market' and entitlements to judge the social results (see Bourdieu, 1984) – but it also presents it as an ongoing reality made possible and ready to burst into full blossom in the climate provided by the free market and the type of governance that supports it with minimal interference. The constant cultural pressure exerted upon parents and young prospective students tends to foster the belief that education may indeed be a magical portal to status, security and economic prosperity in the free-market in an era of expanding 'accreditation' (Amin, 1994; Taylor, 1999). As some of our respondents suggested, university education can often seem like a further step towards an adulthood free from the anxiety and humiliation that characterize low-grade service work or welfare dependency. For them it just seems like the *natural* thing to do, and for others it also offers a parentally approved sojourn from the pressures and responsibilities of 'adult' life. However, continuing education into the early and mid-twenties comes at a significant price. Large numbers of students are struggling through university degrees and accumulating huge amounts of debt only to find that fast-track management positions in the 'creative' industries are for ever out of reach (see Brown and Hesketh, 2004).

The university education that is expected to develop and hone the individual's skills and qualities is also on the path towards full marketization. This has transformed traditional university culture, and some lecturers have recently expressed grave concerns about falling standards (see Ahmed, 2002; Smithers and Curtos, 2005) as the student body assumes the powerful position of the 'paying customer' and the once austere intellectual world of higher education falls under the spell of the market (Brown, 2000; Graham, 2002; Kirp, 2003). The customer is always right, as the market proverb tells us, and because many of these particular customers are painfully aware of what various employers require – and thus what skills and qualities they need to 'buy' at university – they are, sometimes encouraged by vocal parents, becoming very tough customers indeed. The core skills that universities deliver must meet the new focus on 'employability' (see Knight and Yorke, 2003). Higher education is thus increasingly focused on 'outputs' – awards and references confirming knowledge, skills and personal qualities – which students can then take to the market. The more diverse benefits of traditional higher education, in terms of general enlightenment, disseminating social and scientific knowledge (Kirp, 2003) and helping to create the educated and critical population upon which genuine democracy would depend, is forgotten as universities are increasingly seen as machines for moulding young people to fit the labour market.

The time-honoured practices of delivering social scientific and arts education also shifted accordingly, moving away from a principled ends-orientated rationale and much closer to an instrumental means-orientated rationale. All higher education staff are now under increased pressure to grab as many students – or 'further education customers' as they are increasingly characterized (Bok, 2003) – as possible in order to secure funding, and also to allow failing students to pass through assessment processes, thus maintaining student numbers and attaining favourable positions in national 'league tables'. Students who fail are now unlikely to be assessed as uninterested or less capable individuals in their specific field, but rather as consumers who have failed to receive an adequate service for their money (Graham, 2002; Bok, 2003; Stevens, 2004). Maintaining a high student intake and decreasing drop-out rates is now high on the agenda of the formerly rarified intellectual and academic elites (Kirp, 2003) and in the near future it would be interesting to research the effect that consumer-power might be having on the actual intellectual content and assessment methods that lie at the heart of undergraduate degree programmes. Indeed, it is already quite clear that new joint-honours degree routes are proliferating in a desperate attempt to draw in potential students and old academic disciplines are being pressurized to diversify their content to appeal to as many students as possible.

Lecturers themselves are not absolved from the brutal competition of employability and labour markets. Failure to recruit enough students means that redundancies loom on the horizon (Curtis, 2002), and the increased reduction of academic research to the measurement of 'outputs' has created a heated transfer market for elite professors who churn out a large number of publications (in some cases repetitive variations of a single piece of research or a single idea), and increased pressure upon those who have failed to do so (Graham, 2002; Stevens, 2004). Senior administrators must now pressurize their key players to produce publications to secure research funding, which some would suggest has produced a sea of fairly mediocre and often rather obscure work that adds little of originality or importance to the disciplines themselves, but racks up the scores for the next 'research assessment exercise', a distribution process where committees of officials and academics decide how much funding specific subject areas in specific universities will receive, or whether they will receive any at all. As a result, despite the wealth of academic talent and research expertise that many of them possess, some new universities in the less attractive urban areas are becoming primarily teaching institutions. Those with better 'A'-level results select upper tier traditional universities or new universities in 'cool' British cities, leaving these other new universities with a surfeit of less academically interested or able students. These students tend to receive low-grade or mid-grade degrees that carry progressively less currency with corporate employers seeking high-achievers for their 'fast-track' management schemes in an 'employers' market', where in many sectors the supply of qualified young people greatly outstrips demand.

In the classic Mertonian (1938) sense, the expectations that are being implanted in the minds of young people by neo-liberal culture are clashing with the availability of opportunities for their fulfilment. However, today's friction between cultural expectations and structural reality is more profound than Merton's original formulation because the current structure itself is much less clear, and young people have a correspondingly unclear idea about what success actually means, except that whatever it is can be signified by 'performing' well in the marketplace and conspicuously displaying the lifestyle object-signifiers that their satisfactory performance allows them to buy. Most of life's other moral ends seem to have been severely attenuated or sidelined, and for both staff and students the climate in many British universities and colleges is becoming fraught with anxiety and permeated by cynicism and disillusionment. If, indeed, the installation of neo-liberal market principles at the heart of the British higher education system is creating fields of altered power relations in which the nature of the struggle for symbolic and cultural capital is now much more individualized and instrumental, it seems worth investigating the possibility that the attitudes and practices of the young student 'actors' might also be changing in corresponding ways. In the following section we offer some field data from a number of key respondents intimately acquainted with the risky nature of contemporary higher education.

Donna

Donna is twenty-two and studying for a degree in social sciences at a new university in the north of England. She lives with her parents in a quiet suburban estate nearby. She perhaps personifies the middle ground of the 'new breed' of student, with some gender-specific qualifications that distinguish her and the other female interviewees from the young men. From what once would certainly have been regarded as a working-class background, she is surprisingly stoical about her chances for social advancement through education. Although she is uncertain about her specific career, she is quite clear that her main ambition is a job that will provide both underlying security and a degree of disposable income that will allow her to indulge in material comforts and some hedonistic pleasures; Epicurian moderation with the opportunity for the occasional bout of Bacchanalian excess. Lacking a positive vocation, her career ambition is determined by what she doesn't want to do – and that, of course, is work in the lower end of the service sector. She expresses a vague preference for some sort of managerial job, and although a reasonable amount of money is more important than interesting and satisfying work, she is circumspect about her personal ambition. She regards 'less stress' as more important than big money, but a decent wage is still paramount and she seems to be very aware of the possibility of balancing remuneration with dedication to work.

Donna's opinion of her subject is not entirely lacking in enthusiasm and commitment, but it would be more than fair to describe it as lukewarm. She feels that most of the knowledge she encounters is largely irrelevant to work, which says quite a lot about her attitude to knowledge itself and her awareness of the political and social functions of knowledge. She seems firmly convinced that knowledge is associated largely with economic needs and her own function in the economy, but neither knowledge nor work are valuable ends in themselves. Her wish to marry someone with a big wage to provide for her potential children, despite her belief in the proliferation of opportunities for financial independence, betrays a distinctly traditional attitude to gender relations. She was quite clear that the utilitarian principle of maximal return for minimal effort figured highly in her own medium-term personal ambitions:

I messed up at school. I made the mistake of thinking it would be easy to get a job, but when you're at school I don't think you think seriously about that type of stuff. I just thought that I'd get one [a job] whenever I wanted really … My Dad really wanted me to go back to school and he really wanted me to just, like, make something of myself … just move on and do something with my life … and not be one of those people who just sits about all day. I didn't do that well with 'A' levels but I got in at Scarville university and now I'm doing a degree … I did Geography and Sociology [at A level] … Everyone's dead proud about it [getting into university] … I think there is a bit of pressure, because everyone's always asking about uni and that, how's this going, how's that going, but it's not a bad thing because I know everyone's behind me …

With my 'A' levels I should have done better but there was a lot going on in my life at the time and I just didn't put the work in. I wasn't really sure what I wanted to do at university, but I definitely wanted to go to Scarville [university] so I could stay at home. I didn't want to move away … I think it was a mixture of getting homesick and missing everyone and money; I didn't want to pay to live in some crumby flat …

It was a bit weird at first [being at university] but you get used to it and I've made a few friends so it's good … At first you're not really sure what to do and stuff like that, because it's a lot different to school and it can be a bit disorientating.

When I started [at university] I thought I'd get stuck in and work hard, but to be honest there's not that much work to do and so I got a job … just to get some pocket money really … I didn't have to, but it's nice to be able to go out and buy things … I work in an office at the moment, just doing filing and typing and answering the phone and that … [I] work though an agency and get about six pounds an hour I think [circa 2003] … What I'm hoping is that I can just get something a bit better paid once I've finished [at university] … I'd like to have more money. I'm not bother what I end up doing as long as I've got enough money to just, I don't know, buy things and look after myself a bit … I'm not stupid, I know that when I get older six pounds an hour isn't going to be enough, and even if I get married there's no guarantees … really that's what I'm at university for, it's just like getting you up to that level where you can earn more money.

I don't know what I'm going to do. I don't want to work in a call centre, but I think you can earn about fifteen grand a year as a team leader if you've got a degree, which doesn't sound bad. To be honest I haven't really bothered to look because I'd prefer to leave it until I've graduated ... [Ideally] something in retail or sales [would be good] ... I'd like to be on the fashion side of things, but really I think you've just got to be ready to see what comes up ... [My Dad] says I should start looking now, write off letters and stuff ... I know I should but I just haven't got around to it ... Looking into the future is hard. You can't tell how things will turn out. I think I see myself working in quite a good managerial job, something like that, then maybe settling down ...

[The type of job I want is] really a mixture of good money and interesting work, but mostly I'd like good money ... say twenty to thirty thousand would be good ... [I know] there's all kinds of jobs that you can get a lot more than that, but I don't think I want to move away and all the hassle of trying to get those type of jobs. I don't want the stress ... It's probably stressful having a really top job, and I think there'd be a lot of pressure. I'd just prefer an easy life; get a nice job where you get quite good money, but you're not stressed to bits all the time.

Donna's personal ambitions have not entirely displaced her affective attachments to others, but as was the case with all our respondents, her social circle is restricted to family and a small circle of friends. The broad geographical community in which she lives or the rapidly disappearing working class from which she came simply do not exist in her emotional or intellectual life. Rather, and entirely understandably, her interviews were littered with references to money and her own personal security:

I'm not sure if the degree [subject] makes any difference in the types of jobs I'm looking for. Not much I hope. I just think they want someone who's got a degree ... I used to think it would be good to move to London and get a proper career, but more and more I think I'd rather stay at home in Scarville ... It's where my family's from, and I've got a boyfriend and I think there's a lot to be said for staying where I am. It's nice to go off for a holiday, but you feel happier when you get home I think ... I wouldn't want to lose touch with my friends and things like that.

I want the job I do to be interesting. A lot of the jobs I've done through the agency are just boring and I want something that keeps you interested, but really it's all about money isn't it? ... [I think] I'll get a better paid job with the degree than I would've got otherwise. I'd like to get a really, really well paid job, but most likely I'll just get the average ...If I have to guess I'd say about twenty thousand [a year], I want to be earning about twenty thousand. With that you've got the money to do whatever you want, really. Most of my friend who work full-time are on about twelve or thirteen but I think some of them say they're on more just to show off a bit. Obviously you aim to get more, but I think I'd be quite happy if that's what I end up with.

University's all right. The subject's all right. Some of it's interesting. I've learned some things I think, but most of it'll have nothing to do with any job. [My marks have been] mostly 50s and 60s ... [Most of the other people there] seem like me really. There's some on my course that are older and a couple who dress a bit weird but it's just normal people ... I'd say most of them are from Scarville or maybe a bit further out. There's not a lot of different accents, like I was expecting.

Moving out is something I've avoided thinking about. To be honest I don't know what's going to happen. You kind of think it'll take care of itself, like you'll get married and get a place together or you'll move for your job or something, but I'll probably end up staying at my Mam's for a good while ... I don't know, you just get all the comforts of home, don't you? I don't have to do my washing or any of that stuff. To be honest I'm a bit spoiled I think, because my parents give me money to go out and help out a lot with university and stuff, so I'm lucky ... We've got a nice house, or at least I think it is, in a good neighbourhood ... [I know that the cost of houses has gone up], but I just haven't considered moving out or getting a house myself ... It's probably going to take ages to save up enough money to get that sorted out. I don't know. You know these things are out there but you try to avoid dealing with them ... I try to do it one thing at a time: get university finished, get a job then start thinking about houses and the future and things ... If I'm honest, I don't think there's any point in worrying about it. You can make plans, but then things change, and life's too short to be constantly worrying about what happens next. Better to just have a good time while you're young.

I got the full loan and I've got a part-time job so it hasn't been that bad money wise. My parents have told me to save some of the loan but it's gone down quite a bit ... I couldn't have really managed without the loan ... it makes sense to take the full amount because it's such low interest, you can put it in another account and make a profit, but I've just ended up spending most of it ... I went on holiday which was quite a lot, and I've taken bits and pieces out to buy things, clothes mainly ... I pay for nights out out of my wages and sometimes I'll get some money off my parents ... I'm not bothered about the loan. My friend Janet has saved nearly all of hers, because she doesn't want to be paying it back for years, but she earns more than me and so she can afford not to dig into it as much ... she works for [mobile phone company – call centre] and does quite a few hours. I think her parents help out a lot as well ... You don't have to pay it back until you start earning about fifteen thousand a year I think it is, so really it's not that much of a worry. If you're earning that kind of money, say if you get a good job once you've graduated, then I wouldn't have thought the repayments would be that much trouble, and if you don't get a good job you don't really have to pay it back ... There's probably people doing degrees now that just plan to get a low-paid job so they don't have to pay the money back ...

[When I graduate] I'll have about nine thousand to repay, which isn't that bad. I've got friends who've got themselves in trouble with credit cards and loans and overdrafts ... They just think they can go out and buy clothes and go on holiday and don't worry about paying it back ... Everyone likes nice things and going out shopping, but I think people who get themselves in that kind of trouble must be mad. Nine thousand is bad enough at my age I think.

Ian

Ian is twenty-one and studying information technology at a northern university. He is also a first-generation student but sees his involvement in higher education very differently, and for him 'getting out' of the town in which he was born is the key motivation, which is linked to a quite consuming desire to get 'one of those well paid city jobs, something to do with banking'. His desire to work in the general area of buying, selling and profit making is fixed and very powerful, and throughout his interviews he showed no interest in or knowledge of any alternatives. His interest in the technicalities or the politics of information technology appeared limited, and his principal ambition was the attainment of a 'top job', looking to move up towards £100,000 per year as quickly as possible.

Ian's desire to leave his hometown and his disparaging description of it indicated virtually no sense of class or community whatsoever, and few lasting friendships. He was resigned to the fact that his childhood friends would simply evaporate into the Diaspora to pursue their own ambitions, and his totally instrumental attitude to education was that it was the platform on which he was about to launch the rest of his life on the current of a lucrative career. Ian is a glowing illustration of the many capable young people who are being driven by a combination of the advanced capitalist imperative of mobility and a driving personal ambition to succeed, leaving behind decaying communities to decay even further (Wilson, 1987, 1996). It appears that he attended university to attain marketable qualifications and nothing else. He is bright, single minded, determined and totally uninterested in social and political awareness, especially the potential social consequences of the actions of millions of young people like him:

> My plan is to take a year out and go travelling, to Australia probably, and then come back and get a job ... At the moment I'm looking at jobs in banking, which is kind of related to my degree course. Ideally I want to go into trading in the city, but I'm not sure how things will work out ... I'm trying to get as good a mark as possible for my degree, although that's not the be all and end all of it. I might try some kind of postgraduate study or just try and get some certificates or diplomas in banking ... [I want that type of job because] it just interests me. Buying and selling and profit making ... [I imagine] it's very stressful but it's worth it because it'd be so rewarding, wouldn't it, doing that kind of job. I'd see it as sort of a challenge, every day at work ... Maybe it's the money you can make that got me interested at first. At first I wanted to design computer games ... The money is rewarding you for the pressure and how good you are at your job ... I think the average [wage], once you've been trained, is about eighty or ninety thousand at some of the top firms, but obviously you can make more than that if you're really good at it ... [another option would be to] take a job perhaps a bit lower down and work your way up to a trader, but that's really what I want to do ... Yes, I think I can [do it] ... I've been to the careers office

and I've got quite a bit of information about who the key employers are and what they're looking for ...

It probably will be [very competitive], because it's a top job. They can pick from thousands of people. You've just got to try your hardest and do everything you can ... I've thought about [what happens if I don't get in], but you've just got to keep trying. If I have to take something else then I will because you've got to live, but I think aiming for the top is a good idea. If you go for a job that's easy to get, then you're probably going to stay there all your life ... There's all kinds of jobs out there if you're willing to work for it. It'll be competitive and the work will be hard but so what? ... At the moment I haven't really thought too much about back ups [jobs if he fails to get a trading job]. I'd probably go for another aspect of banking, and try and stay in that industry ...

I think going to Riverville university might have set me back a bit because there's probably a lot of people who've gone to Oxford and Cambridge who'll be going for the same type of jobs, but when I started I didn't really think to much about it ... Obviously you know there's some universities that are better thought of, but it didn't bother me ... I didn't really want to move away from home ... I'd do it differently now. It'd move away, try to get into a top university and probably take a different degree. I think they'll pay more attention to grades than which university you went to now ... I can't see why I wouldn't be what they're after because I'm a hard worker, or at least I will be if they give me the job ... I don't think accent and all that makes a difference. It's just either you're good or you're not good now ...

[I'm happy to] move down south. I've got a couple of friends who look like getting jobs in London, and Riverville is a dump and I'm sick of it really. There's nothing here, there's no jobs, or at least no proper jobs, paying good money ... I'll miss my family but you can see them on holidays and stuff or they can come and visit, and a lot of my friends will be moving away anyway ...

I like the job itself, but the money is the big thing because getting that type of money lets you do whatever you want to do. Life would just be so much easier if you've got money ... That's why it's worth the effort [trying to get a job in trading] ... My parents aren't rich and there's never been much money around and so a job like this makes everything better because I can help them out and, just, just not have to struggle all the time really ...

It [university] has been a lot of work, that's why I'm taking a year out before I try for a job. I've worked hard with course work and I've been working weekends in a shop in the town ... I owe about nine thousand or I will when I graduate. I've been trying to save as much as I can and I'm going to take out an overdraft so I've got enough money to have a good year away ... I'm not really bothered about the student loan because it'll come out of my wages so you won't really notice it.

Paul

For Ian's friend Paul, who has chosen a much more non-vocational subject with more nebulous career destinations, the future is a mystery that he has tried to block from his mind. Work, he hopes, will turn up when needed. A history student, Paul shows little interest in the study of history itself or the many important lessons that it can supply to today's politico-cultural milieu. He seems to be a victim of what some academic historians disparagingly name the 'kings-and-wars' version of history (see Carr, 1990), uninterested in the social and political aspects of the discipline and far more focused on the general symbolic capital of the degree qualification itself, and the attainment of the much-vaunted 'transferable skills' that will help to secure what he believes might be a 'better job'. However, it seems that at the time of the interview he lacked the driving ambition of his friend Ian to secure a 'top job' in advanced capitalism's 'fast lane':

I'm doing history at Riverville [University]. It's all right. A lot of it's not what I expected. I thought there'd be more stuff on the wars and things like that but a lot of it's been a bit boring and the assessments have been hard. I chose it just because I did OK in the 'A' level ... My Mam didn't go to university or anything, but everyone goes to university now ...

I don't know [if I wanted to come to university]. It just sort of happened. It's just what people do, and it's expected that you'll go to university, especially if you pass your 'A' levels. A lot of the people I go about with were going to go, and my Mam wanted me to go. It's just expected. [At college] they just get you to apply for universities, and when I got my results I was accepted straight away so really it just sort of happened and I didn't think about it too much ... I think at the back of my mind I was thinking, I don't want to get a job. Going to university gives you three years extra, and at the end of it you should be able to get a better job so really it probably makes sense ... Some of my mates who went off and got jobs instead are working full-time now and I'm completely skint compared with them and it makes you wonder why you bothered ... I suppose you get a better job because you've got a degree, I don't know ... Now though I'm skint ... I've haven't got any money to go out and I get the full grant. I've spent most of it. My Mam doesn't know. She thinks I'm only getting a bit ... I just thought there's no point in telling her because she'll give me a hard time about going out and things like that.

I haven't done very well with assessments but I should finish the degree OK ... [Then] I'll start looking for a job. I haven't thought about it. It's like there's no point in worrying about that kind of thing until it happens and you've got to go and get a job. I'll just end up doing something in an office I suppose ... I'm not bothered ... Obviously I'd like a well-paid job, but you can't tell what's going to happen ... It's a bit depressing [thinking about getting a job]. I've done some part-time stuff in shops and that but I've always hated it. I'd rather be skint than do one of those jobs because it's just so boring it drives you mental ... I get a bit of money off my Dad and some off my Mam but not much ... I can use computers so I might try for something like that, or maybe something in the pub trade. Being a publican or a licensee or whatever is quite well paid I think and that's something that interests me ... I don't know [how my degree will help with these jobs]. It's just something to impress employers isn't it? It's not like most people who do degrees are using the stuff they did when they get a job, it's just trying to get a head start over the people who haven't got one really ...

To me there's just no sense in trying to plan stuff because you could get hit by a bus tomorrow. Just, you know, when you finish [university], have a look about and see what's available and what you fancy. That's what I'm planning to do.

The quotes we have selected in this chapter typified the whole group of more than forty respondents, and the same values and aspirations permeated the group's attitudes to heterosexual relations, friendships and education. Personal ambitions and instrumentalism were dominant throughout, and in an intellectual age where the ability of grand ideologies and economic forces to determine the lives of individuals has been firmly refuted (see Mouzelis, 1995), our data suggested that the fundamental principles of neo-liberal ideology were resplendent across the social landscape and embedded very deeply in mainstream youth culture. Rather than 'narratives of dissent' and 'resistance in the interstices', amongst the majority of our respondents we found dominant culturo-economic principles at the very heart of attitudes, ideas and practices, with a virtually total absence of any alternative way of thinking, a lack of any sense of communal attachment or social injustice, and a seemingly unbroken correspondence between advanced capitalism's macro-economic logic and the desires and aspirations of young individuals. Nowhere could we find anything that looked remotely like an 'oppositional reading' (see Fiske, 1993), or for that matter even a 'negotiated reading' (see Hall, 1980), of any aspect of advanced capitalism.

The classical liberal principle of minimally constrained competitive individualism has been reinstalled at the heart of consumer capitalism's culturally driven economic engine. Popular culture and educational institutions are now in the advanced stages of recruitment into the business of trimming thoughts and practices down to functional essentials and energizing the desire for personal success and hedonistic rewards. Despite ubiquitous feelings of insecurity and anxiety, the young people we interviewed seem to be quite well advanced in the process of adapting emotionally and cognitively to the neo-liberal norm of atomized individualism. However, although their responses to the task of confronting socio-economic insecurity in isolation seemed to contain contradictory elements ranging from fatalism to burning personal ambition, they all lacked a detailed knowledge of the risks and injustices inherent in the free-market economy, a knowledge that might inform ideas and attitudes more precisely. They are uncomfortable and slightly afraid, but precisely of what, beyond a vague feeling of possibly 'falling' at some time in the future (see Taylor, 1999), they are uncertain. At this stage there is certainly enough evidence to suggest that, rather than creating opportunities for freedom and creative forms of self-identity, or being powerless to prevent the inevitable oppositional tendencies from growing in the interstices of its fragmenting structure, advanced capitalism's prevailing ideologies and institutions have quite successfully converged around the task of preparing most young people for its radically altered functions. Rather than acting as comforting and inspiring 'finishing' stages in a general process of socialization, intellectual-emotional development and transition into adulthood, the cultural institutions of relationship formation and higher education are now anxiety-inducing experiences that represent nothing more than the first steps on a risky journey to a mythological place of personal success and hedonistic rewards. If indeed it was Margaret Thatcher's ambition to move beyond economic change in the 1980s and 'touch the soul' of the British people, it seems that she has enjoyed a good deal of success.

-4-

Young People, the Culture Industry and the Night-time Economy

For much of the twentieth century the exploitative and alienating nature of waged labour in the era of monopoly capitalism tended to dominate critical social analyses of industrial capitalist Britain. Post-war sociology, from both revolutionary Marxist and liberal-reformist perspectives, continued to focus on the reproduction of the unjust social system and the degradation of human experience in a society dominated by the unrelenting logical demands of capital accumulation (see Braverman, 1974; Gorz, 1982). However, as the capitalist project progressed through the twentieth century, new technological developments allowed employers to cut back on the huge costs of human labour by reducing the ranks of the massed industrial workforce (see Blauner, 1964). Machines were more powerful, more skilled and more reliable, they possessed a less abstract economic worth and in the long run were far cheaper than maintaining an increasingly militant and cohesive industrial workforce (Blauner, 1964; see also Gallie, 1978). Marx portrayed these new machines and productive methods as the enemies of the industrial worker, denying industrial employment to those conditioned to rely upon this form of economic engagement in a world beholden to the wage form (see Mallet, 1975). Technology provided only a partial liberation from hard physical labour for the industrial worker, and this was scant recompense for a significant growth in competition within shrinking industrial labour markets and the dark cloud of unemployment that constantly loomed above them.

Combining with forces of economic globalization, the onward march of these new technologies contributed to the gradual decline of heavy industry during the 1970s, and its virtual extinction during the 1980s, and thus helped to usher in an age of post-industrial employment increasingly reliant on 'innovation' and 'talent' rather than the manual power of the workforce upon which modern Britain was built. This gradual decline of labour-intensive production methods impacted significantly upon the working classes' experience of industrial labour, but also contributed to the emergence of distinct forms of leisure experience, seemingly divorced from the relentless demands of waged labour. While it would be a gross simplification to suggest that leisure as a cultural and economic sphere was created by the diminishing needs of industrial labour, in advanced capitalism's culturally driven consumer phase the market began to infiltrate cultural dimensions of life

71

that had remained to some extent separate and relatively autonomous. What it meant to be working class continued to be negotiated in accordance with the centrality of work (see Charlesworth, 2000), but the creation of modern culture industries produced new forms of economic relationships that had less to do with labour power and more to do with spending power and the manipulation of 'lifestyle' tastes (Chaney, 1993).

From the mid-1970s sociology began to reflect the profound upturn in the globalization of the capitalist economy and the increasing importance of consumption. As theorists working from a variety of backgrounds observed (Lasch, 1979; Beck, 1992; Chaney, 1993; Bauman, 1998; Adorno, 2002), consumerism's ever-expanding and anarchic commercial media apparatus began to cultivate cultural forms that were either quite novel or intensified variants of traditional forms. Thus, the following decades were characterized by a cultural paradox in which what seemed to be burgeoning opportunities for freedom of expression and identity formation (see Gibbins and Reimer, 1999; Ray and Sayer, 1999) emerged alongside the expansion and consolidation of the means to pump Americanized neo-liberal ideology into the population – especially the younger elements – faster than ever (Chomsky, 1999, 2003).

Sociology took a distinctive 'cultural turn' in the 1980s (Chaney, 1993; Ray and Sayer, 1999). To neo-Marxists influenced by the cultural analyses of seminal thinkers such as Gramsci (2000), Adorno (2002), Lefebvre (2000) and others, this reflected the increased ability of neo-capitalism to exert its mass deception on populations and engineer consensus by means of hegemonic cultural domination and control (see Hall et al., 1978; Hall, 1980), or, in a more extreme version, disconnect individuals from reality altogether and absorb them in a hyper-real semiological system from which there is no escape apart from the eventual collapse of the system itself (Baudrillard, 1983). On the other hand, other liberal humanist and post-modernist thinkers emphasized the 'loosening up' of the rigid structures of industrial modernity and the creation of increased opportunities for dissent and opposition. Neo-liberal thinkers joined the debate by continuing to argue with great vigour that each phase of liberal-capitalist development had made possible increased opportunities for individual freedom, prosperity and identity construction, and this latest phase was the delicious icing on the cake. However, as the debates in the 'cultural turn' raged (see Ray and Sayer, 1999; Cieslik and Pollock, 2002), the underlying logic of capitalist production was mutating rapidly and impacting on culture and identity in ways that had been dismissed by the catch-all pejorative 'economic reductionism', a critical term that was itself far cruder than many of the sophisticated historical materialist ideas that had been hatched in the attempt to understand the ways in which the developing technological forces of production in capitalism's economic base directly affected both social relations of production and cultural forms in its superstructure.

In the midst of these debates in the 1980s, some thinkers realized that as the productive capacities of post-war consumer capitalism transcended basic needs it became driven increasingly by manufactured images and desires that added economic value to objects, and that the need to colonize culture at home was as vital to the project of consistent economic growth as the expansion of markets abroad (see Bourdieu, 1984). Alongside the factory robot, many of the principal technologies of the post-war economy – colour television, the PC, the compact disk and so on – were indeed developed not only to process and communicate information but also to lubricate the communication of styles and images in an economy that was coming to rely almost exclusively on rapid changes in fashion, lifestyle and identity. In other words, the forces of production were now being developed chiefly to enhance the communication of the proliferating cultural styles that were required to accelerate and expand the circulation of commodities. Whilst even the most committed Marxists, such as Gramsci and Althusser, admitted that culture and intellectual life had always been relatively autonomous – at least potentially – this post-war period was unique in that mass consumer culture and the needs of the capitalist economy had become inextricably linked, and the economy was deploying its massive resources to invade and colonize every aspect of human life. The organic intellectualism that had driven some of the working classes as enthusiastic autodidacts to the libraries, workers' educational associations, political meetings and new educational institutions of the nineteenth and twentieth centuries (Rose, 2002) was either diluted in the post-war period by liberal individualist conceptions of radicalism or overwhelmed by a riptide of consumer imagery that colonized the imagination and altered the concepts of freedom and identity to echo the needs of consumer capitalism. Some writers argue that organic, non-colonized 'interstices' remain as a perennial source of autopoeitic 'resistance' (see Chapter 1). Without the essentially inorganic practices of education, politicization and organization, we remain unconvinced.

If working-class women were the essential units of reproduction in capitalism's industrial-imperial heyday, proletarian men vastly outnumbered women as the essential units of the production that drove the industrial capitalist economy forward, and the essential units of organized violence that equipped capitalist states to become colonizing imperialists and further the interests of capitalist elites. The nature of productive and military work in this fundamental economic function was in many cases brutal and dehumanizing (Gorz, 1982), but it was deemed essential to the expansion of an industrial system that, during the nineteenth century, secured for Britain a central position in the world's unstable politico-economic order. On Britain's own shores it produced the most pronounced class system in Europe, which would remain a key feature of British economic and social life for years to come (Byrne, 1989; Milner, 1999). The emergence of communities based around specific industrial concerns, coupled with the powerful ideological dominance of the capitalist class, created a social world for the working classes grounded in the centrality of paid employment, the expectation and acceptance of exploitation, and the drudgery of the working week (see Bourke, 1994; Charlesworth, 2000). Those born into the working class not only accepted the dominance of capitalist production and their subservient position within it, but learned to embrace actively their roles as workers and providers (Willis, 1977; Winlow, 2001), creating durable forms of social structure and class-based culture that patterned working-class life for much of the twentieth century (Bourdieu and Passeron, 1977; Bourdieu, 1984).

Human agency and organic intellectualism were notable features of everyday life (Williams, 1961, 1979; Rose, 2002) but, in the main, cultural practices operated within the parameters set by the economic and social system. It is clear that the inter-subjective constitution of meaning in numerous small groups, along with countless acts of individual decision making, played important roles in shaping biographies, but the pervasive influence of prevailing hegemony, occupational imperatives and the cultures of class-based micro-communities set the context. Some commentators (see for example, Moorhouse, 1989) have suggested that analyses of industrial society that focus on the importance of economic relationships and the perceived deprivations of life for industrial workers have underplayed the ability of actors to construct alternate meanings and find contentment in industrial labour, but it strikes us that to focus on anything other than the economic foundation of working life under industrial capitalism serves only to marginalize what should still be the central focus of sociological analyses of modern British society. Certainly, industrial workers could find a range of consolations within the workplace; work could be fun (Roberts, 1993) and not necessarily as strenuous as some might assume (Mars, 1982); friendships and collective sentiments provided a sense of belonging (Dennis et al., 1969), and work often provided a range of social connections that grounded individuals within locality and community (Bourdieu and Passeron, 1977; Bourdieu, 1984). Yet, work remained central to working-class life and necessity propelled the industrial worker back into work the next day, and in doing so constructed biographical paths for the working classes that had little to do with individually or inter-subjectively ascribed meaning and everything to do with the demands of the capitalist economy. In a competitive and insecure labour market, the physical, cognitive and emotional requirements of labour loomed large in the constitution of very durable identities and *habitus*, bringing the external influences of economy and ideology into every individual decision and inter-subjective conference. What some might see as the failures of individuals to assert their authentic selves could also be seen as the pressure exerted by the 'dull compunction' of labour, aided by the prevailing cultural hegemony, overwhelming the fragile autonomy of the psyche and the micro-community.

The Function of Leisure

+p 110

The combination of consumer capitalism and liberal democracy was, according to its supporters (see Fukuyama, 1992), supposed to free the working classes from the highly restricted work-based identities and *habitus* that populated the landscape of capitalism's industrial-imperial phase. However, commentators such as Clark and Critcher (1985) identified the myth of freedom that permeates both public and academic conceptions of leisure. The myth informs us that leisure is no longer a limited concession but now a reward, an end in itself that has replaced survival as the purpose of work, a freeform sphere of expansive luxury that can respond very quickly to almost everyone's autonomous and creative desires. But, as we shall see, underlying this putative road to Nirvana is a broad range of practical and ideological leisure functions that actively reproduce consumer capitalist hegemony, increase market demand and revive relations of exploitation, insecurity and subservience that had to some extent been rolled back by organized working-class activism in the twentieth century. Now that leisure no longer fulfils the mere function of periodic refreshment but has become a crucial profit-making cog in consumer capitalism's machine, we must consider the possibility that it actually offers little more potential freedom and creativity – possibly even less – than it did in capitalism's industrial heyday.

Historical studies have tended to return repeatedly to what we might call the two flagstones of working-class leisure: sport and drinking (see for example, Bailey, 1987; Reiss, 1989; Blackshaw, 2003; Metcalf, 2005). These masculine leisure options, of course, have tended to overshadow feminine forms, which, during the 'golden years' of post-war capitalism, were largely restricted to community and household (Young and Willmott, 1961; Goldthorpe, 1980). For many industrial employees, drinking with work colleagues tended to occupy a sizable chunk of the hallowed downtime (see for example, Gill, 1977; Roberts, 1993; Bourke, 1994). The bonding and reaffirmation of both masculine and class forms that occurred in and around pubs – a key site for the reproduction of working-class codes and *habitus* – should not be divorced from commercial leisure's more 'serious' capital-accumulating and employment dimensions (Rojek, 1989: 95). In industrialism's ghostly landscapes, the ribald voices of men in bars echo in the memory just as loudly as the jackhammer and the goods train. Rather, the reproduction of the capitalist social system was the soil in which the both the general species of leisure and work *and* the vivid floral foreground of inter-subjective meanings evolved. The homology between economic imperatives, the class structure and cultural meanings represented by the image of working-class male excess in the shadow of the factory suggests capitalism's ability to influence and structure all dimensions of the lifeworld.

Whilst many critical readings of economic and social relations during this period tend to imply a dour, cheerless and mechanical working-class *habitus*, in fact joy, humour and excitement were everyday features of working-class culture (see Hobbs, 1988; Charlesworth, 2000). Not all work was brutal and oppressive, and conditions improved during the twentieth century alongside increasing amounts of time set aside for leisure (see Clark and Critcher, 1985). However, this does not mean that the forms of leisure that evolved were the products of individual creativity, freedom and choice – autonomous creations that reflect the sanctity of the human spirit or the ability of exploited social groups to 'resist'. It is just as likely that the formally durable yet practically adaptable working-class *habitus* evolved a feel for forms of work and commercialized leisure that were established and reproduced by the demands of the capitalist economy (Bourdieu, 1977, 1990). English football, for instance, in the form of professional teams performing in front of large crowds of paying spectators, was not the product of working-class choice – the precursor to football had for centuries been a communal game – but rather the product of legal and economic intervention and modification in the interests of maintaining public order and finding new ways to generate profit (Delves, 1981; see also Armstrong, 1998).

All forms of drunkenness, abandon and rough physical activity within the industrial working classes have been variously portrayed as pathological products of powerlessness and alienation or ineradicable primitive cultural traits necessitating various forms of control and refinement (see Fiske, 1991). The impact of excessive male 'hedonism' upon the family unit has also been highlighted (Bourke, 1994), as has the role of drinking in the establishment and reproduction of class-based masculine codes (Winlow, 2001; Blackshaw, 2003). Yet, the fun and excitement experienced by participants are rarely discussed. Our interpretation of working-class life suggests that the *habitus* of the industrial working classes, which was a durable suite of affects containing orientations towards fun, communality, excess, physical fortitude, restricted mental focus and many other human qualities, was grounded in economic functions that were not chosen but forced upon the multitude of cultural groups that came together during the urbanization process. For our purposes here, the two most crucial functions were the expansion of opportunities to generate profit from all human activities and the maintenance of public order in a way that secured property rights and reduced interpersonal violence in order to facilitate the safe circulation of commodities; an economically driven *pseudo-pacification process* (see Hall, 2000; Hall and Winlow, 2005).

As Elias and Dunning (1986) have stressed, the evolving nature of both work and leisure served to refine and civilize aspects of working-class life (see also Dunning et al., 1988), although we must stress here that refined and civilized sensibilities were very probably not ends in themselves but means of pacifying and stabilizing competitive market economies (Hall and Winlow, 2005). The structural bedrock of these processes suggests the need for a strong critique of the role of the economy in crafting social forms, but most working-class individuals experienced incrementally increasing forms of pleasure, revelling in the opportunities for novelty and excitement offered by the leisure industry as it developed throughout the twentieth century. The post-war growth of the media and the arrival of regular national television broadcasts further moulded the supposedly unstructured and autonomous world of leisure, as millions tuned in to be entertained and distracted by the revolving spectacle of news, drama and pop culture (Mattelart, 1980; Tomlinson, 1991; Louw, 2001). During the post-war period, sitting in front of the television soon became by far the most common leisure pastime (see Eagleton, 1991), prompting the further development of modern critical theory that stressed the 'hegemonic' ability of elites to manipulate consciousness, maintain the status quo and reproduce faith in the capitalist system (see Poulantzas, 1978; Williams, 1979). The upshot of decades of study is that whereas the audiences of national television are not the entirely passive drones that various structuralist thinkers once suggested (see Fiske, 1987; Gray, 1992), the ability of media forms to influence popular opinion and identity remains a largely uncontested fact of modern sociology and media studies.

As Clark and Critcher (1985) have suggested, the respite that leisure provided for the industrial workforce actively aided the goals of the global economy by returning them to the shop floor 're-charged' and relatively secure in the belief that their lives were not simply a constant monotony of work and rest. Leisure essentially offered a 'time out of time' (Presdee, 2000: 33), a break from all the disappointments and frustrations of everyday life, where all the rich symbolism of the Carnival could be re-enacted. Presdee (2000), however, perhaps does not stress quite hard enough that the volatile symbolic inversion in the traditional Carnival, and the dangerous political undercurrent that it represented, was swiftly domesticated and commercialized throughout the capitalist period. Burgeoning leisure pursuits were strictly regulated and permeated by formal and informal rules to the extent that they became crucial supports for the civilizing process (Holt, 1989). As the night-time economy cut loose from its moorings in traditional before-midnight drinking and dance-hall culture (see Clark and Critcher, 1985) mimicking the previously exclusive metropolitan 'night-life' scene to expand rapidly throughout the 1980s and 1990s (see Chatterton and Hollands, 2003; Hobbs et al., 2003), the marketing industry successfully hyped this new venture by juxtaposing the image of a riotous and unrestrained night-life with the mundane world of work and the repressive regimentation of daylight comportment. This powerful marketing strategy seduced the massed ranks of youthful weekend hedonists, who, as we explained in Chapter 2, had become disassociated from modernist forms of work culture and community and had adopted increasingly individualized and instrumental approaches to numerous aspects of their lives.

The growth of leisure promulgated the belief that happiness was within reach in that realm beyond the magic portal, a taste of the heavenly afterlife that could be bought and experienced in byte-sized instalments. Thus the intensified exploitation, alienation and drudgery that many felt whilst working in the new casualized labour market (Cappelli, 1997; Bauman, 1999), along with the pressured existence in the competitive field of higher education (Bok, 2003; Stevens, 2004), would be easier to bear if the weekend held the promise of enjoyment and self-realization. However, as commercialized leisure culture developed over the final third of the twentieth century it ate away the traditional world of autonomous private leisure, and the numerous private clubs that had grown around pursuits that ranged from cycling to sado-masochism were absorbed by the commercial sector. As the profit motive spread throughout mass culture and increasingly organized 'free time', the gratification of desire through consumerism became a central tenet of the modern world (see Bauman, 2001), despite the fact that the 'ultimate hedonistic experience' – that, thanks to the marketing hype, had replaced the simple, diverse and concrete pleasures of traditional leisure pursuits – was illusory. The perpetuation of the myth of ultimate gratification through consumption had become the customary business strategy of the modern culture industries (see Horkheimer and Adorno, 1972), and the often eccentric diversity and autonomy present in traditional leisure forms have been discarded in favour of the formulaic spectacle that the mass audience craves and the principle of capital accumulation demands (Horkheimer and Adorno, 1972; see also Debord, 1998; Adorno, 2002).

Leisure is now inextricably connected to spending money, and lots of it. The post-industrial economy, with its declining reliance on the actual physical labour that could be bought but never entirely owned, manufactured or controlled, has now ushered the workforce onto a domesticating and energy-draining treadmill of symbol-driven economic and cultural life, while simultaneously constructing a myth of self-determination and meritocracy, which has been propagated resolutely and effectively by the neo-liberal hegemony that now dominates the political stage. Contemporary workers are now exploited in all spheres of work and manipulated in all spheres of leisure, as their every waking moment is experienced in direct relation to the demands of the consumer economy. As the actual production of tangible goods in Britain slowed to a trickle during the 1990s, the increasing importance of the service industry led the increasingly nervous elite political classes to question whether we could survive as a society by simply selling services and symbols to each other (Gray, 1998). That remains to be seen but, in the meantime, while manufacturing productivity and its attendant social relationships have declined in importance in the post-industrial economy, which could be interpreted as a relaxation of pressure, the hand of the economy can be discerned invading every sphere of social life, exerting the pressure to consume where before it had never been felt.

Neo-liberal political orthodoxy bound up all of these processes in a dogma of liberty, opportunity and gratification, where the growth of commercialized leisure was presented as a creative world in which hedonistic pleasure and self-discovery could be combined legitimately and often dialectically (where one meets what one has not experienced and turns into a synthesis of the two), and the staggering array of consumer items produced by the onward march of technology were presented to the public as the new tools of self-definition on the beautiful journey – with the uncertain destination – out of modernist drudgery and repression. Consumerism placed an almost dreamlike hue over everyday life, and we seemed to levitate above the wreckage as the growing cult of hyper-individualism and the process of social fragmentation battered away at traditional forms of social capital. In the midst of this, consumerism's incessantly probing and suffocating marketing industry imbued manufactured objects with an almost mystical lifestyle symbolism, to the extent that the acquisition of these objects – along with the cultural competence demonstrated in choosing and displaying them – became essential building blocks in the construction of status, identity and self-worth. As celebrity and extreme wealth defined the only social hierarchy of universal significance under market capitalism, the perpetual pressure to consume and discard in ways similar to these wealthy celebrities (or even the icons of the allegedly oppositional 'alternative' styles) to some became all-encompassing. Constant immersion in the cultural 'logic of practice' (Bourdieu, 1990) in this totalizing field of power set the feelings, tastes, dispositions and languages that were necessary to survive or succeed within it, constituting the durable *habitus* of millions of young consumers.

Freedom increasingly meant the freedom to shop. Shopping increasingly meant the freedom to be (Morris, 1993). The imagery on the TV, with varying degrees of subtlety, told the viewer that to buy was to be included, to be valuable, to be living life on one's own terms. Your house could be literally 'invaded' (see for example the BBC show, *Home Invaders*, or the more popular *Changing Rooms*) by self-declared style gurus who would condemn your interior decorating skills and simultaneously propel the masses towards the nearest DIY store. We were told, brutally, *What Not to Wear*, as if the 'right' clothing instantly signified intrinsic worth. Travel was constructed as a kind of experiential nirvana, a spiritual journey of philosophical self-discovery, without which the construction of the truly rounded being could not be accomplished. Incorporated in this general commodification of leisure life were a number of media trends, which eroded what inclusivity and security had been allowed to flourish in modern industrial societies (see Presdee, 2000), selectively demolishing or retaining and intensifying the moral agendas of modern media narratives according to the dictates of neo-liberalism, and spreading energizing waves of anxiety and self-interest amongst the population, the significance of which has yet to be fully analysed and explained by social science.

As if the colonization of the private world wasn't enough, the staggering growth of personal debt attests to the seductive power and unavoidability of active involvement in consumerism (British household debt is now estimated at £1050 billion –

Branaghan 2005). The power of the message is such that the traditional Bohemian wish to stand on the outskirts sniggering like Diogenes at the drones who have been sucked into the vortex of rampant consumption is increasingly impossible. Diogenes found a free tree to sleep under, and his anarchic eccentricity was considered enlightening and amusing, neither of which are possible today. Surviving socially now involves a constant, informed display of cultural knowledge, and all the cultural trends that one is supposed to be knowledgeable about are increasingly defined by the sign-value and exchange-value of the market. Thus, as we progressed through the later half of the twentieth-century, leisure joined all other cultural forms to constitute a manufactured world of relaxation and excitement, no longer functioning simply to rejuvenate jaded employees, but rather layering itself over the top of industrialism and service work (see Baudrillard, 1993) as the dominant form of economic engagement. As the dawning of the twenty-first century prompted some to question the commercialization of football, the Olympic games and so on, a broader trend could be discerned within contemporary social life: not simply the commercialization of sport or even leisure, but the commercialization of all social life.

Consuming Leisure

> The culture industry perpetually cheats its consumers of what it perpetually promises. The promissory note which, with its plots and staging, it draws on pleasure is endlessly prolonged; the promise, which is actually all the spectacle consists of, is illusory; all it actually confirms is that the real point will never be reached, that the diner must be satisfied with the menu. (Horkheimer and Adorno, 1972: 139)

Although definitions of leisure remain contested (see Rojek, 1989), throughout the era of its commercialization it came to be regarded as the site of personal pleasure and happiness. Yet, as Rojek (1985) has suggested, the idea that leisure is inherently liberating may be well off the mark. The prevailing cultural orthodoxy suggested that leisure delivered fulfilment, relaxation, contentment and even self exploration, yet leisure and its ideological connection to liberty and pleasure appear to have been a component part in a complex process that has gradually produced an increasingly divided and polarized contemporary social life, which we will address in more detail later. Whilst the ideological reading of 'leisure as potential liberty' seemed to be accepted by the bulk of the population and affirmed by many libertarian and post-modernist commentators (for example, Bennett, 2000, 2001), some Marxists (see Clark and Critcher, 1985) positioned leisure as an elaborate compensation for the arduous demands of capitalist employment. Others (see for example, Brohm 1978) have argued that it was expanded and commercialized by the bourgeois class as a distraction to prevent the growth of class consciousness, thus diverting energies that would otherwise have been focused on rectifying the fundamental inequities of life under the capitalist system.

Much remains to be said about the form and function of leisure in both the industrial and consumer phases of capitalism, but a new generation of left-humanist writers abandoned the traditional critical perspective and portrayed working-class leisure cultures as a reservoir of radical styles indicating cultural awareness and resistance against the tyrannies of capitalism (see Hebdige, 1979; Fiske, 1991). Within the sphere of leisure, working-class youths could allegedly produce autonomous forms of meaning and understanding in opposition to the 'legislated mainstream' (De Certeau, 2002). Here they could remould the meaning of style, re-contextualize consumption and, in a process of bricolage where they re-worked the meanings of consumer objects, create new forms of culture and lifestyle on their own terms (see also Widdicombe and Wooffitt, 1994). The development of distinctive forms of youth sub-cultures seemed to validate the suggestion that young working-class people were not the passive pawns of capitalism that some structural forms of analysis seemed to indicate. Young people, we were told in sociological works too numerous to mention, had access to cultural forms of self-definition that could not be depleted by reliance upon paid employment or appropriated by the developing consumer market. By adopting distinct forms of style, young people resisted being ushered onto capitalism's treadmill. They could communicate something about themselves to others of a like mind and simultaneously distance themselves from the status quo and the dominant meaning system. These processes are often portrayed as causing alarm within mainstream adult culture, prompting a range of punitive responses, and whilst these young people remained very much a part of capitalist society, the constant bubbling of resistance and creativity seemed to indicate that a light still burned within the downtrodden working classes.

This kind of politicized sub-cultural analysis remains popular to this day (see Redhead et al., 1997). There is obviously something intrinsically appealing about the idea that in youth culture a persistent wellspring of resistance continues to reproduce the youthful *condotierres* that can challenge such a dauntingly totalizing system in an era when all traditional, organized attempts to resist it appear to have failed. To some, this 'bottom-up' view of cultural constitution relies on the political significance of the constant reworking of style and symbolism within distinct forms of youth culture. The generation of new forms of music, new ways of wearing clothes and new forms of expressive codes indicate the ability of 'the street' to innovate and resist, to remain fleet of foot and avoid being crushed by the ponderous boots of the capitalist Goliath, and left idealists especially appear taken with the notion that some suppositious 'spirit' of working-class youth will forever remain anarchic, unbridled and potentially transformative. In some cases this has involved the active celebration of developing forms of youth culture (Redhead,

1993), while others have accentuated cultural resistance as an indication that the capitalist project remains far from secure, and the ability of consumer capitalism and neo-liberal ideology to crush resistant voices from the interstices has been overstated (see Ferrell, 1996, 2001; Stanley, 1996).

However, our research findings indicate that consumerism has become an important component in the active constitution of youth leisure cultures and identities. As we shall see, our focus on the centrality of weekend nightlife and circuit drinking indicates that consumption and its associated imagery is at the very top of a hierarchy of youth cultural concerns, and tends to suggest that although the maintenance of superficial differences between individuals remains important, the vast majority of young people are successfully manipulated into engaging actively and enthusiastically with consumerism's principle dynamic of rapidly changing fashion, in order to establish a sense of identity and social inclusion (Bauman, 2001). Throughout the analysis of our data, it became apparent that many of our respondents believed that they played an active role in the creation of youthful forms of style and individuality, yet at the same time constantly expressing the pressure they felt to fit into lifestyles based on the acquisition and competent display of consumer symbols. A number of respondents, although clearly accepting the unavoidability of and devotion to consumerism, saw themselves as negotiating a path through the pressurized world of ornamental culture (Faludi, 1999). They saw themselves as *bricoleurs* (Hebdige, 1979), essentially picking through the offerings of consumerism with a keen and critical eye, accepting the significance of some goods and rejecting others. They would not become devoid of critical reasoning and simply accept the symbolism of high fashion as meaningful and worthwhile. Many were quick to highlight that people they knew fitted into this category, simply buying what they were told to by the sinecured style deities of popular culture, yet none of our respondents placed themselves in this category; fashion slavery was always something that afflicted the other and not the self, despite the fact that both groups were spending the bulk of their incomes buying manufactured goods. They believed they possessed the ability to decide, to create an identity by choice, self-definition and agentic action within the broad field of consumerism, and therefore talked up their ability to create an individual identity and influence currents within youth culture. As Justin comments:

[I'm into] Hip-Hop, since I was at school really. I don't know [what drew me to it]. Just the style of it and that, just the music. I started buying CDs and then I got into the vinyl side of things because I started getting interested in DJing … I think it changed me gradually because I just used to be one of the beer boys, down the town, and then you start going to particular clubs and stuff, and you just pick it up … Just the clothes and everything, you don't even think about it … I'm not bothered about all that fashion stuff, to me it's just stupid. You see all these people and all they care about is clothes … No, I'm not [like that] … I pick clothes based on what I like not on what society says I should wear ... The clothes I wear just go along with the music and what I'm about ... They don't tell you to wear these clothes, you just want to, that's just what you end up liking isn't it?

Emma suggests:

[I like] just pop music really, dance music, stuff like that ... I think I pick the clothes I like. I just go shopping and see things that I like and things I think will go with other things I've got ... [I don't think I'm] influenced that much by magazines and that kind of thing. I mean, I might sometimes pick up ideas, but it's not like I rush out and buy things because I've seen them on TV or whatever. It's just up to the individual ... you just end up working out your own style for yourself ... You don't think about it much, it just sort of happens ... I'd say I'm quite fashionable. I don't pay much attention to it but it just happens. Clothes are just about who you are really.

Ray observes:

I mean ideally you want to be wearing all the best gear, if money was no object. You'd have a Rolex watch, Stone Island, Jill Sander, the lot ... It's the quality, isn't it? If you've got the money why would you want to be wearing just boring high street gear? ... It's just flash isn't it? That's just the kind of stuff I'd want to be wearing ... I don't know why it is, it's just the kind of stuff I'm into, the stuff I'd wear. If you can get the money together to get something top class, it's just like a boost really, you feel better about yourself.

Today, the persistent and paradoxical demands of individualism and belonging, the unstable realm between liberty and community that we all inhabit, appear to promote active involvement in consumerism, and many of our respondents voiced the belief that they felt a degree of pressure to both 'fit in' and 'stick out' (see Miles et al, 1998). Consumerism, to them, was not simply a part of life that could be avoided or re-worked freely according to individual needs. Consumerism was complex and fraught with difficulties and dangers, and it seemed to draw out deep feelings of insecurity in many of our respondents. Wearing even the most popular designer labels, for example, did not immediately bestow status, and could in fact cause the young person to be a target of sly mocking. Donna believes:

You want to look fashionable I suppose, but you don't want to look like a fashion victim. It's sort of, looking good without trying to look good if you know what I mean.

I'd never wear something that was, like, obviously a designer label. I don't agree with buying things just because of what's written on them. It's a bit naff really, it's like saying 'look at me, I can afford D&G', or 'I'm really fashionable', but it just isn't I don't think. It's more like saying 'I can't think for myself'.

The meaning of a designer label, even one that on the surface of things can produce significant esteem within the general consumer culture, can be transformed in the increasingly fluid contexts of youthful consumer culture; but not necessarily in a positive way that indicates freedom and creativity. Our respondents felt pressure to be conversant with the latest fads and try to remain abreast of the contextual meanings that can be applied to such overt forms of signification. Our research appears to indicate that young people must not only be aware of mainstream cultural meanings that are applied to consumer signs, but also be reflexive enough to constantly rework the presentation of self in relation to context and audience. High fashion, in certain bars and with certain people, was in some cases anything but, as the meanings applied to consumer signs constantly changed trajectory. In some cases irony seemed to be the order of the day, as people sought to mix high fashion items with cheap high-street accessories or second-hand goods picked up in charity shops or from local markets. As the meaning of specific forms of consumer items remained in virtually constant motion, young people to a certain extent were forced to take chances and guess, and as a result the overwhelming message that came from our respondents was that consumerism produced risks and anxieties that weighed heavily upon their minds as the pressure to appear competent impacted directly upon identity and self-identity. Some could afford to make the odd mistake, as their place within friendship networks had been previously solidified, whereas others placed crucial importance upon always looking good, maintaining an adroit grasp of culture and appearing constantly on the fringes of mainstream fashion and culture. While it would be a slight overstatement to suggest that all of our respondents had elevated fashion and overt consumerism to a paramount importance within their daily lives, all appeared to feel significant pressure to play out the roles demanded by the market and to accept the social values of consumerism. These young people seem to have been drawn into a Saussurian world of social division and the endless dynamic fragmentation of negative meaning, an anxious world in which one desperately requires a never-ending procession of fashion signifiers simply to be who others are not, where one can be differentiated from others from a distance, without any intimate knowledge of distinguishing characteristics. Joanne comments:

> I like to be a bit daring with the things I wear when I go out, but you've always got that doubt about what people are going to think. You don't want to look like you just crave the attention, you don't want to look like someone who's completely into themselves, but you want people to look, just so you stick out a little bit … I've seen my friends try something new, and the others can just be unmerciful, you know, making fun and that.

The tools at their disposal to actively craft innovative cultural forms and differentiate themselves from the sea of others who populate this anxiety-laden cultural terrain are those offered by consumerism and the culture industries, and while this has been the case for some time, actual innovation, for this group at least, usually means voracious consumerism and immersion in popular culture. Whilst the specific meanings of consumer items changed in time, consumerism remained omnipresent in their everyday lives. Sarah suggests:

> What I do is just see what I fancy and go with that … I listen to a lot of music, and I suppose you could say that that has something to do with it, but you just don't know. It just happens. I'm not that bothered about being the first to get certain fashions. You just kind of buy stuff you like when you've got the money.

The consumer market has now become so diverse and the cultural trends created by the market display such a multiplicity of ever changing meanings that what might appear to be trends of disassociation might be anything but. The message that comes from the interview data is that many young people appear to cling on to the idea that they are not being manipulated by the culture industries and they independently possess the power to change their identities by utilizing individual consumer signs. Yet this strong desire to presume independence from the dominant means of identity might well indicate an understandable desire to believe that the individual exerts a significant degree of control over the active display of identity when, in fact, that control may not exist. Instead, individual forms of self-determination, and the post-modern idea of the 'self-created persona' may be a powerful mirage that has long been part of the capitalist project.

Some of our respondents, for example, highlighted the shifting meanings of consumer products, and portrayed themselves as independent style critics with the ability and means to create innovative fashion trends that worked in virtual opposition to the dominance of the mainstream culture industries. However, the idea of a kind of anti-fashion operating within the parameters of an increasingly 'mix-and-match' fashion industry cannot be ruled out; 'retro' and 'vintage' (see Crewe et al., 2003), for example, have become increasingly powerful trends within contemporary fashion, and in fact position themselves in opposition to *haute couture* fashion. Indeed global fashion houses now produce new and branded clothes designed to look old and revel in the suggestion of combating mainstream style, yet the idea of constructing an informed identity by dipping in and out of a diversity of fashion markets may become not a radical departure from mainstream consumerism, but in fact a further indication of submersion within its semiological system. Magazines have picked up this trend and tip off readers about which charity shops tend to stock 'quality' used clothes, and newspapers fawn over superstars who appear to embody the fluidity of 'mix-and-match' fashion culture, wearing old ripped jeans with a designer jacket, or hideously expensive shoes with a battered old handbag. Ann:

I buy my clothes from anywhere I see something ... You might get ideas from magazines, or seeing someone else wearing something. It's all mix and match now ... You want to look different, but, you know, not too different.

My clothes tend to reflect the kind of music I'm into and style and attitude, whereas I see some other people and you can tell they just buy whatever everyone's wearing down the town.

Although many tended to see their involvement in consumerism, and especially fashion, as a means of expressing their individuality (see Galilee, 2002; Guy et al., 2001), the pressure to be involved, to cultivate an individualized yet culturally acceptable style remained palpable. As Miles et al. (1998) have noted, exposure to advertising may not be as influential upon consumption as we might have presumed, as many young people appear to draw from an apparent diversity of influences that reflect their social and cultural environment. This might indeed be a form of 'bricolage' and redolent of a certain degree of creativity, but the claim that the individual exercises free choice *over* the items chosen rather than *between* sets of socially acceptable manufactured items seems to be something of a myth. Darren comments:

I don't think I'm that affected by advertising really. Maybe a little bit by adverts for trainers, but that's not really the advert, it's just telling you something new is out. I get my ideas, just little things I see on other people, like a style of jeans, and you think that would look good if I do that to them, or wear them with that ... but I try to change it around a bit so it's a little bit different.

Joanne:

I suppose, if you didn't know, you'd say we all [friendship group] dressed about the same, but it's not like that at all, it's more complicated. You probably wouldn't notice the details, but we all do and I think we're still a little competitive about it.

What were once considered to be clear demarcations between, on the one hand, sub-cultures characterized by mutual experience, taste and style and a sense of grounded belonging, and, on the other, attachments to the signifying aspects of consumer markets, have clearly been challenged not only by the 'fragmentation' of social life (Bauman, 1995, 2001) but also by paradoxical processes of homogenization. Evidence now seems to indicate that this homogenization of key aspects of youth culture (see for example, Chatterton and Hollands, 2001; Winlow et al., 2003, on 'mainstream' nightlife), increases as media and consumer culture, leisure, and the various complexities of incorporation, exclusion and risk pervade the everyday lives of young people. It seems that most young people are no more fluid and changeable than the rapidly reorganizing society in which they live, and that they are 'malleable' in ways that the remorseless need for sanitized differentiation and novelty at the heart of the consumer marketplace prefers. This is not homogenization in the sense that young people are slowly becoming virtual clones and ideological dupes, or that individuals are being denied their means of 'individuality' and 'resistance' against prevailing orthodoxy, but that the specific means they are employing are themselves products of the consumer market that they are pressurized to engage with rather than relatively autonomous sources, such as traditional class-based cultures. Clearly, aspects of social division and inequality play a part in shaping ways in which young people engage with the consumer market, but the experience of the unprecedented pressure to buy and flaunt the various trappings of consumerism – yet do it in a way that represents substantive 'differentiation' (see Lasch, 1979) – appears common.

The ability to pass a constant style test, where failure impacts heavily on the psychological security of a self that constructs its identity and achieves its status in consumption and forms of waged work within its circuits, is now a crucial part of everyday life. Proving to others that we are sufficiently attuned to recognize the sign value of Ralph Lauren or Prada shares prime importance with the ability to differentiate the unique self from the ubiquitous 'others' attempting to navigate the same path. As Tonnies (2001) observed, the market needs to be in constant motion to prevent stagnation, and so, in the magic moments between creation and absorption, the next wave of consumer styles at once appears to fragment popular culture whilst further reinforcing the vital importance of consumerism. The core value of 'individualism' pressurizes many young people to seek out specificity and differentiate themselves as 'cool individuals' from the 'mass' who appear to have been absorbed into the mainstream; in this way conformity, like ideology (Eagleton, 1991), can be perceived as something that the self has avoided and others have not.

However, if everyone constantly seeks to create the self as a true differentiated individual, then a form of uniformity remains that cannot be understood without a penetrative and critical analysis of the relationship between consumerism and identity. Despite the persistence of significant social divisions, young people appear to be ever more united by the ethic of compulsory individualization as market capitalism tightens its strange hold on the 'means of identity'. Underneath these processes lies the same old economic bedrock: the corporate ownership and control of the means of producing and circulating both physical commodities and the social 'lifestyle' signifiers they carry.

A further dimension to this story of the consumerization of youth leisure can be seen in the growing importance of body concern within youth identities and the display of these identities in the night-time economy's social world. Virtually all of our respondents were aware of the growing significance of body shape in relation to identity and mainstream status hierarchies, although some were clearly more preoccupied with this pressure than others. The importance of possessing an admirable physique is yet another structural pressure borne by contemporary youth (see Boni, 2002; Duncan et al., 2004; Williamson et al., 2004), and has been related to the growth in a number of worrying medical and social trends (Nettleton, 1995; Hesse-Biber, 1997; Williamson et al., 2004). The rather perverse pressure to display a slender physique in consumer culture preoccupied with eating and cooking was keenly felt by some of our respondents (see also Jacobs Brumberg, 2000; Boni, 2002; Brownell, 2004). The construction of culinary expertise as a form of high cultural engagement has now become part of mainstream entertainment, and the cornucopia of choice presented in supermarkets across the country tell us of the pleasures of eating. Global culture also constructs idealized body shapes and perpetuates the extreme pressure to embody high status personas by subscribing to the rigorous regimes of diet and exercise, which of course have also been commercialized. Simultaneously the market constructs solutions to the obesity that results from sedentary working lives in the service economy (see Frank and Engelke, 2001). Michael reveals:

> I go to the gym as often as I can. I think I do it more for myself than other people really, because it makes me feel good, and just, I don't know, gives you self confidence maybe ... There's a lot of pressure to look a certain way, especially when you're young, because there's just so much importance on looking attractive, and not looking fat ... [My main worry is] putting on weight, because of the way it's seen by other people. I doesn't bother me if other people are fat, but healthwise and looks-wise you want to be fairly slim.

> I'm trying to put on some bulk at the moment ... Just to put on a bit of weight so I don't look as skinny ... I've been going to the gym lifting weights and having protein shakes and generally trying to eat more, chicken, eggs, things like that, so you put on weight but not fat. You've just got to keep exercising regularly ... [I know] a lot of people would like the problem [of actually having to put on weight], but it's not like that, it's not easy ... [Men] have to look kind of muscular don't they, so being to thin is like being to fat in some ways.

Emma admits:

> I try to get to the gym but really that's isn't too often. I'm always on a diet as well ... because you want to be in good shape ... I don't know [why]. I suppose you just want to be good looking, but it's not just about men it's more than that. You want to look good for yourself.

And Peter claims:

I'm going to try and loose weight. It's just the fast food and all that, and drinking, I've put on a bit ... I'm not the type [to go to the gym]. I'm not in to all that muscle business ... [I want to loose weight] just so I can get into my jeans really. My clothes are getting tight, so I think it's about time I cut out some of the rubbish [I eat].

Young People and the Transformation of Friendship in the Night-time Economy

As we've already stressed (see Chapter 2), the emergence of new forms of post-industrial labour and the decline of distinct forms of biographical development have generated serious forms of anxiety in youth cultures regarding the construction of identity in a cultural world where the ability to see oneself as a part of a broad historical process has been virtually eliminated. The unpredictability of contemporary labour, the growth of new management practices and new market ideologies have worked to erode traditional social hierarchies. Yet, by rendering social and cultural survival increasingly precarious, consumer culture has replaced traditional social hierarchies with a process of shifting and rolling cultural hierarchies that has impacted upon young people's lives with extreme force. The growth of service sector employment of course directly relates to the growing importance of leisure as a social sphere, and was by far the most common form of employment for our respondents. Although 'service employment' is increasingly diverse, the remorseless market logic of late capitalism has on the whole driven down wage levels in comparison with the 'family wage' of modern industrialism (Westergaard, 1995). All of our respondents who worked in this sector tended to gather on its lower reaches.

If work is to be endured and forgotten, its sole purpose is to fund forays into the consumer market, which for many seems to be saturated with the communal symbolism that was once found in traditional religious, geographical and class communities. Leisure personas appear to be attributed with considerably more significance than other dimensions of life (see Banks et al., 1992; Cappelli, 1997). Who they were, it appeared, was who they were on a weekend, away from the pressure and mundanity of work. On weekends they could be with their 'real' friends rather than the acquaintances at work to whom they presented a one-dimensional, instrumental and rather unsociable persona (see Chapter 2).

Work may not be particularly rewarding but the weekly big night out appears to offer a 'time out of time' (Presdee 2000: 33), a functional respite of carnival to sooth the pains of daylight frustration and prepare workers in these low paid consumer industries for what lies ahead. Joanne describes the weekly routine:

On a Saturday we'll usually start at one of our houses. We have a drink to save a bit of money and then go into the town ... Paula's probably my best mate, she works at [shop name] in the town, Karen's a travel agent, Gemma's a student, but I think she's got a job now, and Angela, I'm not really sure; she's Gemma's mate rather than mine ... We talk about the usual really. Mostly we try not to talk about work cos it's boring isn't it? You want to have a laugh not hear about someone having a bad day at work. We talk about clothes, who's wearing what, where they bought it ... boyfriends, who fancies who ... stuff on TV maybe. When we get out we might talk about men in the bar, we might have a laugh at a few of the weird people out. Then it's clubbing, and by that time everyone's usually completely pissed so it doesn't matter.

Although we accept that close personal relationships continue to exist amongst many young people, we are suggesting that it is a different, highly selective, competitive, fragile form of 'closeness' that, because bonds are not rooted in anything more profound than the instrumental display of style and cultural competence in the circuits of consumer signification, in the medium-term might have a corrosive effect on the deeper, broader and more enduring friendships on which the communal, social and political solidarities of the past were built. To reinforce this point, our research suggests that instrumental attitudes are beginning to be displayed in the construction and maintenance of friendships as well as work relations. For some respondents, friendships provided an essential platform for making a personal 'impact' and achieving a sense of significance and distinction in nighttime leisure cultures. As 'going out' is the most important activity in the lives of most respondents, friends were often seen primarily as a *means* of facilitating the 'right' type of cultural engagement. As Dan explains:

We'd go all over the place [clubbing], and I can remember I'd always offer to drive, or book trains or whatever, because I really wanted to go and you're trying to get all your friends to go ... We sort of stayed together because we all wanted to go clubbing together. If they didn't go I couldn't go ... Slowly but surely we started to drift apart.

Knowledge of friends 'going out' selves can be significant:

I know who's going to get pissed first, I know who's going to be on the score all the time, I know which ones are going to sneak off to meet their girlfriends, I know who's going to get chucked out of nightclubs ... The sense of humour you have to know because you need to know how far you can push certain people, like Eric, he'll stand for a bit of piss-taking but not too much or he'll go mad, whereas someone like Andy just takes the piss all the time ... Eric, guaranteed, is going to have the worse clothes ever, Ian like trainers, and he keeps getting dodgy hair cuts ... and Tony, he's probably the best looking and most likely to score.

These types of assessments of friends, grounded primarily in mutual knowledge of night-time leisure culture, can occasionally be starkly different to more practical and traditional knowledge of apparently close friendships. Joe's knowledge of key aspects of the personal histories of his friends don't trip off the tongue in the same way his stories of their nights out together did:

> Eric works in a factory somewhere in Northville ... I'm not sure what he does really, something to do with car parts ... He still lives with his Mam ... I'm not really sure what happened to his Dad. He grew up in Yorkshire somewhere so I'm not sure where he went to school ... I think he likes his job, the money's not bad, but he doesn't talk about it much ... Tony is a car salesman, he did OK at school I think, but we didn't go to the same school so I'm not 100%. He's got a girlfriend and he's just got a flat in town. He used to live with his Mam and Dad. His girlfriend is called Karen, and that's about it really.

As we mentioned in Chapter 3, the night-time economy is now not only the primary arena for consumption and 'identity-work', but also the primary arena for the construction and maintenance of friendships. Within the marketized carnival of the night-time economy traditional class-based identities appear to have become virtually meaningless as identity is increasingly rendered a task rather than a certainty, and crafted with the tools supplied by consumerism.

It must be emphasized that some respondents occasionally talked at length about their attachment to friends, but, for most, traditional friendship seems to have been largely displaced by superficial, temporary and fragile alliances based on competence in the competitive display of consumer-lifestyle symbols. Whilst the current mode of individualization becomes accepted or in some cases celebrated by some sociologists and cultural theorists, most of this data seems to suggest the need for much more circumspection and a less hasty dismissal of traditional critique. Commercialized leisure, for most of our respondents at least, was woven into the fabric of everyday life and imbued with crucial meanings, hopes and fantasies, and as it becomes so central to their sense of self and belonging it also becomes diffuse with a complex range of anxieties, tensions and pressures that directly reflect the increasingly fragmented, unpredictable and isolating nature of the society in which they live. Making an analogy for something as complex as this is difficult, but for us it was something similar to a crankcase in an internal combustion engine. Here, the frenetic energy of individual cylinders struggling in a harmonized rhythm for dominance and distinction at the same time as trying to escape their connections – an energy that was initially released by keying deeply into the highly combustible anxieties and desires of young people – was converted into a smooth form of forward motion, propelling that specific sector of the consumer economy forward. As we shall see later, it is this complex climate of hedonistic promises and disappointments, tensions, insecurities, competitive instrumentalism, volatility and combustibility in a physically and culturally enclosed area with a tendency to 'overheat' that sets the crucial context for the forthcoming analysis of violence.

Alcohol, Violence and t
Drudgery of Seeking Pleas

Recent media coverage of interpersonal violence in the night-time economy has had a significant impact upon popular perceptions of how young people behave when they go out drinking. Growing public awareness about the sheer scale of violent crime on our after-dark city streets has tended to confirm a number of suspicions about the night-time economy and the young people who populate it, and the fear of violent crime looms on the horizon as a possible thorn in the side of those who support the transformation of inner cities and former industrial locales into leisure economies based on the sale of alcohol. Despite the influx of numerous cultural groups from around the globe in recent years and the alleged proliferation of youth sub-cultures, Britain's night-time economy remains stoically British, and for most young people the dominant activity is weekend circuit drinking (see Hadfield et al., 2001; Hobbs et al. 2003: Chapter 1; Measham, 2004), although mid-week drinking is increasing as marketeers attempt to lure young people into the city centre during the working week with a range of drinks promotions (Hobbs et al., 2000). Put simply, this is just a re-branded, extended and re-contextualized version of old-fashioned pub crawling.

Neo-capitalism's core logic of profit maximization has rationalized key sites of leisure and socializing around the central activity of alcohol consumption. Thus, weekend leisure experiences that in the past were distinguished by local, regional, cultural and class-based variations have, for a significant majority of young people, become homogenized (see Winlow et al., 2003). As we have suggested elsewhere, the ability of the market to structure the financial, regulatory and cultural aspects of contemporary night-time leisure has not created an entirely bland and homogenized vista – although a minority of our respondents made vague complaints that things were going that way – but also forms of rather superficial diversity that are very much a part of market led culture rather than antagonistic voices against it (see Eagleton, 2000; Hall and Winlow, 2005). As some of the more complex and circumspect readings of globalization have recognized (see King, 1991; Scott, 1997; Gray, 1988), homogeneity and heterogeneity need not be considered mutually exclusive. Rather, our suggestion is that the market's relentless monopolization of the means of identity and meaning creation creates a homogenized drinking culture in which a diversity of colourful cultural styles can

ated, enacted and reproduced. However, the styles displayed by most ng people tend to be 'off-the-peg' rather than authentic and, more importantly, the everyday lives of these ostensibly diverse groups and individuals are now reticulated around a number of shared and constantly problematic experiences and contingent risks that are beginning to determine *habitus* and practice at a much deeper level. Our data suggest that the powerful nexus of alcohol misuse, violence and fear has become the principal common experience and contingent risk in the night-time leisure economy.

The mass intoxication and frequent eruptions of interpersonal violence that can be witnessed in most of Britain's city centres on weekend nights is now more readily understood by some commentators as a further indication that the problems facing young people today are changing and also, in many important ways, intensifying (see Pearson, 1983; see also Currie, 2004, for an interesting assessment of the pressures facing white, middle-class youth in America). Excessive alcohol consumption and violence in densely populated urban areas are, of course, two traditional problems that have tended to intensify the social concern and fear that places enormous popular pressure on the methods of social control that governments have attempted to implement throughout the history of industrial capitalism (see Taylor, 1999; Lea, 2002). There is also little doubt that, although for some members of the public they might fade into virtual insignificance compared to the threat of mega-risks such as war and global warming, they further darken the cloud of uncertainty and risk that Bauman (1999, 2002) and Beck (1992) suggest is hanging over Western life today.

Despite the general climate of trepidation, if violence in the night-time economy is indeed the regular and well-known occurrence that our data suggest (see also Day et al., 2003; Hobbs et al., 2003), it has not dissuaded the multitude of young people who flock to city-centre pubs and bars during the weekend and the 'cheap nights' during the week. Nor has it galvanized the state authorities into resolute action. Policing of the night-time economy remains sparse (Hobbs et al., 2002) and legal regulation remains tentative and focused on individual premises. If violence becomes a persistent problem in a particular bar, it might have a detrimental effect on trade, and eventually it might mean the revocation of the license by local officials who are keenly aware that the maintenance of the locale's 'brand' image as a safe yet exciting place is crucial to economic development in consumer societies (see Lister et al., 2001). Concerted efforts directed at large-scale prevention of alcohol misuse seem to have been rejected in favour of a piece-meal 'fire-brigade' approach of stamping out individual incidents when and where they occur and an accompanying 'micro-surgical' approach of targeting legal regulation on individual premises that appear to be persistent trouble spots. Business and the forces of regulation seemed to be caught up in the '... paradoxical demand for orderly disorder' (Hall, 2001), a complex double bind between the essentially contradictory imperatives of economic development via the expansion of hedonistic opportunities and the preservation of an image of safety and order that enhances the attractiveness of the 'brand name' of city centres.

However, whereas most of our respondents were keenly aware of the frequency of violence in the night-time economy, they seemed less concerned than the image-conscious authorities who purported to 'look after' their safety. Yet, at the same time, their direct experiences or observations of serious violence were frequent enough to dispel the claims of optimistic commentators that the persistence of quite serious violence is an urban myth or a sensationalized media construction. This, of course, puts into question exactly which social groups the market-state partnership is trying to attract. Oblivious to these political machinations, our respondents tended to play the percentage game in the full knowledge of the possibility of encounters with real violence. Yes, there was a chance of it happening, but given the overall population of the weekend bar scene, the chances were that they would make it through the night safely. A rational calculation of benefits was added to a rational calculation of possible costs in the overall risk assessment, but the 'benefits' were a concatenation of prospects of hedonistic pleasure that, paradoxically, included the possibility of encountering violence as observers, victors or brave victims who 'gave their all' before succumbing to impossible odds (see Chapter 6). Some of our respondents seemed to regard violence as Janus-faced: a cost if the risk of personal injury was too great but a benefit in the sense that encountering it and dealing with it in specific ways seemed to have certain attractions. We will elaborate this odd paradox in Chapters 7 and 8, but suffice it to say here that the risk calculation does not seem to be based on the standard, simple utilitarian dichotomy of pleasure and pain or the standard moral dichotomy of good and evil, which means that the consideration of safety was always made problematic in the meaning systems of young people who really preferred a bit of 'edge' that might interrupt the monotony of their working and consuming lives.

The artificially created world of hedonism and abandon that is believed by so many young people to be available for purchase in the night-time economy thrives on the palpable reduction of daylight forms of social control, and this reduction in moral and behavioural regulation is closely related to the regularity of violence and ubiquity of disorder that is clearly and constantly exhibited (Hobbs et al., 2005). But, it is also a part of the risk, a generator of fear and, paradoxically, part of the seductive attraction of the whole night-time scene. In this chapter we want to begin our exploration of this paradox of meanings and emotions by outlining the complex relationship between young people, mass intoxication and violence. In order to illustrate this discussion, we have incorporated snippets of interviews that highlight young people's understanding of, and emotional relationship to, the regular interpersonal violence that typifies this milieu.

Experiencing 'Adventure'

Acutely aware of the visceral pleasures and seductive hedonism of the night-time carnival, our respondents overwhelmingly held the opinion that violence was simply a part of the show in the same way that it has for a long time been an organic 'fairground attraction' in village shows and traditional village 'football' matches (Delves, 1981). It was perhaps an unwanted digression from the central business of purchasing and consuming pleasurable experiences, seeking sexual encounters, soaking the psyche in the coherent ideology that equates neo-capitalism with freedom, prosperity and pleasure and engaging in the practices of consumerist identity formation and display, but for the most part the young people we talked to accepted it as an unavoidable aspect of the night-time scene (see also Tomsen, 1997). Most of our respondents started 'going out' around the ages of fifteen or sixteen and had seen a significant amount of violence over the years. They regarded its constant presence in a rather fatalistic manner: violence was, to them, an effect of alcohol consumption and therefore, in a 'liminal' dimension of life based on the loosening of rules and inhibitions to which alcohol was the essential lubricant, quite unavoidable (see Hobbs et al., 2000). Some respondents – overwhelmingly men – moved beyond the notion of 'edge' and openly expressed their enjoyment of the spectacle of serious physical violence, seeing it as an unrestrained expression of the viscerality that has always been a legitimate encoded aspect of traditional proletarian culture (Hall, 1997) and one of the 'main attractions' of history's various 'liminal zones' (Turner, 1969).

> Yeah, you see it all the time. Pizza shops, taxi ranks, inside pubs, bouncers running all over the place, police vans, it's just part of it really ... No, it's just you see it all the time, so it's not like a shock to see it happen ... It doesn't bother me. As long as it's not you then you can just sit back and enjoy it.

> It's just one of those things, there's nothing you can do. You can't stop it happening, because people are going to be pissed aren't they, and then there's going to be trouble ... You're not worried about a camera if you're pissed are you? People just accept it, especially if you've been going out a while ... If you're out with your girlfriend then maybe you don't want to be next to it, but if it's just the lads then it's a bit of a laugh.

For some it seemed that as long as they were not the direct focus of aggression by other users of this liminal urban space then the spectacle of conflict became simply one of the multitude of behaviours that positioned the night-time economy in virtual polar opposition to the regulated world of daylight comportment and the silent fatalism of the working week. Here the night-time carnival *appeared* to offer such a dazzling array of transgressive adventures that the weekly Saturday night 'down the town' appeared to become far more than an opportunity to recuperate from the rigours of the working week, reaffirm friendships or meet a member of the opposite sex. It also offered or displayed a range of cultural activities that appeared immediately seductive in their opposition to everyday behavioural protocols and traditional forms of moral being. Carnival revels in carnality (see Presdee, 2000), and the ability to lose oneself in the recklessness of the night, to momentarily discard the restrictive social conventions of sociability and normative identity is a significant seductive attraction for most young people (Presdee, 2000), although we would argue that the traditional temporary inversion of political power that featured in traditional carnival no longer takes place in this quite systematically depoliticized consumerist simulation. Nevertheless, the intensity of easy availability of hedonistic experience offered by the night-time economy was a constant and eagerly sought attraction for most of our respondents. The possibility of seeing blood spilt and experiencing the brutal actuality of interpersonal violence created a heightened sense of excitement that propelled the night out on the town beyond the stereotypical 'beer-fest' to a real adventure and interconnects with narratives of identity and the risky nature of contemporary culture (see also Tomsen, 1997). Others were more critical of those who become embroiled in violent conflicts, and while they generally appeared to situate violence within the cultures of drinking and mainstream night-time leisure, their views revealed substantial differences in perception (see also Chatterton and Hollands, 2001):

It's just the pissheads, they get drunk and start kicking off. Let them get on with it far as I'm concerned ... We steer well clear of it. You've just got to pick bars and clubs that don't attract those types of people I think, although there's always the danger when you come out, that someone's going to start something for no reason ... You just get used to it, the charvers and pissheads, and stay out of their way.

You see it every weekend. Some people just like fighting, and you see them staggering about pissed out of their head, and it's just not a nice place to be sometimes ... There's loads of bars I wouldn't go near on a Saturday, and we just tend to stick to the same places.

It's down to drink. I think they should change the licensing, so people aren't trying to get drunk before eleven ... It's just the way it is and you can see it happening, they go out at seven and just try to drink as much as they can before the bell goes. It's got beyond a joke ... I don't know where they get the money from ... Sometimes you get a bit edgy being out on the street, but a lot of the time it doesn't matter because you're drunk as well. If we see a fight we just dash on... It's certain types of people who cause trouble. People who go out to listen to music and see friends and just socialize aren't the ones getting arrested for fighting.

Others were keen to point out that going out did not necessarily involve contact with violence:

I'm mean yes there is violence. I've seen it loads of times. But I go out like, pretty much every week and it's really not that often I've seen anything serious. You see people getting kicked out of pubs and things, but actual fighting, to be honest you don't see that much ... If you're half way sensible it's not a problem.

No I think most of those who end up in fights and things, it's just the type of person they are. If you want to stay out of trouble then you can stay out of trouble.

Some however were keen to point out what they believed to be the random and unpredictable nature of much of the violence:

It can just happen, out of nothing. Someone comes up and bang! That's it.

It's like a lottery, because you can just be in the wrong place at the wrong time.

Those who were keen to highlight distinct cultural 'divisions in the dark' (Hollands, 2002) and position themselves as external to the mainstream drinking culture often acknowledged that violence is an integral part of night-time leisure, but appear keen to differentiate themselves from it:

No I wouldn't go. I mean, I've been in the past, loads of times, but I think as you get older, I just, I can't be doing with it. Getting served at the bar and all that, people pushing and shouting and pissing in the street, it's just not for me ... What we'll do, we'll pick bars where there's just good music really, that's maybe a bit away from the crowded bits [of the city] ... There's a good mix of people, and you can tell no one's going there to get into a fight or anything ... People still get pissed, and there's still a lot of the rest of the stuff that goes on, it's just, I don't know, more civilized if you like.

While this particular group appeared to value their 'outsider' status, they appeared very much a part of mainstream after-dark leisure, although their actual behaviour and appreciation of that leisure may be marginally different. They tended to populate the same streets, drink alcohol rather than water (see Redhead, 1993; Measham, 2004), and value much of the overall attraction of night-time leisure. The construction of a kind of pseudo-high culture within the night-time economy, often based around music and fashion (see Chatterton and Hollands, 2001) and implied behavioural and moral protocols, reinforces the suggestion that neo-capitalism's consumer economy is an important site where new moral order is being created. In its processes of social distinction based on the moral and aesthetic judgement of the other (Bourdieu, 1984), this has distinct similarities to the cultural aspect of industrial modernity's class order. Dance music culture, in particular, is deeply enmeshed within the diverse forms of signification created by the consumer economy, and the competitive urge to differentiate themselves from the ubiquitous others who populate the night-time economy suggests to us not the autonomous and inter-subjective constitution of cultural form but rather the ability of neo-capitalism to nurture superficial diversity and create forms of status and identity via processes of distinction within consumerism's reticulation.

For those who considered themselves to be the radicals on the margin, what was once the aesthetic critique of capital has been somehow diluted and reworked into the aesthetic critique of the disorderly and violent consumer, and the romantic elective affinity that once existed between radicals and the 'underclass' has evaporated. The once-feared political radical is now a being out of time, like the famous photograph of Che Guevara on corporately manufactured and distributed clothing, a parody divested of meaning and absorbed into the superficial realm of fashion, or an ineffectual buffoon to be lampooned, like Wolfie Smith. Indeed, our morally superior respondents were fully incorporated in consumer capitalism's *doxa*, and within its parameters seemed to be creating an important aspect of their identity by distinguishing themselves *negatively*, in the standard structuralist manner, outlined by Saussure (1974), Bourdieu (1984) and Lévi-Strauss (1999), against others who were equally incorporated but who displayed different habits and dispositions. These consumerist pseudo-radicals identified themselves as *not* disorderly and violent consumers, rather than *not* consumers, and became quite vociferous and judgemental when defending their preference to consume the signifiers of their 'alternative' lifestyles in peace. However, at the most basic level their *positive* identity was still as consumers of manufactured styles and – if we remember that the pacification of the internal territory and the outlawing of interpersonal violence has been one of the bourgeois state's crucial functional norms for over 600 years (Elias, 1994) – rather than being alternative they constituted the orderly consumerist norm.

The depoliticized and ahistorical processes of identity formation in which our respondents were absorbed seemed to be shot through with novel forms of competitive snobbery, misrecognition and denial, yet this was contained quite comfortably within the normalized *doxa* of consumer capitalism. Despite this, those who favoured various dance music cultures implied that they had seen through the vacuity of youthful mainstream drinking cultures in a Nietzschean moment of self-actualization, and occasionally spoke in rather evangelical terms about the pleasures of cultural awakening (see Malbon, 1999). They tended to see themselves as latter day *flaneurs*, a culturally adroit and stylistically discerning groups of bon vivants and distinct from the hard-drinking barbarians (see McDonald, 1997b; Purcell, 1997) who had yet to awaken themselves and pick their way through the fog of unquestioning cultural conformity:

I used to be like that, just going out with the lads and getting drunk … I don't know what happened, things just changed … You get into different things, and then you realize, what was I thinking of? It's just part of getting older.

However, at the basic level of taste and practice, for this group the attractions and opportunities of the night-time economy were very similar to those of the beer-soaked metropolitan barbarians from whom they sought to distance themselves:

You just want to go out and have a good time, just enjoy yourself and that. Get drunk, have a laugh with your mates, maybe have a couple of pills [ecstasy tablets], just the usual.

It's all about having a laugh isn't it? It does you good to get yourself out on a Saturday night or whenever, get pissed, that type of thing … You always end up regretting it the next day, but before you go out you don't care.

You get the excitement before you go, the build up, because you know that you can go out and have a really good time. You're kind of thinking about who you might meet, about clothes, just about the fun you can have once you get out … There's times you just want to go out and get off your face cos you've had a bad week or something.

In common with most other respondents, they seemed to be very keen to exercise the consumption of hedonism as a right, an opportunity not to be missed and an end in itself. Their determination to consume in peace did not drive them into separate spaces outside the city, or exclusive enclaves in favoured parts of it, although many did express a preference for specific bars and clubs. While this group tended to pick its routes through night-time leisure with a little more consideration, contact with mainstream consumers was unavoidable and distinctions were often unclear:

There's some bars we go to, like if we go for a few cheap drinks, and you see lads who look a bit rough. I mean, you've got a bar full of people, you're going to get different sorts.

As long as there's not loads of charvers in the club it doesn't really bother me that much. Bars, you kind of expect there's going to be all sorts.

Sometimes it bothers me and sometimes it doesn't. I think there's a beer monster in all of us really.'

Yeah, I mean, it's not like we're snobs or anything, and we go out to have a laugh; we're not posers, nothing like that. We like a drink and all the rest of it … It's just when things get a bit dodgy we try to steer clear.

Some of the bars are just crap, the music, and all that, just really, really corny, and everyone's really pissed … Sometimes you can go somewhere like that and you say, I'm never going there again. Other times, it's good just to go in and have a laugh.

Witnessing Violence

The vast majority of our respondents could recount tales of violence that they had witnessed first-hand in the night-time economy, and indeed it was one of the key themes that emerged in the early transcription and analysis of our interview data. It was a topic upon which many were keen to expand at length.

[The worst thing I've seen], just like a stand up fight between a bunch of bouncers and this bunch of lads outside Jimmy's Bar. It was just amazing, honestly. There were loads of these lads and there was just complete hell on, people running all over, people getting kicked to bits … We could see this one bloke, and he's just getting kicked about on the floor, and I saw this other bloke just get knocked out cold off this bouncer.

I was in this pizza shop, about one-ish, and I was drunk and didn't see what happened, but then I turned around and there's these two girls, and they both kind of knock into me, so I moved, and one's got this other one like that, and she's pulling her hair, it was just mental.

The relish with which some of these stories were recounted clearly displayed the highly charged pleasures that can be gleaned from witnessing violence, up close and personal. This was not the rather alien media version of violence, but actually cast the observer right there in the middle of the action, amid the grunts and the groans, the breaking of bones and the splattering of blood. The glee with which these experiential adventures were described occasionally contradicted claims from the same respondents that they found violence distasteful, regarded the perpetrators as barbaric and attempted to avoid it at all costs. Some of our respondents became quite effusive, and recounted the blows and injuries in minute detail, even though, in some cases, the violence had been witnessed some time ago. The violence was deeply memorable, and spoke of the subtle attractions of base and brutal forms of transgressing the doxic norm of a society geared towards sublimated competition and the codified repression and control of interpersonal physical conflict. Enjoying the carnality of violence, being appalled by the injuries and yet unable to look away, seemed to typify male readings of night-time violence. Being on the periphery, for most of our respondents, remained far more appealing than being actively involved in violence, and yet many seemed to exhibit the same adrenalin-inducing reactions to conflict noted in regular participants in violence (see Chapter 7). The witnessing of this violence at first hand removed the diluting effect of watching boxing on the flat screen of the television, bypassed the moral and stylistic insulation of fictional cinematic violence and the political and religious function of the staged auditorium violence of the past, and allowed witnesses to become briefly immersed in the brutality, physicality, proximity and spontaneity of real live violence. Male witnesses seemed to be especially fascinated by the details of the melee, which they committed to memory and could quite easily recount:

It was just amazing, claret [blood] everywhere, you could hear it [a nose] break.

His eye came up like this, I'm not kidding, you could look at him and watch his face change.

He must have had rings or something, because when he stood up he's got these gashes over both eyes, really wide. It was horrible.

The horror, for some, came with an element of glee:

I've never seen anything like it ...

I'm not kidding, it was unbelievable ...

You've seen nowt like it, it was like off a film ...

The degree of pleasure derived from witnessing acts of serious violence was partly determined by their ability to maintain a safe distance and protect themselves from physical harm. For the most part, these brushes with violence were a 'walk on the wild side', perhaps the chance to experience activities that were generally outlawed by the political, ideological and cultural forces that constituted the *doxa* they inhabited – activities that had been decreed out of place and out of time. The expression 'like a film' was used on a number of occasions, and it indicates the ability of this sort of real encounter to perform quite adequately the function normally reserved for the media representation; to transport the audience to other places and times, but of course without all the moral and ideological baggage that subsumes the violence in a narrative. The chances of being inadvertently dragged into these conflicts also appeared to inflate the emotional reaction to violent incidents, as all of our male respondents who had witnessed violence in the night-time economy were aware that it could often be haphazard and often lacked the traditional build-up and warning-signals. Seeing serious violence at close hand, and passing safely through this highly charged situation, made the recounting of the tale all the more dramatic. As we were to discover, when violent situations changed and witnesses became victims, the effusive narratives of violence were often replaced by far less passionate and detailed stories (see Chapter 7).

Not all of our respondents were enthralled by the spectacle of violence, and although there wasn't a clear gender division, those who expressed distaste for violence were often women:

> Yeah I've seen it loads of times, people getting punched … It's just stupid drunks really, spoiling everyone's night. You just get tired of it.

> The police should just go in there and arrest them because they bring it on themselves … No it's disgusting when you see it, it's just awful. You get ready to have a night out, see friends or whatever, and then these blokes just bring it down to their level.

However, some women displayed attitudes similar to the men, and the perception of 'spoiling it for everyone' seemed to be related to levels and forms of sensibilities (see Day et al., 2003). Different methodology with a much larger sample than ours would be required to discover the proportions of various sensibilities and attitudes towards real violence present in the young female population and correlate them with various social and cultural backgrounds. All we can say at the moment is that some young women were not appalled by violence:

> It's amazing isn't it, to see it, shocking really. As long as they don't come over to me, then it gives you a bit entertainment.

Drunkenness, Disorder and Violence

The sale of alcohol is perhaps the most obvious feature of the night-time economy (Hobbs et al., 2000; Hadfield et al., 2001) and its consumption seems to be inextricably bound up with the night-time economy's attempt to establish and maintain its reputation of pleasure, sensuality, freedom and excitement. As we have discussed in previous chapters, the promise of hedonistic release from the stifling monotony of service work, the pressures of education and career building, the moral restraints of parents and the gloom and isolation of decaying communities has been crucial in the remoulding of weekend leisure to fit in with the shifting dynamics and the basic profit-maximizing demand of consumer capitalism (see Mullins et al., 1999). Hedonism, which is such an important characteristic in the construction of consumerized identities (Chaney, 1993), and the ceaseless search for experimentation and 'experience' in the night-time economy, should be understood against a broad backdrop of individualization, social fragmentation and the gradual marketization of social life (Hall and Winlow, 2003, 2005). However, the form of hedonism that has become normalized in this particular milieu is also inextricably linked to chemical intoxication, chiefly drunkenness (Hobbs et al., 2000; Measham, 2004). The abandonment of virtually all sense of normality and reason – getting 'out of your head' or 'off your face' – has become virtually a pre-requisite for the active search for individualized hedonistic excess. For many young people the night-time economy has become the sole site for hedonistic excess, and it is becoming less common for young people to express their quest for freedom and identity in artistic, intellectual, political or outdoor pursuits, although it must be said that sport remains central to many lives and global 'travelling' has become very popular, but of course alcohol consumption is far from absent from these activities. Not only are a range of conventional youthful concerns increas-ingly played out on its shifting terrain, but the imagery of the night-time economy has become the exclusive signifier of the pleasurable and hedonistic experience, attracting millions of young people into a mutually understood realm of excess, freedom and debauchery predicated upon the physical delights of sex, drugs and dance (see Presdee, 2000; Sanders, 2005) and spiced even further with the risk of violence or some sort of encounter with the law. However, for the vast majority of young people the required lubricant that enables all of this to become a real poten-tial is alcohol.

For our interviewees, drinking alcohol in the company of friends made up the vast majority of time spent in the night-time economy, and while our sample was rather limited, we found little evidence to suggest a diversity of alternative intoxi-cants, natural or chemical, in night-time leisure (see Redhead, 1993). Certainly, there was evidence of drug use, but those who admitted to regular drug use always included alcohol in their list of intoxicants (see Measham, 2004; Sanders, 2005). Each one of our respondents drank quite copious amounts of alcohol, often far in excess of the limits prescribed by the medical profession, and they saw it as a crucial part of their night-time experience. Going out and not drinking was anathema, and it was very revealing here that, without intoxication and the alter-ations in perception and the loosening of inhibition that it allows, the sober reality of the night-time economy was occasionally seen as just dull and tacky as other aspects of life:

> I've been out and took the car before because you're skint or whatever, and it's a total nightmare. You just can't get in to the crack; everyone's laughing and that and you don't know what they're on about. You can just see how crap everything is … I'd rather sit in the house and watch the box.

Alcohol has, of course, played a key role in the evolution of night-time leisure, as pubs have gradually been transformed into wine bars and super-pubs, and our industrial centres into commercial and consumer-orientated business districts (see Chapters 4 and 5). The specific environments that our respondents found more appealing than any other existed purely to make money, and their primary means of doing this is alcohol sales. Yet the appeal of the drinking strip is far more than mere intoxication. The cultures of the night-time economy and the signs that float in its atmosphere are inextricably tied to the cold, hard world of capital accumulation, yet this fact is often forgotten because, at first glance, young people seem so active in the construction of their own cultural meanings and individual identities that it seems to confirm the liberal doctrine that freely negotiated inter-subjective meaning creation is the cultural bedrock of society. However, our data consistently suggested that the allegedly meaningful and expressive cultures that add colour to the night-time economy are moulded by the neo-capitalist economy, and while the construction of these cultures clearly involves a range of broader processes, the sale of alcohol remains firmly established as the *raison d'[ecircumflex]tre* of the supply side and the crucial prerequisite for the pleasurable experiences that constitute the demand. Alcohol is the economic and cultural backbone of the night-time economy, and although its sale is the primary means for corporations and entrepreneurs alike to make money (Hobbs et al., 2003), the cultural activity of alcohol consumption remains an important means of understanding the nature of contemporary night-time leisure.

Intoxication is attractive for a number of reasons (MacAndrew and Edgerton, 1969), and alcohol provides a socially sanctioned means of altering everyday perceptions of the world and an individual's place within it. For the most part, it is that altering of perception, the ability to *imagine* oneself briefly discarding the regimented world of daylight comportment, casting off the frustration of the working week and releasing oneself from normative identity and behaviour, which makes the night-time economy so appealing. As we suggested in the previous chapter, for many the attraction of the night-time economy is the relaxation of social control after dark in a 'liminal cultural terrain' (Hobbs et al., 2000), but, of course, this relaxation cannot be perceived with any real intensity unless it is contrasted with the monotony and repression of daytime existence, so in a very important way the very different nature of the two sides of life in the consumer economy – the pleasure and sociability of consumption and the monotony of service work in the absence of communality – make the reproduction of each other's existence possible in the realms of both the real and the perceptual. The continual control of expression makes the opportunity to experience simulations of alternative and transgressive social behaviours all the more appealing, and to a psyche whose perception has been altered by alcohol to mistake the menu for the meal, these simulated behaviours can be perceived to be given free reign in the allegedly unrestrained (but actually controlled by privatized violence specialists) carnival of night-time leisure.

The marketing strategy of the night-time economy generates the impression that the weekly night out can potentially involve wild and unrestrained personal pleasure, and for the most part young people's selective memories of nights out confirm that this is indeed always seen as a possibility and experienced as such whilst intoxicated. This inducement contributes to the social importance of the environment to youth culture and youth identities, and also goes some way in explaining the continuous seduction of the night-time economy and the Bacchanalian cultures it promotes. The socially accepted means of distancing the self from normative reality and realigning perception, emotion and the body to the more appealing world of hedonism and abandon encapsulated by the night-time economy is drinking alcohol. As a visit to our city centres at around two o'clock on a Sunday morning will reveal, the signs of often excessive alcohol intake are exhibited in abundance. The historical and economic importance of alcohol to night-time leisure (Clark and Critcher, 1985), and its place within carnivalesque cultural forms throughout history (Bakhtin, 1984), suggest that 'alcohol consumption ... is the necessary social lubricant that aids the slide of young people into this quasi-carnivalesque and consumer-orientated world' (Winlow et al., 2003: 177).

The social acceptance of alcohol's 'disinhibitor factor' (Room and Collins, 1983) allows a legitimate simulation of the rapid abandonment of daylight behavioural protocols as it is ascribed properties similar to a 'get out of jail free card'. Alcohol's tendency to release individual desires from their normative straitjacket means that focus tends to remain on the self, and thus the traditional forms of ritualized transgression or the symbolic inversion of social power that characterized traditional Saturnalia are often absent from the night-time economy. Society generally, and perhaps young people in particular, imbue alcohol with mystical properties that are in no way an inevitable consequence of 'ethanol entering the blood stream' (McDonald, 1997a: 13). Most of our respondents subscribed to the belief that alcohol revealed a culture-free, natural self:

> You say things that you wouldn't normally. There's no ... you don't constantly watch what you're saying, you just say whatever comes to your head and you just do things that normally you wouldn't dare.

> It gives you a bit of confidence, so you do things you normally wouldn't. You're just not bothered, you don't think twice, you just do it ... It gives you the bottle to go up and talk to women, just act like an idiot and not care.

> It helps conversation because once they've had a drink everyone's got something to say, everyone's got an opinion about this or that, everyone just becomes completely honest and tells you exactly what they think.

Most of our respondents were also aware that alcohol use offers a socially acceptable explanation for what would generally be considered unacceptable behaviour, a 'technique of neutralization' as Matza (1964) might have described it:

You say things, I've said things to friends that I didn't mean, and really it's because I've had too much to drink and I'm just not thinking ... It always gets sorted out because we all get a bit like that when you've had too much to drink, and I think everyone just assumes you don't mean it, and when you wake up the next day it just gets forgotten.

I got thrown out of this nightclub and it's all started because I'm off my face and I've just gone up to this lass and said something, and she's standing with her boyfriend and it just went from there ... You wake up the next day and you laugh because it's just amazing what happens. I mean, it's embarrassing really, and you get the piss taken out of you but then it's all forgotten because someone else does something daft the next week.

Some of our respondents suggested that while the general attitude appeared to be that behaviour while drunk should be forgiven, it shouldn't necessarily be forgotten:

I think you're more truthful when you're drunk because you're saying things which normally you'd stop yourself ... There's been times when we've been talking and people have said things, and you think, oh, that's what you really think, because normally you know they wouldn't say anything, they'd stop themselves ... There's times its just confirmed what bitches women can be.

As MacAndrew and Edgerton (1969) have suggested, the social behaviour of intoxicated individuals tells us far more about the organization of culture than the properties of alcohol, and explorations of the social construction of drunkenness tend to confirm the idea that many young people find the transgression of restrictive norms an attractive and exciting proposition, perhaps even more so when it involves danger and risk. As the respondents above seem to indicate, alcohol 'frees' them from normative behavioural codes and enables them to engage in or witness forbidden activities. The condition of 'drunkenness' gives individuals the courage and confidence they normally tend to lack, and this is also true of communicative as well as physical interaction. Intoxicated young people are more likely talk to others without formal or informal introductions, or without practical and rational justification. However, if the approach is rebuffed, 'drunkenness' provides a means to significantly lighten a situation that may have otherwise resulted in loss of face and self-esteem. Drunkenness allows forms of behaviour that may be immediately appealing but are usually appraised and rejected, not only because of alcohol's ability to temporarily suspend the inhibitions of the super-ego but also because the culture of the night-time economy encourages disorder and hedonistic fulfilment. Minor infractions of the vague rules of social interaction within the night-time economy are not only forgiven but expected, and the exciting prospect of spending time in a liminal zone where there are fewer rules than normal – and where even those that exist are minimally and ineffectively regulated – is the genuinely powerful marketing attraction that lies behind the official rhetoric of 'safe and harmless fun'. By partially neutralizing the traditional agents of public order at the same time as removing responsibility from the individual and placing it at the bottom of a pint glass, the night-time economy can promote itself as the main attraction to the consumers who populate the highly lucrative youth market.

This culture of drunkenness, which has been incorporated into the general hedonism of night-time leisure as an indispensable commodity, is crucial to any attempt to understand the overwhelming sense of disorder and dangerous excitement that exists in Britain's night-time economy. Forms of behaviour that would, during daylight hours, be met with immediate social and legal sanctions have become normalized. This is not simply a division between night and day, a reflection of the fluidity of contemporary moral codes or an indictment on the ability of today's agencies of law enforcement to maintain public order (see Hobbs et al., 2000). More importantly it also represents a widening chasm between the economic spheres of production and consumption and the behaviour required to keep them profitable. Without the *potential* pleasures of hedonistic abandon – and, as we will discuss very shortly, potentials do not need to be made real consistently to keep the consumer hooked – or the tacit acceptance of transgression, the night-time economy would hold much less appeal for the huge numbers of young people who populate the multitude of city-centre bars across the country every weekend. The perceived ability of alcohol to release psychological inhibitions and alter perceptions, together with the ability of the 'culture of drunkenness' to legitimize minor transgressions and expose individuals to 'risky encounters' that can be mythologized, creates a psycho-cultural portal. Through this portal millions of young people can be led each weekend towards the wider spectrum of seductive commodities, and without it the prosperity and continued expansion of this section of the consumer economy would not be secured.

Prominent amongst the potential 'minor transgressions' that the night-time economy dangles before bored and restless young people who work and study in a climate of traditional 'dull compulsion' and repression, where the bourgeois project of 'pseudo-pacification' (Hall, 2000) still performs its utilitarian operations and truncates emotional life (Elias, 1994), is of course interpersonal violence. Given our analysis of the development of the night-time economy in the previous chapter and above, it seems that an increase in the rate of real violence is an inevitable by-product of the ineffectively regulated cultures of transgression and hedonism that support the logical demand of the continuous economic growth of the night-time leisure scene. Whilst these cultures are indeed a useful way of understanding the context of alcohol related violence in the night-time economy, beneath the surface lies a tangled web of social, economic and environmental factors which are the root cause of interpersonal violence in this cultural context.

The night-time economy creates and thrives on a seductive *potential*; the expectation of possible transgression and disorder in the interstices of orderly consumption, and accessing narratives of and justifications for violence within this context is far from difficult.

Most of our 'perpetrators' (see Chapter 7) alluded to the expectation of encountering violence as a participant, and most were aware that that minor confrontations often rapidly escalate to vicious brawls that can cause serious injury (see Polk, 1999). Our interviewees were describing the nuts and bolts of the normalizing process, or at least *a specific normalizing process* that seems to operate in this environment. This general acceptance of the likelihood of violence occurring somewhere in the vicinity at some time (it does not need to be certain or constant) generates internally a climate of risk and trepidation. This has the tendency to heighten sensitivity to slights, taunts, disorderly decorum and other warning signals that tend to place all but the most unworldly (or the most drunk) individuals in an adrenalin-fuelled 'emergency mode', a potential bio-psychological condition apparently common to all human beings (Ehrenreich, 1997). Experience tells the alerted individual that in this environment such minor incidents often escalate and might both need and justify a response of immediate violence. If this very real situation of alertness is coupled with the expectations and experience of audiences, the acceptance that minor confrontations tend to end in violence creates actual violence, not only as a defence of self-identity and status (Winlow, 2001) in front of a judgemental audience of both sexes or as a retribution for over-stepping moral and behavioural boundaries, but because actors are sensitized to the inescapable fact that violence often moves beyond its potential and its mythological status to *actually happen*, so of course ignoring warning signs may result in serious injury. Violence has established itself as *doxic* in this environment, generated in the dynamics of the prevailing logic of practice (Bourdieu, 1977, 1990) and highly active as a formal cultivator of the *habitus,* the repository of dispositions and habitual responses in the psycho-emotional make up of the individuals who inhabit the *doxa.* This, as we will explore in more depth in the conclusion, is a more adequate explanation of the generation and reproduction of the violent male *habitus* in this environment than the rather one-dimensional notion that violence is a transhistorical strategy of male domination reproduced by a 'hegemonic' masculine form.

Thus the culture of the night-time economy adds a crucial layer of context to the over-used and misunderstood concept of 'alcohol-related violence'. Whilst a biological causal relationship between alcohol and violence remains unproven, the role that alcohol plays as a psychological disinhibitor in a culture of expectation that has evolved in the night-time leisure sector of the consumer economy provides a number avenues to address serious violence on our after-dark city streets. We must stress here the cultures of expectation and disorder that are an integral part of the night-time leisure scene are not the only contexts in which the habit of physical violence can be and have been normalized and reproduced, and lack of space restricts us from offering a more comprehensive analysis of violence causation. However, the evidence from our interviewees here supports the evidence and analysis from earlier stages of our work. The deeply ingrained visceral dispositions and identities of those who have lived their lives in micro-climates of insecurity, fear, aggression and violence, which are the products of functional economic and ideological imperatives in specific phases of capitalist development (see Horne and Hall, 1995; Gilmore, 1990), should form the basis of theories of the tendency to violence within the night-time economy and other dimensions of contemporary Western life.

The Drudgery of Pleasure-seeking

Despite the powerful, seductive and ubiquitous message that hedonistic excess is constantly in stock and ready for immediate sale, many of respondents felt that the night-time economy resembled Adorno's consumer capitalist restaurant, in which customers were left all night to peruse the menu, but the waiter never came and the food was never delivered, a confidence trick that could 'perpetually cheat its consumers of what it perpetually promises' (Horkheimer and Adorno, 1972: 139). Whilst the vast majority of younger respondents recited passionate stories of fun, pleasure and excitement, a few jaded old hands near the top of our eighteen to twenty-five age range were beginning to see through the ethic of compulsory enjoyment:

> To be honest, the last few weeks, it's been a bit shit. Sometimes there's just not the same crack ... The thing is you can't stay in because there's nothing else to do really on a Saturday.

> You go out, and you're hoping it's going to be a great night right, but then it ends up just the same old shit ... You can't tell. You can go out for ages and then one night you have a great night. And it's like every week you're hoping it's going to be the same.

> I think some of the time you just keep going out because you can't avoid it. I think under the surface is wanting to meet somebody, and so you go out on the off chance, but sometimes you think it's not worth the bother, another night down the town.

Turning a series of events into a mythological narrative always necessitates omitting the mundane parts and editing the exciting parts together into a time-lapsed thread. Indeed, many of our respondents were wrapped up in the process of mythologizing their experiences in the night-time economy, indicating that the alcohol- or drug-influenced perception of the pleasure gathered from a particularly good night out was such that the mediocre nights in between could be set aside as they privileged the unbridled pleasure of the original 'good night' in their individual and collective memories. The gradual accumulation of 'good nights' tended to merge into a single idealized experience of night-time leisure that permeated youth culture in general, and it was this mythological ideal that kept these youthful consumers coming back. Every weekend offered the chance to recreate the cherished memory of the idealized night out, where the entire friendship group appeared to be in the mood for good times, where jokes were funnier, the alcohol and the atmosphere more intoxicating, the music better, the opposite sex more attractive, and so on. It wasn't simply the culture that advertised hedonistic excess – experience told them that hedonism was on offer and could truly be experienced in the night-time economy, and so they came back every weekend to try and seek it out:

> I stay in on a Friday, and when I get up Saturday you're in a good mood because you know you're going out [on Saturday night].

> Going out on a Saturday, you know everyone's going to be out, and you just look forward to having a laugh.

But what they found week in week out was not necessarily unbridled pleasure:

> No it's not always like that. Sometimes it's just not the same crack … it's still good, and you can still have a laugh, but just, it's not always the excellent night you think it's going to be.

Every weekend was the chance to start the search for the 'good night out' anew, as the extreme pleasure gathered for just one such night out would quickly overshadow the rather mundane business of weekly leisure. And yet the search for hedonism was not simply an individual urge:

> You don't want to miss a Saturday night, I wouldn't miss a Saturday. It's just, that's what it's all about, going out and enjoying yourself.

> You have to go out on a Saturday night. You just have to really. It's the only time you get to see everyone, and you know you've got to get the money together to make it out … If you miss a week, then everyone's talking about what happened last Saturday and you don't know what they're laughing about. If you miss too many weekends, people just stop phoning you.

> I wouldn't want to miss a Saturday because that's where it all happens really. You look forward to it all week, thinking about what you'll wear, where you'll go and things like that … If I've bought something new, you always want to go out to wear it … If you

don't go out you miss all the gossip. You miss being able to just go out and enjoy yourself really ...

Many of our respondents felt pressurized to engage with night-time leisure, as it incorporated such a broad array of youthful concerns, and weekly involvement entailed a significant financial commitment:

[I spend] About eighty quid on a Saturday, about, I'd say, fifty on a Friday.

[I spend] at least a hundred quid a week on drink.

That's where all my money goes.

Some of our respondents also appeared to be reconsidering the various attractions of night-time leisure:

There's times you think, I've spend too much. You think, bastard, [I've spent] sixty odd quid and it's been fucking shit.

I was spending too much, just going out drinking, and a lot of the time there'd be things I wished I'd spent the money on instead ... It just feels the thing to do, and you don't want to stop in ... Now I try and pick my nights out. I ring around to see who's out ... [there's some of my friends] who you know are going to have a laugh, and if there's a bunch of you, or it's someone's birthday or whatever or you're going somewhere different, then you go out then, but if they're just off down the town then I won't bother as much.

It's like, sometimes you haven't scored, you're pissed, you wake up in the morning and you're bad off the drink, you wish you could just go back, stop in and keep the money.

The five principal reasons for this edginess seem to be the excessive intake of alcohol (the night-time economy's main legal commodity); the constant eruption of flashpoints in the queues and melees formed as large crowds of intoxicated consumers struggle for finite resources such as taxis and fast food; the tendency of some door minders to use confrontational methods of regulating the behaviour of consumers; the infiltration of violent criminal groups distributing both legal and illegal commodities; and the aggressive tendencies that seem to permeate certain individuals and cultures amongst the predominantly young consumer group and find release in an environment where hedonism and lack of inhibition are systematically encouraged to increase the attraction of the environment and boost profits. Thus one of the major risks for consumers and wage workers in the night-time economy is the constant possibility of encountering criminality and violence.

However, it must be noted that the first four phenomena permeate the night-time leisure economies of other places, such as most of Europe or Canada, yet levels of serious violence tend to be higher in the United States, Central and South America, Australia (Homel et al., 1991, 1992; Tomsen 1997; Zimring and Hawkins, 1997) and, in our case, Britain (Hobbs et al., 2003). This tends to suggest that there are certain peculiarities about youth culture and the consumer economy in Britain that need to be explored in the anthropological depth that ethnographic research allows before theorization can proceed with any confidence. Having said that, it is of course well known that most ethnographic research into the relationship between culture and economy tends to be heavily informed by pre-existing theoretical paradigms, which in turn are driven by a variety of often quite unyielding political ideologies and cultural or personal interests (see Chapter 1). One criticism is that the proliferation of these conflicting views has diversified social science to the extent that it risks stalling in a gridlock of perspectival relativism, conceptual incompatibility and intellectual alienation, unable to explain anything in ways that can be understood, let alone inform or criticize politics and governance at either the micro or macro levels. In one single study we cannot possibly explore and assess the explanatory power of the significant number of theoretical positions that surround this problem, and we also acknowledge straight away that, as we put it elsewhere 'individual acts of violence have complex micro-cultural and psychological aetiologies' (Hall and Winlow, 2003). However, distinct socio-cultural patterns also exist (Hall and Winlow, 2003), and although the Americas and Australia are obviously outside the scope of this study, what we can do here is to explore the mutually observable fact that in Britain there is something – more complex yet paradoxically more fundamental than standard explanations such as intoxication, poor regulation, socialization, labelling, enclosed sub-cultural norms and destructive masculinities – about the relationship between young people and the night-time economy that produces comparatively high levels of violence.

–6–

Victims' Stories

Our interviews revealed that roughly two-thirds of our male sample and one-fifth of our female sample had experienced serious violence at first hand. As we have already indicated, the 'dark figure' of violence in the night-time economy is extremely difficult to estimate (see also Lister, 2002) but the data here suggest very strongly that the violence rate in this dimension of everyday life is significantly higher than anywhere else and that violence cuts across the traditional class, gender and geographical lines of differentiation that characterize other forms of violence. Very few will be from socially excluded backgrounds (see Hollands, 2002) but the night-time economy is something of a 'melting-pot', where individuals from a number of social and cultural groups mix freely in the same space, seeking the same hedonistic adventures, attaining the same states of extreme intoxication, experiencing the same problems and risking the same potentially volatile encounters in this bustling, deregulated and minimally policed environment.

The lines that differentiate meaning between allegedly diverse cultural groups and individuals here appear to be faded and broken as the inhabitants of the liminal zone engage with the symbolism of the ornamental consumer economy with great enthusiasm and growing expertise. Although there are small distinctions based on music and fashion, nowhere, in our experience, apart from in uniformed organizations, do individuals appear and act less 'differently'. This is partly the product of the night-time economy's utilitarian environment, which is geared up to sell its principal commodity – alcohol – in the most efficient manner, ushering in masses of young people, supplying them with alcohol, feeding them with hot snacks and then transporting them back out *en masse* in the most unceremonious way imaginable (Hobbs et al., 2000). The dominant ethic of this massed population appeared to be extreme intoxication; very few of those we talked to and observed restricted themselves to mild intoxication, exchanging anecdotes over a glass of wine. There is nothing genteel or cosmopolitan about the homogenized drinking strip. Drinks were imbibed standing up, quickly, before moving on to the next bar. This is a world of slammers and shooters, powerful lager, alcopops and loud music. Drinks promotions reflect and sustain this ethic of the rapid removal of all that is humdrum, routine, boring; doubles for singles, trebles for singles, free shooters with every drink. Before long, progressing around the drinking strip involves side-stepping piles of vomit, dodging drunks slumped in the street, and edging past the various threats that are scattered around the after-dark urban environment. There are few places on the youth-orientated drinking strip to engage in meaningful discussions. When people talk, they do so at volume and directly into the ears of their companions. Being served at the bar involves triumphing in the battle to get the bartender's attention and then screaming your order. Those too sober, polite or inexperienced to engage in the melee are condemned to thirsty and prolonged wait, a highly undesirable diversion from the central business of becoming rapidly submerged in drunkenness. Those who elevate the importance of music and particular fashion trends may go to fewer bars, steer clear of the main drinking strip and head off to a club earlier, but the vast numbers of night-time revellers tend to progress gradually along the well-trodden drinking route like a happy, intoxicated and disorderly rabble. Each an individual, displaying highly particular aspects of character, moving agentically through the night, but all participating in this created culture, all imbuing it with value for much the same reason, and, to the sober observer, uniform in so many respects.

The interpersonal violence that erupts at specific points in this process (Homel et al, 1992; Homel and Clark, 1994; Tomsen, 1997) is, of course, one of life's great social levellers and cultural de-differentiators, unifying individuals, and the complex, fragile psycho-cultural baggage that both differentiates and civilizes them, in moments of visceral hatred and frantic physical activity. The following interview data are indicative of the types of violence regularly encountered by many of the young people who frequent the night-time economy and the way it tends to be experienced and understood.

Paul

Paul is 21 and works part-time in a sports shop in north-east England while studying for a degree in psychology at a local university. He lives with his mother and father in a quiet and fairly affluent neighbourhood in his native city.

Paul describes himself as an 'average young bloke'. He enjoys sports, goes to the university gym regularly and 'loves a night out with the lads'. Paul coyly admits to a keen interest in fashion, regularly uses sunbeds, dyes his hair and is considerably removed from the traditional forms of masculinity that predominated in this region in the not-too-distant past. Indeed, any theoretical explanation based on concepts such hegemonic masculinity, machismo, patriarchy or the loss of dominance-rights immediately runs aground on the paradoxes that permeate the complex suite of affects and meanings that constitute Paul's personality and social being. His ostensible 'attraction' to the 'exciting' prospect of violence might lead towards essentialist and individualist explanations based on the 'sensual attraction' of transgressing the norm, such as those offered by Katz (1988). However, Katz's thesis neglects the sociological fact that this alleged 'motivation' – even if it is hard-wired into the human psyche – is manifesting itself in actual violent acts in a specific context where, as we shall see, a higher rate of violence is itself the norm. Someone wishing to transgress the norm in this environment would have to do something like sit quietly on a doorstep reading *The German Ideology*. We must consider the possibility that consumer capitalism has become – for its own instrumental purposes – a multi-normative environment of simulated cultural sectors built around a unified and ubiquitous economic logic. Consumer capitalism has learnt very well how to elicit desires and feelings of excitement without risking any genuine transgression of its normative core (see Žižek, 2000.

Of average height but quite slim, Paul is not too different from a lot of other young consumers of the liminal night-time experience that is sold by the network of pubs, bars and night-clubs that clutter the centre of the post-industrial city that he calls home. Whilst he readily admits that he is 'no tough guy', and points out that he has had a good upbringing and 'isn't one of those people who goes out purposely looking for bother', Paul regards his involvement in a number of violent incidents over the past few years as something of an 'adventure'.

> You get the feeling, before you're going out, that it's like an adventure or something, when you're young anyway. Even now we always ring around and see what's happening, and it's like a build up to a football match and that. We use to say we got 'pre-match tension', like before a night out, like the anticipation of it, coz you want to have a good time and you're wondering what's going to happen.

> [ex]I think I probably had my first fight when I was 17 or something ... It was someone from school I didn't get on with and I saw them down the town and it just happened really. It was about even I'd say ... I can remember being really, really nervous, shaking and everything, but it just seemed like one of those things that happens. I'd seen fights before but there's nothing really to prepare you for it. I cut my lip, but afterwards I felt great ... It's a bit like losing your virginity ... it's something you know will happen and you're happy to get it out of the way really. In a couple of days you kind of forget about it ... but you know, it comes up when you're talking to your mates and that ...

Paul recalls peripheral involvement in a number of other violent incidents while out drinking with friends in the city centre. He stressed the normality and routine of petty violence and the adrenalizing aspects of this type of physical engagement:

> When I first started going out it's a bit scary really because you'd always see these blokes getting into fights and that, and it's all a bit mental ... It didn't stop me. It doesn't put you off because you kind of think it isn't going to happen to you, and these, and all this other stuff that you've got to go out for that it doesn't really bother you. I think it's just expected and no one really cares about it [the violence]. You just get so used to it that it's just normal ... Like every night, guaranteed, you can see a fight or

something. It's either bouncers grabbing people in a pub, or there's a fight in the street or if you get a taxi, it's just the way it is and it doesn't bother people.

Mimetic admiration for 'experienced' and 'battle-hardened' older men still held a time-honoured place as a reproductive process, and the emboldening feelings of invulnerability and imminent victory that strength in numbers generates echoed, in a miniaturized sort of way, Canetti's (1987) famous study on crowds:

Mostly just little things. We used to hang about a bit with these older lads ... [who some of Paul's friends] knew from the match, and they'd get into fights. They'd start [trouble] with people for no reason really, but when you're out in a group and it's not you it's kind of exciting ... I can remember watching people get hit, knocked out and that, and it's kind of like a joke, because you know you're with this big group of lads and nothing can happen [to you] ... Some of them might start with people in bars ... the bouncers would come over and that but mostly nothing happened. Pizza shops and that ... I think we [Paul's close friends] quite liked it, or at least some did, because there's the safety and stuff of going out with a bunch of [older] lads like that, but I was always a bit wary because I didn't know them that well and you just know something bad's going happen soon or later.

Paul regards himself as having matured out of that old scene, and tries to distinguish himself as an individual from the violence-seeking crowd that he once found so attractive, yet there is an underlying fatalism about the inevitability of violent encounters:

But even then, it's not like you can avoid it, because it [trouble] just seems to find you. Usually it's nothing much, but mostly I'm not really the type to get into fights. I try to stay out of the way of those types of people ... [who] you can tell like fighting ... You pick the kind of bars you go to and the nightclubs and that. It's basic commonsense really. There's some bars and nightclubs where you know fights are going to happen, so you just don't go. And, you know, be careful in pizza shops and trying to get taxis and stuff. We usually don't go to those type of places anyway, so normally it's OK.

The description of his encounters reinforces the view held by a number of researchers (see Polk, 1994; Zimring and Hawkins, 1997) that violence between young men is often an escalation of trivial arguments and altercations. Inebriation is the normal condition in the night-time economy, but because violence is not ubiquitous or constant this is an inadequate explanation in itself. However, the emboldening and disinhibiting effects of alcohol cannot be taken lightly:

Paul: It was just a normal Saturday night out really. We've started at about seven o'clock in *Dino's*, and it was just like most nights really, but for some reason I was really pissed. I can't remember why. It's a bit blurry really until there's just like an argument or something starts while we're walking between pubs and all of a sudden we're getting chased down the street.

Q: Why, what happened?

Paul: I really don't know. We [Paul and his friends] didn't really talk about it afterwards. You just kind of take it for granted that an argument started over something. Not really an argument even, just, like, a couple of words and then that's it isn't it? … My guess is someone said something, it happened behind me, someone's said something and this group of lads have just gone after us. I remember running, but I was drunk and my head's all over the place and I see my mates going past and going off in different directions and then I get grabbed by the shirt and they start laying in to me … I got hit mostly on the side of my face, but I stayed on my feet so it wasn't that bad.

Q: what did it feel like, while it was happening?

Paul: It didn't really hurt actually. I was drunk so it didn't really kick in 'til the next morning … I was shocked mostly I think. I put my hands and arms over my face like this and just kind of waited for it all to stop really. [I must have been] hit maybe a dozen times on the side of my head. Something like that. I got hit in the ear and it went really, really hot, and I got hit beside my eye there. I think it was mainly one lad laying in to me, and I think someone else must've joined in because I got kicked in the legs and on my arse a few times, and then that was it really, they ran off, going after the others I think.

Q: What did you do?

Paul: I just made my way back onto the main street. My ears were ringing a bit and the side of my face was sore, but I felt OK really … I walked up the street and I think it was in my mind to get a taxi, then two of the lads showed up and I went off with them.

Paul's reluctance to report the incident was typical and reinforces the view (see Lister et al., 2002) that, although confident quantitative estimates are very difficult, the 'dark figure' of violence in the night-time economy must be very high indeed:

I didn't even think to tell the police or anything. It just happened and I just thought I'd get on with my night and forget about it. I must have looked a bit of a mess because I got knocked back from the nightclub we went to because I was a mess … My shirt was ripped and I was bleeding a bit from my eye … I had a cut just above my eyebrow there.

The next day it hurt though. I was covered in bruises all over my legs and I'd cut my lip inside a few times and I had a small cut over my eye … I had a hangover [and] felt like death. I couldn't believe I wanted to stay out [after the attack] … my Mam and Dad were asking what had happened and that and fussing and I just had to beg them not to call the police … They told me I had to go to the hospital to get my eye stitched but I just went around to my mates because I didn't want to sit there for ages … I think I just wanted to forget about it … A couple of my mates got a kicking as well, Ian was the worst off because he got his tooth knocked out and had to go sit in the hospital all night.

The need to avoid humiliation is a principal reason for the extreme reluctance of young men to report incidents of violence, especially if their physical conditions might indicate that they have come off worse (see Newburn and Stanko, 1994):

> I think we were a bit embarrassed about it really. You don't want to admit that you got beaten up, and it got to me a bit because I felt angry because I'd let it happen I think … My stomach, you get that feeling in your stomach … no, no I wasn't scared it was going to happen again or anything, far from it … I think I wanted it to happen again so I could kick the shit out of them this time. You go through, thinking about what you should've done and you shouldn't have been that drunk and maybe blaming your mates a little for being mouthy, but really I was angry at myself.
>
> We didn't talk about it at all really it was like we just wanted to forget about it. No one took the piss or anything, because we were all to blame a bit. I think it toughened me up a bit that though, because you just think if it happens again I'll just to go nuts and get in to them, not just curling up and letting them get in to you.

However, Paul was the victim of a second assault shortly after, and the location of the incident reinforces the view that fast-food outlets are 'hot spots' of casual violence:

> The second time was nothing really to do with me and there's nothing really I could have done about it … I come out of a nightclub with this girl and we're both a bit drunk and we go for a kebab before we get a taxi. She was talking to some people in the queue and something happened, I'm not sure what, and this big lad, like a bodybuilder type has just started slagging everyone off and starting arguing with this girl I'm with, and I'd gone to get her hand to kind of move her towards the counter and this lad has just said something to me, and kind of put his hand out and then just punched me in the face.
>
> I got up and people are fussing all over me and I just sort of felt groggy. The police came and took me to hospital and I must've waited about four or five hours before I got to see a doctor … I broke my nose. I had to give a statement but there wasn't much I could really say … I just told the truth about what happened. I could only give them a sketchy description of what he looked like. The girl I was with sat with me at the hospital, but she didn't give a statement because I couldn't get in touch with her. As far as I know nothing else really came of it. The police came around and said they were investigating it and said I could apply for compensation but I just wanted it forgotten.

This incident belies the assumptions that most violent incidents tend to occur between people who know each other, and it suggests that unpredictable 'stranger violence' is becoming more common (see Riedel, 1993). Paul's reluctance to have anything more to do with the girl who seemed to have a peripheral involvement in the incident indicates the powerful alienating socio-cultural role that violence continues to perform in the maintenance of specific interpersonal relationships and the prevention of others:

> I suppose I felt the same as the first [time] really. I suppose I was a bit upset, a bit angry … just going over it and over it and making it worse, but this time I think I kind of knew there's nothing I could've done. It was just some arsehole really, and if someone is just going to hit you for nothing, with no warning or anything, there's nothing you can really do … I didn't see her [the girl] again. Well I saw her, and she asked what had happened and are you all right and that, but I think I just wanted nothing more to do with her … it [the attack] must've had something to do with it.

Throughout our interviews Paul understandably avoided emotional issues and a more direct analysis of his feelings about the two attacks. Having said that, he was quite happy to talk about fear and foreboding before the incidents actually occurred. It was the result of the incident – in this case a 'loss' – that demanded a specific emotional response, which contrasts with the often more self-deprecating and honest responses after 'victory' or before the incident actually happens, when of course coming out on top is always a possibility. The general culture that forged Paul's *habitus* seems to have the distinction between winning and losing at its core. For the most part he talked generally about feeling angry, for men perhaps one of the more acceptable emotional responses to violence and loss of face. He tended to direct his anger inwardly, in contradistinction to theories that posit this as a gendered trait of the traditional 'repressed female', and although there was no direct discussion of masculinity, Paul appeared to be commenting on an internal dialogue with his masculine identity in light of socially expected scripts about male violence and male victimhood.

The painful physical wounds were important only as signifiers of his victimhood. Indeed, he would not show himself socially until the outward signs of his perceived ignominious defeat had healed. He was more conscious of what he expected of himself than what he believed was expected of him by his peers, his father and the massed audience of night-time human traffic that populate these city streets, which suggests that these cultural codes were strongly internalized in the *habitus*, and therefore not entirely dependent on the constant external judgement of peers for their reproduction. The blows that caused the most pain were delivered retrospectively upon his ego and his youthful masculine self-identity. When pressed for details, and forced to relive the incidents in his mind, Paul became mildly upset and, because our interview was first and foremost a conversation between men, we skirted around issues likely to reveal the full extent of Paul's psychological injuries. As he indicates:

> I did go over it a lot. I still do really. Now, talking about it, just makes me wish I'd, you know, whacked the bastard, just tore into him, and the more I went over it the more I decided I wasn't going to get caught like that again.

Apart from the understandable need to fall into the standard self-congratulatory masculine repertoires about violent potential, Paul clearly made a connection between being the victim of these assaults and a victor in others. He talked about 'growing up a lot' as a result of being beaten up, of it being 'a learning experience' and it 'toughening [him] up a bit'. At the bottom of Paul's personal discourse lay the fear and insecurity of living in what he perceived to be a hostile world populated by a significant number of potential assailants. However, this perception was not the 'social construction' of a mass-media out to propagate what Taylor (1999: 224) named a 'hyper-active moral panic' amongst the population, but rather an understandable and rationally filtered response to the bitter experience of real life in advanced capitalism's most common form of youthful leisure activity in Britain:

> It just makes you think that really there's some proper nasty people out there and you've got to be wary about what's happening and what's going on, and I suppose you've got to expect the worst to happen. It can happen to anybody. Someone can just pick you out of a crowd and that's it.

Despite the mass media's undeniable ability to influence perception at the broadest of levels, real-life experience continues to be the anvil on which the individual identity and *habitus* of young people are forged:

> I think I probably just starting to think about it more and more. I went to the gym a lot more and just changed a bit really overall ... It might have just been me growing up but I think my mood changed a bit ... I'm not sure how. Like I say, it could've just be part of getting older and it might have had nothing to do with that [the assaults]. One thing I think pissed me off is that I could tell my Mam was upset, and I suppose I just kind of thought I wouldn't let that happen again.

However, stranger violence has compounded rather than displaced the type of violent incident that occurs between people who know each other and have a history of antagonism:

Paul: One time we were in this bar and my mate got into a fight. It was over something that had been going on ages since we were kids and they'd had a fight before and we all kind of knew each other. He was getting the better of my mate so I just whacked him really.

Q: Why?

Paul: Just happened ... I just saw him there and then I hit him ... I suppose I just felt angry, just angry and then hit him ... People sort of jumped in and then the bouncers came and threw them [the original protagonists] out. We went outside and they had another fight but someone said the police were coming so it just broke up ... I don't think I felt good but I didn't feel bad ... [I think] maybe people might have thought about me a bit different, and that was kind of good, but I didn't feel good about hitting the lad.

Paul had waded in to maintain the friendship with his friend, which again relates back to the 'safety in numbers' motivation. This is unlikely to have been an entirely altruistic gesture, however. A subtle form of status acquisition also appears to have been working its charms as Paul would have been aware that proactive violence of this type can bestow a measure of esteem even within Paul's rather pacified segment of masculine working-class culture. An act such as this is, of course, unlikely to catapult Paul through the variegated ranks of fistic repute that continue to develop in the remnants of localized working class communities, but those who witnessed the act will have quickly added it to the list of information available on Paul, and a small realignment of perception may have taken place. On the surface of things, this was a generous and impassioned attempt to help a friend in need, an act likely to bond the two to a greater degree and reinforce the expectation of reciprocity. This, of course, is another example of an instrumental friendship that is maintained specifically for its defensive capabilities, the sort of 'mutual back-up' principle that pervades police cultures (see Manning, 1977; Hobbs, 1988). Again, personal insecurity at the basic physical level and the imperative of developing defensive capabilities overrides the standard explanations of the maintenance of masculine dominance and patriarchal rights:

> I think it just made me think I could do it if I needed to. I didn't think I was some hard case because it's obvious that there's loads of people who could flatten me down the town. But I think it was really thinking about the other stuff [assaults] that made me not want to be soft if anything happened.

Other incidents of violence can be heavily ritualized, engaged in to establish and communicate – internally and externally – the courage and fortitude of the group and its members in the face of hostility. A lot of football violence falls into this category (Armstrong, 1998), and there is a tendency towards a lot of aggressive posturing but very little physical contact:

> There was another time when we got into a fight with some lads at a taxi rank in Northville and I really liked that. It was just kind of funny really, running around and hitting people. No one got hurt ... [and] we won and they ran off. Another time I hit someone in a nightclub and got chucked out, so I think I didn't feel as bad because if it's all one way it's not good.

However, in the face of the true 'professional warriors' represented by the bouncers (see Winlow et al, 2001), whose bodies, occasionally enlarged and strengthened by gym training (see Monaghan, 2001), make them virtually unassailable opponents to the average young man, the whole cultural system of honour, victory and loss is instantly suspended without even the slightest indication of the traumatic loss of face. Loss is inevitable, and 'black humour', the traditional working-class tactic of coping with the long-term loss and humiliation experienced in the position of constant subordination to a monolithic power that is unassailable yet at the same time hamstrung by legally enforced rules and its sheer visibility in the crowd, returns to rescue and re-humanize these young men.

> I've been hit only once since that last time and that was by a bouncer in Studio 21 [a local Northville nightclub], so there's not much you can do is there? ... My mate was getting thrown out for being lippy to the barmaid or something, arguing about change, and as he was getting chucked out this other bouncer just came up and started throwing me out, and I hadn't done anything. So I'm saying, look, I've done nothing wrong, and he's just pushing me really hard at the door, at this fire exit. So I've kind of gone to get out of the way, which I shouldn't have done. I was drunk, and I should've just gone outside, but I tried to like drag my arm away and he's just slapped me really hard and I've kind of stumbled down the stairs ... [After that] he's just dragged me towards the door at the bottom and said I was barred. Outside my mate started laughing because I had this red hand print on the side of my face.

> I wasn't really that bothered about that one. It just happens. It was funny after, but at the time I can remember thinking he's going to kill me or something. He just slapped me but he's enormous compared to me so it's not like it's nothing ... It was funny because you can't really do anything, can you, if that happens, so you can see the funny side. I've known people get proper good hidings off bouncers and ... I think I got away quite easy.

Phil

Phil is a twenty-three year-old contract employee in a maintenance firm. He lives at home with his mother and younger brother in a small terraced house in a fairly nondescript area of his hometown. Phil's first interview was dominated by discussion of his experience of night-time leisure and his attitudes towards identity and consumption, but he agreed to a further interview after hinting that he had experienced violence first-hand. His first experience was at comprehensive school:

> I had my first fights at school. I had a few fights with this one lad who I know quite well now, and another couple just with other kids my age. There was a group of us and we'd get into gang fights I suppose, nothing serious though. Just running about and shouting really.

Phil claims to have been a bit of a party animal during his late teens, going out as much as he could afford. His early perceptions of violence amongst older and larger men were almost like those felt whilst watching a cartoon:

> When you go out all the time you just get used to seeing fights all the time. I think it used to add to the excitement, that you might see a fight, especially when you're young like I was at first ... We'd be trying to get in [to bars] at maybe sixteen and that, trying to look older by dressing up a bit ... You'd see fights all the time, especially in the types of bars we used to go in. You'd see these big blokes just whacking fuck out of each other and it was kind of funny watching it.

Phil reiterates what in this later stage of our research had become the ubiquitous 'strength in numbers' explanation, but adds to this the distress predicated on the failure to keep the group together in the transition to adulthood and the ensuing feelings of isolation and insecurity that permeated individuals. The fear and risk of 'stranger violence' comes back to the fore in Phil's accounts:

> We'd just get into fights when it came up, it's not like we went out really looking to get into some trouble. I knew a lot of quite hard lads from school and round the doors and we kind of all knew each other and would back each other up and that if anything happened. When I was like seventeen or something it was amazing because we'd go out in big groups and if there was a fight we'd always win easy because there's just so many of us, and you're just kind of really game at that age I think ... [As we got older] there wasn't as many of us and there'd be fights with other lads who could handle themselves ... I got knocked out, clean out, one time outside Studio 21 in the town when I was about eighteen or something, when we got into this fight over pushing in a queue I think ...
>
> It was nothing major really. Just a small scuffle and then the shouting and that, and my mate Mike, who can handle himself, having a go with this other lad. I just kind of jumped in because they were all in to him, just kind of ran in and started throwing punches, and it all kind of drifted off because it's right outside a nightclub and the bouncers came over. So me and a couple of others go back to the queue and I can see Mike walking off the other way, I think just walking around the block so the bouncers don't see him [rejoining the queue], and so it just starts calming down and this lad's come up from the back of the queue and just whacked me.
>
> I just sort of saw him out the corner of my eye but there's people all over the place and I didn't know what was going to happen. Just hit me once I think on the side of the head. After that obviously I don't know what happened.

For Phil, recounting this story causes little obvious emotional distress, at least a partial reflection of his more practical and tougher habitual dispositions. Indeed, in places, he seems quite amused by the unfolding story, which indicates that either he is not heavily immersed in the cultural codes and psychological motivations of 'machismo' or destructive forms of 'hegemonic masculinity', or has ascended to a level where defeat need not impact upon his sense of self or his place and reputation within his friendship network and the broader culture. Indeed, he seems less heavily immersed in the pervasive code of honour related to winning and losing violent conflicts that seemed to figure heavily in the accounts of some of the other interviewees. Phil's knockabout, slapstick sense of humour seems to override the allegedly serious business of masculine codes and identity:

> Well, I'm not that bothered by it because I'm all right. It hurt at the time, but what can you do? … It's the knocking out bit that was kind of funny because I'd never been knocked out before and it's just kind of unusual … you just kind of wake up kind of confused a bit … I didn't really know what was happening at first, and slowly you kind of piece it together. The police were there and they're asking questions and then take me to hospital, but I just went home after a while … I didn't think there was much point in waiting … I felt OK and I just didn't think it was that serious really, it's not like anything's going to happen, so I just went home.
>
> I had a throbbing headache in the morning, right behind my right eye, but that was it. It was a bit of a joke for a bit but then it was forgotten … well that's just the kind of thing that happens and there's no sense in worrying about it once it's happened. I mean, I was a bit upset about it, and I can remember we were all looking around for these lads [whom they fought with] for a couple of weeks after. But that was it … There's a bit of piss-taking I suppose but really a lot of the lads had come off worse in a fight before so there's not much they can say really … I had headaches for a couple of weeks afterwards but that's it.

However, there were occasions when violence asserted itself as the serious and dangerous business that it can often be. Once again, the altercation occurs between strangers for no apparent reason, certainly no history of antagonism:

> A worse time was when I got proper done over by this lad and a couple of his mates. It was definitely the worst … He tried to bite my fingers off … It's just a fight that happened. Me and my mate John and these lads. I got knocked over and I was getting kicked, and then one of them starts pulling at my hands, and I'm thinking he's sort of going to get a good shot in my face, so I'm pulling, and then he just sinks his teeth in … Oh yeah I was shitting myself obviously. He didn't get his mouth all the way round but it fucking hurt and I've just gone all the way nuts, like screaming and lashing out, but I was on the floor so as soon as I move my hands I'm just getting booted in the face, so I go to cover up again and he has another go … This is on a pretty crowded street. It must have been about midnight maybe … This time he's got my left hand with two hands like that and he's going to bite my finger off … My heart was jumping out of my chest, just pure panic. I knew this lad who had his ear bitten off, and I'm just thinking, shit, this is going to happen to me … One of them's just gone [meaning said], the coppers are coming, and they've all drifted off, and then this women's come over and got me sat up, but I was wide awake, and John said run so I just ran off after that.

It was just cut really, but when his teeth went in it really hurt. I'm talking really hurt. It bruised up quite bad and swelled up to this size or something and I had it bandaged up for a couple of days. The rest of it didn't matter because all I was thinking about is losing my finger ... Yeah, I suppose I was a bit pissed off about it. I really wanted to find this cunt and get him done over, big style. John saw one of them in a club a couple of weeks later and we pasted him and John done him with a bottle. It wasn't the one that went for my finger, but I just wanted to kill the bastard anyway ... if the bouncers hadn't come I think I'd still be there now, booting in to the bastard.

While Phil's finger managed to remain attached to his hand, this kind of incident reflects the real human costs that can result from interpersonal violence in the night-time economy. This is not the media-sanitized, jocular, knockaround version of barroom brawling, and nor is this a form of honorific combat, in which both parties agree to fight by rules, remove their coats and step outside. Here, disputes arise quickly, occasionally for seemingly minor reasons, escalate rapidly, and few if any rules apply. The violence is real, destructive, and its repercussions occasionally highly significant (see Shepherd, 1990). In the above passage, Phil's violent intentions and actions seem to be motivated by revenge, and appear to be grounded in his perception of righteous anger. The involvement of his closest friends in the revenge attack is an expected but deeply symbolic reflection of masculine identity and friendship within the culture in which both Phil and his friends were raised, but it also reflects the manner in which enclassed identities and dispositions interact with the cultures of the night-time economy. Revenge attacks of this kind are of course a standard topic in the anthropological study of serious interpersonal violence (see for example, Trompf, 1994). Cycles of violence and revenge can often establish and reproduce themselves, but the act of revenge can often be a means of affirming the solidarity of the defensive group. Miniaturized, temporary and unstable variants of the traditional defensive community seem to be struggling for a brief but spectacular existence in the atomized and individualized world of consumer capitalism, like rare forms of Durkheimian social matter that need the intense energy of a particle-accelerator to allow them to exist briefly in a Weberian legal-rational, individualized world that is otherwise hostile to their existence. Phil went on to relate how this attack ultimately resulted in the arrest of his friend, John. Phil said:

I don't know [how I feel about it]. I just think that these things happen when you're young. I try to avoid that type of thing more now, and you just kind of grow out of it a bit. I wouldn't do half the things I did when I was a young 'un ... I don't feel bad about it much ... sometimes a little thought will flash and I'll think, you cunt, and want to beat the shit out of him [his attacker], but it's just the way it goes ... you can't win them all and I've done all right and I know that I can look after myself because you've lived through it really ... I'm not saying I'm dead hard or anything, it's just you kind of get used to it a bit and I know what it's like and how it happens and you know what to do a bit.

Now I think I can kind of spot things a little better ... well, like before, you get so scared and so excited when you get into a fight but now it's not really like that and I can see things happening and, well, get out of the way and that. A lot of the time ... [when I was a kid] you wanted to get in to a fight for the laugh, but now you just get tired of it and you just grow out of it.

Harry

Much like the nocturnal biographies of Phil and Paul, Harry's victimhood is couched in an assortment of anecdotes about friends and fun, about the centrality of evening entertainment and peer group judgements of self-identity, and occasional acts of violence as a peripheral participant and occasionally as an aggressor. Harry is nineteen, and lives with his mother and father in a reasonably well-to-do neighbourhood in a northern city. In his first year at university, he also works part-time in a small supermarket. Throughout his narrative is a nagging concern about the danger and risk extant in the night-time economy:

> Everyone loves going out ... and it's just a good laugh to go out and get drunk and behave like an idiot really ... You save up and just blow all your money on a weekend ... [It's where] I enjoy myself the most because we'll just be taking the piss out of each other and going on like nutters ... I think a lot of it is to try and score, at least for some people, but mostly it's about mucking about with the lads and having a laugh ... you can see that there's a bit of a risk going out. Ever since we started going out there's always a bit of trouble and you can tell that once some people get really drunk they just want to go out and start fights ... There's always trouble, it's just all over the place. I'm not saying that everyone is out there looking for trouble, but you can tell some people do, and so you see it a lot. A lot depends on where you go, and in the good clubs there's usually no trouble ... I think it's mostly because you get different kinds of people going, and there's people using drugs and stuff, so they're not bothered about fighting or acting macho or any of that. You go into the rougher bits though at eleven o'clock and it's like Gladiator [the film], just fights all over, and police, and ambulances and all that ... It makes you think why they do it, but it doesn't really bother me. Some people are just into that type of thing.

Again, Harry's perception of the night-time economy as a risky arena is not based on a socially constructed and mass-mediated 'fear of crime'. We do not deny the immense power of the mass media in Western culture, but we are convinced that its seductive and incorporationist methods are much more subtle than simply creating an exaggerated, general atmosphere of fear. Even when this method is employed, it tends to label a specific group as the object of fear, an internal or external 'other'. Harry's quite understandable suspicion, disillusionment and caution about modern life, his fellow human beings and their behaviour in specific circumstances is the result of a sustained beating he received as he rather gallantly and misguidedly intervened in a dispute between a man and a women on a dark city street. As the Left Realists were at pains to point out, much fear and caution has a rational, experiential core (Lea and Young, 1993). Nor does Harry seem to be motivated by a quest for excitement or an ambition to exercise 'patriarchal rights' and reproduce male dominance:

I'm not really much of a fighter. I only had one fight at school, but I wouldn't say I was soft, I'm no softer than most of my mates. It's just I'm not one of those lads who get into fights and are always talking about fighting and stuff. It's just straightforward really. I don't like to think about it much and I suppose to a certain extent what happened was brought about by me. It just wouldn't have happened if I hadn't have been drunk ... I wouldn't have done what I did and I wouldn't have been in a position where someone can do that to you ... We were just walking past and we saw this couple rowing ... there was a few people just kind of standing and watching ... he screaming at her and she's screaming at him and he's kind of banged her against the shutters like that ... the shutters at the front of some shop [that's shut for the night] ... some of the people have said, woah! But really people were treating it as a joke. They were arguing and we were ... slowly walking towards the corner, looking back at them. She started slapping him, over and over and he just stood there taking it, and she started pulling his hair and then he slapped her across the face, like really hard. You could hear it echo down the street, and she went flying, into this barrier at the side of the road.

It was just stupid and I don't know why I did it ... I just didn't think really ... Maybe I wanted to show off or something but I can just remember thinking that, well, he shouldn't have done it basically. She seemed kind of shocked and I just think I thought I had to do something or it's going to get worse. So I walked over ... [I] must've been expecting other people to say something, because there's a lot of people standing around and a lot must've seen what happened. I just said something like, come on, leave her alone or something, just something daft. He had her against the shutters. She's crying and he's shouting dead loud, and he's just turned and started screaming something at me and I could tell straight away that I was in trouble.

I think ideally I wanted him to just say OK, and just let her go, but looking back you can tell she didn't want to go anywhere. It was both of them ... [I don't know if I] wanted to play the hero or show off. I kind of backed off as soon as he started coming towards me and I turned to run and he's hit me in the face, about there, and I was on the floor and I think I expected him to start kicking me but he didn't ... I wasn't unconscious. My face was just bruised, but he really hit me. I could hear some shouting and then a couple of my mates have sat me up and they [the arguing couple] weren't there. It was a bit weird because you can feel loads of people looking at you but nobody does anything. I expected the police to come and arrest the lad but it was like nothing happened ... They [Harry's mates] were asking if I was all right ... I looked in this shop window, expecting to see my face all over the place but I was just really red and my face was sore and my ears were ringing ... Some of the lads put me in a taxi home.

[I didn't tell my parents] because they'd have blown it out of all proportion ... [I didn't phone the police] because I just wanted to forget it. The next day I just had a bad head and a sore face ... [I think] mainly it was the drink. I'd had a lot to drink and I would never had gone up to someone like that if I was sober ... [I was] to blame in a way because I shouldn't have done what I did, but that's no excuse. There's just people like that in the world, just nasty people, and I should've stayed well out of his way. I was trying to help but really I should've minded my own business ... I think there's an element of hate there ... I'd like something really bad to happen to him ... because look at what he did. Look what type of person he is ... I haven't thought anything about her [the perpetrators female companion]. She's probably getting slapped around [off him] right now.

[I feel] anger mostly, at him and at myself ... for being so stupid. Afterwards I was a bit angry at Scott [Harry's closest friend] for just putting me in a taxi ... He just went out afterwards, just stuck me in a taxi and left me, but that was just because I was mad about what happened ... I don't blame him. I suppose a bit at the police for not doing anything ... They've got all these cameras all over place but it didn't do me any good. Her [the female companion] a bit because she wasn't just standing there, she looked like she'd started it [the confrontation]. Just everyone. People who stood and watched, everyone, because I might have been stupid for doing what I did but that [the attack] shouldn't have happened ... [I think I learned] not to get involved ... I wouldn't do anything like that again. I learned that you've got to be very careful all the time, but I might have known that to begin with ... now I very rarely go down the town [after dark] because it's full of these people and I don't want to have anything to do with them ... It's just not me, all that getting pissed and falling about and fighting ... Now I'll go to bars where you know things like that aren't going to happen.

Harry's intoxication might well have released him from inhibitions, but it says a lot about the sort of inhibitions that our way of life encourages individuals to internalize, the rather impoverished state of the super-ego in advanced capitalism. Weber and Durkheim both wrote about the individualization of disputes in modern rational societies, and it is quite obvious that this atomization process erodes the solidarity of groups and is indicative of a general condition of alienation. Status enhancement might have been informing his actions, but Harry chose to intervene in this individual dispute, a form of traditional behaviour that is now increasingly discouraged in all circumstances. In his intoxicated state, Harry temporarily forgot that he is supposed to be an alienated, self-interested individual and that other people's fate is not his concern, but the salutary lesson learnt by being a victim of violence might psychosomatically reinforce the cultural norm that the fate of others is really none of his business. Indeed, perhaps this is simply another example that interpersonal violence and alienation in many ways seem to operate together in a downward spiral, and thus high levels of interpersonal violence amongst the population, as evidenced in the Anglo-American world, perhaps does not seem to worry the ruling elites as much as it would do if they attached a higher value to the social solidarity of their populations.

Lee

Lee is part of a small cohort of friends who were interviewed initially to ascertain their views about night-time leisure and consumption. Lee was also part of a focus group discussion, but the following incidents were recounted in an interview at his friend's house while his friends sat in another room waiting to go out on another weekend drinking sortie into the city centre. He is 25 and works for his father, a plasterer. Lee attended a local comprehensive school and lives with his girlfriend in a small rented flat in an outlying suburb of the city in which he was born. A thin white scar of around three inches in length is testament of Lee's various encounters with violence, and the initial route into the following discussion of 'fighting':

I had the usual fights and stuff when I was younger. I had my first fight outside my Mam's house when I was ten or something, and then I had a few at school. We [Lee and his friends] had fights after that, the lads I used to go to school with. Just daft things that would happen and all of a sudden people are jumping all over the place [throwing punches] … We'd get the bus over to other estates and get into fights, or when we had the money we'd go down to town and get into fights with bouncers or blokes coming out [of the pubs] pissed up. Someone would start it and then everyone would jump in. You take a few [punches] and you give a few. We always came out on top but there'd usually be someone with a fat lip or a cut eye or something. We had some really big dos [fights] where there'd be people getting kicked all over … It was a laugh most of the time … it's just messing about when you're young, getting into fights.

I got this scar here [a small scar above his left eyebrow] off a ring I think … I've just caught one [a punch] when we were having a fight outside Deconstruction [a local nightclub] … No, it never really bothered me. You get into a fight, you've got to expect these things to happen. I got a bad cut on my bottom lip once, it was really bad, a lot of blood, but I wasn't really bothered by it because there's probably people who been cut up and stuff by the things I've done so you can't really complain and most of the time it's just forgotten.

This one [points to the scar on his cheek] is a glassing. I got smacked with a glass in The Imperial [an old style pub in the city centre] about, maybe two years ago I think it was. A half glass in the face … It's [the background is] sort of complicated. Mac [Lee's friend, sitting in the next room] was having bother with this lad who lives round ours [estate]. There's a bunch of them, about four brothers and cousins and uncles and all sorts, and it grew out of that.

Lee was present when Mac, his friend, had had a fight with a member of a large, well-known family in a local pub on the estate from which they all hail. Reinforcing the 'cycle of revenge' explanation, the fight had ended in a stalemate, but with vows that hostilities would be resumed in the near future:

> These people are just bullies, the lot of them. As soon as you stand up [to them], they bottle it or run off to get back up. You get them on their own and they're nothing ... I won't lie to you, you get a bit worried because there's talk to them doing this and doing that, and you know they can be a bunch of psychos, especially his uncle. But there's a few of us and Mac knew we'd have a go with them, and as long as it's a straight fight then that's all you can ask ... It does my head in a bit when you hear people saying this and that, and there going to kick the shit out of you and stuff, and I didn't want me Dad to hear about it because he'd go mental. But we just got on with it, we didn't hide or owt like that, so it died down a bit after a while.
>
> It was about a month after, when we were in the town. We were in The Imperial to start off ... We usually meet in there and have a game of pool or something before we go into the town proper, and it kicked off in there ... there was four of us: Me, Mac, Phil and Jackie. He [Mac's rival] just started shouting and screaming and throws a bottle at Mac, and they start getting mucked in to each other. It's just them at first, but then this bloke starts kicking Mac when they're on the floor, so Phil's smacked him and then it just turned daft. I didn't know there's so many of them. I didn't recognize half of them so I thought they were just blokes, and we had a good go but we just got the shit kicked out of us basically.

Despite Lee's rather vague and half-hearted expectations, the old codes that throughout modernity attempted to govern physical encounters between males appear to be breaking down (Hall and Winlow, 2005). The use of weapons – as in most other cases quite needless and not deployed out of desperation to rescue a losing position – is becoming routine in certain environments:

> *Lee*: Phil had his nose broke and was covered in blood; Jackie didn't get anything really serious, but I can remember him getting knocked about a bit; and Mac was in a pretty bad way. He had like, nose busted, both eyes cut, and his lip I think, and his shirt was ripped to pieces ... My eye got cut, and then I had this cut on my face. It just felt like a punch to be honest. You can only feel it cut a bit, mostly it's just like a bang.
> *Q*: What happened exactly?
> *Lee*: Ah, I couldn't say really [exasperated]. It was just nuts. Everyone was just into it. I can remember I had my head down, and I'm getting punched on the top of the head, and then I've come up and caught it on the side of the face ... I'm a bit pissed off about it obviously. I'd love to find the person what done it and fucking murder him. I think it's bang out of order using glasses and that. You have a fight you have a fight, you don't go around fucking hitting people with glasses, it's just, it's just, it's just not the way you're supposed to go on.

Q: Did you expect them to use weapons?

Lee: I don't know. It does happen like that. You don't have to time to think about that stuff because when it happens like that you're just in the middle of it and there's nothing you can do. One minute you're having a drink, the next people are wading into you and smashing glasses over your head ... I didn't even realize it was that bad until we got outside and Phil said I better go to hospital. I just thought, fuck, you know, because you know you're going to spend hours waiting around to get stitched, and then you've got to listen to all the shit ... You've got to listen to the coppers, do this do that, all the rest of it, and then, like me Dad going on about what's happened and me Mam and all the rest of it.

Lee refused to give evidence against those who had assaulted him, as did all of his friends. This is one of an unknown number of nocturnal assaults that never enter the record books. Fortunately, in many cases the codified habit of refusing to extend hostilities beyond two or three encounters still appears to hold firm, perhaps because of the fear of eventual prosecution or the fear of 'ending up burning each other's houses down':

It's just not the thing to do is it? You can't get a name as a grass, and even then I just wouldn't want to do it. I just wouldn't ... we were talking about sorting it out ourselves, and getting a squad together and all the rest of it, but in the end it just died off.

Contrary to some popular accounts of male attitudes to violence, Lee was quite forthcoming about his own personal feelings of fear and trepidation, which throughout our research showed only occasional signs of being repressed by 'macho codes'. On the contrary, Lee delivered his vivid descriptions of his personal fear and the 'scariness' and briefly spectacular nature of the encounter with a good deal of enthusiasm, in the same way that many people would describe a traumatic experience. It was endurance that figured highly in his descriptions, rather than the transgressive excitement at the centre of Katz's notion of the 'seductive attractions' of violence. Lee's general attitude offers some support to the idea that *fortitude* is the ability still being valorized and reality tested in this particular culture (see Horne and Hall, 1995; Hall, 1997):

When you first realize that you're going to get the shit kicked out of you, it's just shock I suppose. You don't think, nothing really ... Yeah I was scared. Your heart's banging and that and you're thinking, fuck, but really you're looking about and looking for people who're going to start getting in to you. You're trying to react. Especially then because everyone there was getting stuck in to us. I squared up and kind of backed away towards the door, and then you're just trying to get out of the way of punches and hoy [meaning throw] a few digs back. I got punched a few times, and I whacked a few people but then the punches were coming from all over and I put my head down which I shouldn't have done ... when you're standing up, you can see what's happening, what's going on, when you put your head down, well, you might not get caught flush [in the face], but really anyone can have a free short at your cos you can't see or get out the way or anything.

I could hear Phil kind of screaming, and I'm getting whacked round the head, and it seemed to go on for ages, cos most fights I've been in only last a bit. It's like you kind of hope they're going to pack in after a bit and leave you, but they just kept on going … I was just trying to stay on my feet, and then you just get scared and I thought I've got to get out of here, and I've stood up to go for the door, and that's when he's glassed me. Not kidding, but at the time, it's like, shit, they're going to fucking kill me, and you just go into overdrive like, steaming towards the door. To be honest, after that, I'm not sure what happened. I think the owner's come over or something, or I don't know, and I've just stumbled out the door. After that the others [his friends] have come out, and then the coppers have come down the back lane and stopped us. I couldn't even tell who's done it [glassed him]. It's just faces, and I only recognized a couple of them. You're just not thinking about things like that. You haven't got time to think, who's doing what, think, what should I do, what's going to happen, nothing … It feels like someone's squeezing your guts, like you're in shock or something, just blank.

[Now I just feel] what a set of cunts, really. I'd have had a go with any one of them really, just a straight fight. They're the type of people though who if one of them's fighting they've all got to jump in … I wouldn't say I was upset about it. I get kind of tingly thinking back, and I'd love to get them properly sorted out, but sometimes you've just got to leave it alone … Tingly like angry, wanting to fuck them right up, you know? When it first got done [his face, the stitches] it looked really bad. Our lass was proper not happy, me Mam and Dad were going on and that. When you look at it in the mirror, well, I'd be grinding me teeth, just mad at what'd happened. I though the Doctor what done it had made a right mess of it, but when I got the stitches out, the nurse said he'd done a good job cos it's difficult to do a cut like that… It was about fourteen stitches, and if you look, it goes all over the place, and the stitches made it look worse than what it was. Now you can hardly see it. If I get a tan the scar looks worse because it's like a dead white line, but mostly you can't hardlys see it.

The onus on fortitude is often accompanied by fatalism, and being seen to survive eruptions of physical violence is still part of the traditional – if not ancient – initiation rite that prepares the male for survival in inevitable encounters with violence. It might have something to do with learning how to control extreme fear, a ritual that is at once pedagogical, functional and cathartic as well as status-establishing:

Now I'm not bothered. Fuck it, you know. It happened and there's nowt you can do. It doesn't bother me … I'd say I hate them, and I'm angry, the only problem is there's nothing I can do about it … I don't know if you'd say it affected me, it's difficult to tell. We went out, maybe ten of us, a couple of weeks after, and I just had it in my head that we'd find them and if we had, I might of done something daft cos I was that raging about it. Mac as well, kind of made us a bit edgy, like waiting for something to happen all the time. Before we'd just turn out for a laugh, after we'd have a go with anybody, but that kind of dies off after a while and you get back to normal and forget about it ... [Me Dad] says it happens to everyone sooner or later, and mostly I'd forgotten about it until you started asking questions ... Learn anything? Nothing really that I can think of. Maybe it might have toughened ez [meaning 'me'] up a bit or something or made ez more careful, but I can't really tell. It's daft to think about it and go over and over it, and it's not like it's the only time I had some bother, so it only really sticks out a bit because of the glass and the stuff that happened. We have a laugh about it, saying it was like a film, but that's just part of the crack.

Lee's other assorted anecdotes about life on the frontline suggested that his reactions to and feelings about violence are at once a reflection of his enclassed socialization and his ingrained feelings about identity and social life, and the turbulent cultures of the night-time economy. In this liminal and marketized culture resides an expectation of violence, and correspondingly heightened reactions to potentially conflictual situations. Violence, for men like Lee, clearly produces a degree of fascination and a powerful dose of adrenaline, but violence within the night-time economy has become the norm, and in its actual enactment lies a range of other considerations that have been somewhat neglected by criminology in recent years. Lee displays a deeply internalized expectation of violence; he knows it's out there, and he knows what it feels like and what it means. His father's observation, that 'it happens to everyone sooner or later', is telling. Growing up with a distinctly practical *habitus* that values endurance, fortitude, fearlessness, stoicism and so on has patterned Lee's reaction to the threat of violence and violence itself, and thus structural, historical and experiential influences – rather than mass-mediated culture or freely negotiated meaning – continue to be the main platform upon which so much violence occurs, and upon which the meanings and sentiments that surround it are forged.

Andy

Andy is twenty-five and works in a call centre in north-east. He lives with his sister and brother-in-law in what used to be a traditional industrial village on the outskirts of one of the region's major cities. Like Lee, he is yet another respondent who seems painfully and fatalistically aware of the ubiquity and unavoidability of violence in the night-time economy, especially that meted out by the 'professional' door-minders, whose specific remit is to prevent it:

I can't even remember how many times we've had bother down the town ... I started going out when I was sixteen and there's always been fighting down there, you'd see it every weekend, especially a couple of years ago before they got all the cameras and everything ... You just get used to it. You get used to seeing it mainly, but the more it happens you kind of work out how to stay out of the way and stuff ... Like groups of lads, baldy heads and muscles, tattoos, pissed up, you walk the long way around, stay out the way. Just let them get on with it. Stay out of kebab shops by yourself, watch it when you get a taxi, never argue or anything with the bouncers, just stuff like that. It's never really put me off going to the town because it's just always been like that, but it's not as bad as it was ... When you get that many people drunk together there's going to be things like that happening ... It's not like every time you go out you're going to get in trouble. Ninety-nine times out of a hundred nothing happens and you have a laugh and that's it ... I don't know why I like it. It's just where you go to see your mates. You have a pint and a bit crack and it's just good.

I got a kicking in a pizza shop when I was about seventeen. I've got slapped off a bouncer, I've had a kicking off a bouncer, had fights all over, and it's all when I've been pissed. I turn into a bit of a dick when I'm drunk, and I can get a bit mouthy and when I'm in front of the lads I might act up a bit ... I had all kinds of fights. We'd get into big gang fight in taxi queues and that or outside nightclubs when there's a lot of us ... It's the kind of thing you do at that age, with your mates ... The kicking in the pizza shop was me working myself with this lad, over some lass, and I didn't realize he was with this big lad who's put me straight on my arse and the two of them's booted me about and then legged it. This is when my mates aren't there. I got slapped off this bouncer in Studio 21 [nightclub] after I'd got thrown out for throwing a drink at my mate ... He's pushed me out the fire doors, and cos I'm pissed, I thought I could get back in by kicking the door and trying to get it open. The bouncer's come back into the back lane and slapped me. It fucking killed me, open handed slap, my face was knocking for weeks.

The worst was off another bouncer in Deconstruction [nightclub]. My mate got caught with some pills [ecstasy tablets] and they've dragged him down the stairs, I mean really throwing him about, I kind of jumped in saying leave him alone or something, and they've thrown me out as well. We're in the fire exit bit, and they're making him turn out his pockets, and they get hold of a bag of pills, and then one of them's smacked him in the face. He just kind of crumpled up, and he's booted him, so like an idiot I've said something and gone to help him up, and I've bumped this other bouncer, and they all just went nuts ... I was kind of trapped against the stairs and one of them's got hold of me shirt and he's just nutting me over and over, and then he throw me down towards the door, and this other one's kicked me in the face and then punched me in the side of the face. We both got pushed out and that was it ... I'm still barred, because one of the bouncers recognizes me every time I try to go back.

Mostly I blame myself but really everyone's got their stories haven't they? I could tell you about some other times when I've been in fights when I won if you want ... It's just what you expect when you go down the town. When you're growing up, these things are going to happen ... A few people might get a shock if they go around here, but most people know what it's like ... Some of them enjoy it, that kind of scared feeling when you know people are going to start fighting. It's part of a night out for a lot of people, and there's nothing you can do to stop it. I know people that honest-to-God enjoy fighting, even when they lose, they just love it, love getting in to trouble, love starting bother, love kicking the shit out of people. The town's full of them, and when you've got people like that all over you've got to expect things to happen.

Bobby

Bobby is twenty-six and has just started his first job as a bouncer after years of being on the other side of the velvet rope. After a stint as an amateur boxer, Bobby is now largely welfare dependent and spends his days in the gym and trading in the North East's various illegal economies. He splits his home life between his mother's house and his girlfriend's house, with whom he now cares for two young daughters. Bobby has an established reputation for violence, and he is loosely connected to various criminal networks operating in his home city and across the region. His upbringing is more stereotypical than the other respondents, and his attachment to violence seems to be the product of the sort of long-term socialization that produces 'violence specialists' (Hall, 2000, 2002; Winlow, 2001):

> I always loved fighting, ever since I was a boy. It's just something I've always enjoyed, everything about it … Me dad always told me never to back down and now I never back down, no matter what happens, because I'd rather get blown away than be a little chicken shit who lets people walk all over him … People who know me know that I'm not bothered by reputations or any of that pretend gangster stuff that happens all the time around here. If someone pushes me, then I'm not going to fuck around.
>
> I've hit people at work [as a bouncer]. If they work themselves then they get hit, I don't care if I lose my licence or any of that.

Whilst Bobby talked extensively about his various violent adventures in the night-time economy, the focus of this particular interview is an incident outside a night-club in which he was beaten unconscious by a group of doormen:

> It happened around two years ago when we was on a night out through Scarville. There'd been a bit of previous going on for ages about a couple of mates of mine, and we're in there giving it some, properly pissed up, and it just came on top and we end up outside in this car park.

The 'previous' to which Bobby refers involved a tangled web of drug dealing and unpaid loans, about which Bobby is unwilling to elaborate. Again, the fatalism that pervades the perceptual world of most young men who frequent the night-time economy – and always seems to intensify in the run-up to a violent encounter – is noteworthy:

> I was sitting down and I can see what's happened. People are drifting off, and I'm left sitting there with this group of birds. Chris, Dino and Pete had gone – turfed out or tapped down for money. People are looking and you can just see it coming. There's going to be bother and there's nothing that could stop it. James [the bouncer] comes up and sort of bends down and says, you've got to go outside. He says it sort of polite, but

I'm thinking fuck them you know? I says, what for, and he says, you know what for, and I'm drunk and I just think fuck it. He says, get up, and goes to grab my arm, so I gets up and they've all just jumped me, about five of them. They get me to the door and I'm giving it everything because I'm really pissed off, you know? I take a couple and I think we're going outside, then they kind of hold me up and one of them nuts [head-butts] me, like three or four times, and they're just all in to me, and as I'm going down I take a couple in the face. And that's it really. I was out cold for a bit and I woke up and it's pissing down and there's just people going out of the club, like not even bothering, me just fucking lying there, fucking blood all over.

I knew I was in a mess, so I just walked straight up to the door and said, there's not one of yous could have a go by yourself, and all that, and just like this isn't the last, cos I'm gonna be back and back and back and back.

Bobby did return, and return again, to settle the score of what was done to him on this rainy night in Scarville, but despite his best efforts, the memory of the violence that was inflicted upon him has not been erased by his search for vengeance, nor his burning sense of injustice appeased. He shows none of the stereotypical 'pride' in his wounds, only deep resentment that fuels and sustains his hatred for the assailants:

Angry, oh angry like you wouldn't believe. Fucking cowards, you know? I knew as soon as they grabbed hold of me that that wasn't going to be the end of it. When I'd sorted myself out, and just knew that whatever it takes, whatever it takes, these cunts aren't going to get away with it. I'd do time for them. I just wanted to murder them ... For weeks, I was like an animal and no one could talk to me. Nothing else mattered. My face was the worst. My nose was literally over here, teeth was out, eyes and cheek-bones. Either they've had a knuckle-duster or something or they've had sovs [sovereign rings] on, cos I had to have a few stitches. My sides was all purple, and they cracked a rib and my feet were all bruised ... they must've jumped about on my feet. I was angry but it's done with now. It's been sorted so I'm not bothered by it too much, but you still get that crazy feeling like wanted to get them properly done in.

Again, this serious violent incident has not entered the record books:

I couldn't apply for the compo (compensation) because I never made a statement to the police, and I could've got a few grand. It's just the way it goes I suppose.

The fatalistic attitude displayed by almost all of our respondents seems to suggest that criminology's rather hasty adoption of standard explanations for inter-personal violence needs to be reconsidered. The ubiquity of violence in the night-time economy suggests that many young men are living a significant part of their lives in an emotional climate characterized by a '... constant background static of aggressivity' (Horne and Hall, 1995). Violence and the distinct probability of encountering it exists 'out there', as the perpetual outcome of circular networks of inevitability, fear and revenge, not as a media construction or a compendium of urban legends, rather as a reality that pervades the memories and discourses of young men and shapes with great intensity their emotional lives, their practical lives, and thus their *habitus* (Bourdieu, 1984). Although standard explanations such as patriarchy and male dominance, destructive and hegemonic forms of masculine culture, sub-cultural codes, surrogate politics, negotiated meaning, seduction, transgression and others, which have helped criminology to understand some of the sociogenetic and psychogenetic processes that might generate and reproduce violence amongst young men, our evidence suggests that they create more questions than they answer. If positive agentic desires do operate in this climate, rather than dominance, honour, winning, losing or lusting after excitement, it is simply fortitude, survival and the prevention of an intolerable degree of humiliation that seems to be at the forefront of many young men's minds, especially those that come from lower working class backgrounds. The proven ability to get through dangerous and traumatic experiences with a modicum of competence and dignity, perhaps even panache, is deeply ingrained in their sense of self and the wider cultures from which they hail. The ability to relate a tale of real endurance seemed very attractive to these Salty Dogs, and how they felt about themselves was often understood in reflection of their conduct in violent situations. The building blocks of masculine self-identity lie is these encounters, and the ability to make claims about the internal self, to compose and display narratives of encultured masculine identity, can be all-encompassing. Victory and skill are by no means the be all and end all. To display an unwavering stoicism in the face of adversity is often as effective as a highly proficient display of measured brutality. Over and above individual perceptions and motives, and feeding back into them, is an objective environment of routine violent incidents and potential enemies that seems to connect otherwise atomized subjects in brief social alliances and archaic cultural practices, which form an overall *doxa* in which a durable *habitus* is constantly being forged and reproduced.

–7–

Perpetrators' Stories

Researching violence is a complex task. Even when a workable definition can be negotiated in a divided social scientific community that varies its definitions from the extremely broad to the extremely narrow, the issue of varied perception still remains problematic. However, there is a tentative consensus about the issue of 'interpretative rights', which outlines three principal groups as the most important regarding the collection of research data: victims, perpetrators and third-party observers (Jones, 2000). Victimology has exerted a powerful influence upon criminology since the early 1980s, and consequently the victims who were said to be 'silent' in traditional criminological research increasingly appear to be a privileged defining group. However, although we fully support the victimologists' aim of revealing violence that has hitherto been concealed, in order to achieve an interpretative balance and appreciate the complexity of the meanings, causes and contexts in which violence takes place, we have included both perpetrators and third-party observers along with victims in our sample of respondents. The following chapter will focus on data collected from police officers, third-party observers who witness a fair amount of violence – or at least its immediate after-effects – and can offer us descriptions and interpretations that might differ from those of the young people themselves. However, in this chapter we will explore the meanings and motivations of some of the young people who perpetrate violence in the night-time economy.

Ray

Ray is 26. By today's standards, at around six feet tall and thirteen stones in weight he is by no means excessively large. He was born and raised in one of north-east England's former industrial cities where he attended comprehensive school and now works short-term contracts in the building trade. Since leaving school at 16 Ray has found it hard to find a permanent job but he has still immersed himself in night-time leisure culture with great enthusiasm. Indeed, for Ray, life without a regular foray into the manufactured delights of the night-time economy would seem drab, depressing and virtually meaningless. Much like the 'victims' discussed in the last chapter, night-time leisure is an important end in his life and work is the instrumental means to acquire the money required to consume as much of it as possible. Alternative cultural pursuits, such as family activities, education, politics, art or sport did not seem to figure in his everyday life:

> When you leave school, and you start to earn some cash, but you're still living with your parents or whatever, it's like your full week's wages is just there for you to go out on the piss. When I was seventeen, eighteen, I'd be earning, like two hundred and seventy odd quid a week, just labouring or off contracting, and it's like a lot of money because what are you going to spend it on? You're down the town on a Saturday, buy some clothes, and then you're out … When I was out of work it's just so depressing because there's nothing to look forward to because you've got no money … A lot of the time you can still scrape around and get a few quid for a drink [down in the city centre]. The rest of the time you're just going out your mind, watching TV and listening to my Ma moaning on all the time.
>
> Working is better, even when it's like hard work, it's just better to be out the house, but mainly it's down to the money … Money lets you go and do stuff, just go out and buy clothes, just do whatever you want to do. When you're just on a Giro it's the worst thing in the world because anything you want to do is going to cost money … I'd do bits of fiddle and stuff, just to get the money to go out, just because otherwise you're like stuck by yourself because everyone else is off down the town … They [Social Security] push you at these daft jobs answering the phone all day, but you've just got to keep looking and a proper job will turn up.

Ray displays disdain for the service work that provides the employment opportunities for most young people in the post-industrial economy, and his preference for traditional, rugged physical labour with the possibility of higher wages compels him to occasionally take on contract work outside the region:

> When you're away it's like being on holiday because you're living in digs and that, and your out with the rest of the lads pretty much every night you're away. Obviously some of the older blokes don't, but mostly it's young lads anyway so everyone's out.

When he can't get a contract, Ray often finds fiddle work with a local building firm while claiming benefits:

> Sometimes you can't do it because of all the bullshit about finishing contracts, but mostly it's just labouring, mixing cement, filling skips, odd jobs, just for a bit extra cash … He [the owner of the building firm] knows most of the time I'm claiming, but it's best off for everyone really. He's not paying you good money, so really as long as I'm doing a bit graft there's no bother. It's good work and to be honest a lot of the time I prefer it to contracting cos you can go down the town and see all the lads and that. Either way I don't mind as long as I can get out of the house and earn enough to get meself out … It can be hard graft, labouring, like filling skips or something, but a lot of the time there's a lot of sitting about. Like Harry, the bricklayer I work with, and

Jimmy who runs everything, they don't really put themselves away with the graft that much unless there a rush on for something, so you can only really do what's there – if there's nowt to do, there's a lot of sitting about.

Aside from conventional work, Ray seems to have transposed his preference for a physically rugged and visceral existence to his leisure time, where he seems to relish the possibility of encountering violence. Alongside his penchant for night-time leisure, excessive drinking and occasional drug use, Ray has developed a small but deserved reputation for violence within his extended peer group. In previous eras, his ability to fight might well have secured him a number of tangible rewards and a high degree of status in his local culture (see Winlow, 2001), but Ray's chosen arena has little to do with financial reward, parochial neighbourhood reputations or the perverse pleasure of instilling fear in others. Instead Ray favours the increasingly faceless world of night-time leisure culture, as he blends into the throng of revellers who descend upon the city centre at weekends. Here, those who actually know him are aware that Ray can fight well, but this is a city of hundreds of thousands, and Ray is a long way short of being propelled to the Olympian heights of local fistic mythology. Some of the bouncers around the city know him, most do not; some people know some of the assorted violent anecdotes that accompany him and others like him but, again, most do not. Ray is not driven by reputation and has no interest in the gangsterism that tends to overlap localized cultures of violence, and no wish to use his propensity for physical violence to aid more acquisitive forms of crime (ibid). He has little interest in riding the waves of dread and sycophancy that excessively violent men can generate in their locales (ibid). On the surface of it, he seems to belie all standard explanations of male violence that are associated with status, instrumentalism and reward, and the rather flat, mundane way that he describes his routine expression of violence indicates virtually no expectancy, excitement or seduction. He is simply one of many young men who can on occasion be extremely violent, and he expresses his brushes with physical violence in the same fatalistic manner as the victims in the previous chapter, except that he plays a percentage game and expects to come out on top in encounters more often than 'getting a hiding'. Although he accepts the possibility of losing a physical encounter with the stoical resignation that might accompany losing a job or a bet on the horses, Ray seems to focus on the strategies and technicalities associated with encountering inevitable violent incidents and coming out of them with dignity intact and as little injury as possible:

There's a load of shit what's talked about fighting. First of all, the most important thing is, it happens quick. People do all this training, talking about this that and the other. The most important thing, always throw the first punch. Never miss and make it a good one. After that, nothing matters, if you're still in to it, just go daft and do whatever you like.

But that shouldn't happen, if it does you didn't do the first bit right. If you miss, and you're into someone who knows how to properly fight, then they're going to get you on the floor and you don't want to be rolling around with that type of bloke.

Times when I've been done over, it's always been you get whacked and after that you're fucked. There's nothing you can do really except don't get too pissed and stay off the cowies [ecstasy tablets] ... You've got to look about and try and see who's going to do what, but really, if I'm going to hit you, there's nowt you can do about it. Some people come over and start talking first, but most people these days are just going to smack you straight off. No arguments, no nothing like that, just, smack! And that's it.

These days you've got to watch for cameras, watch for Old Bill, and be careful with bouncers, cos there's loads of them and they all stick together. If you've got bother with a bouncer, either tell him you want a go one-on-one, or come back later when you're sober and you've got some back up ... If you have a go with most bouncers, you want to just whack them because otherwise nine times out of ten you're going to get beat ... I know a lot of lads that can have a fight and I know there's all these bouncers who are nothing, but it can get a bit gangy with bouncers and the main thing, they're sober and you're most likely pissed out your head.

People might had told you I've had a few fights, but I don't think I've had that many. Most lads like us end up having bother [down the town] sooner or later ... It's just what happens ... I just got told, never bottle out [lose nerve], stuff like that all the time when I was coming up. It's just a usual thing, but I can remember bottling [losing nerve] a few [fights] when I was a young'un', because it's just a scary thing when you're young. My first fight was at school, just silly really. Then there was bits of bother when we started to go down the town, a big gang of us. We had some bother on holiday, just all sorts when you're out on the lash.

The cultural capital handed to Ray by his father is of course highly significant, and reflects important aspects of the *habitus* that frames Ray's personal understanding of violence and his self-identity, and motivates his excursions into the liminal night-time leisure culture. The broad principle 'not to take shit' – which, it should be noted, is not a detailed technical instruction about how to fight, how to 'do masculinity' or how to exercise power over others but rather a plea to prevent power being exercised over the self in a violent and humiliating manner – is very often handed down from father to son, disseminated within local lower class cultures, and often couched in defensive and cautionary terms rather than instrumental or status-enhancing terms. As many of our respondents who admitted regular engagement in acts of violence, 'not taking any shit' involved a highly complex internal debate about potential responses to direct and indirect threats that reached the very core of self-identity. The self-identities of many of our perpetrators, grounded in a *habitus* emphasizing physicality, survival, honour and respect, appeared to steer them towards proactive, but to them entirely justifiable forms of violence. While they clearly recognized external influences, such as audience reaction, peer judgements, chances of success and potential repercussions, one of the most telling factor appears to be how much they will allow their preferred moral and cultural order – and their own position within it – to be profaned and disrupted before they take violent action.

For us, the suggestion that interpersonal violence of this kind represents a metamorphosed and atomized vestige of an old rebellious politics is excessively romantic. Nevertheless, one can still hear faint echoes of the more dignified amongst impoverished workers, who were ripped away from the autonomy of their traditional agricultural lives and forced into an urban labour market, reacting to the violent agents of a domineering indigenous class or the competitors within one's own class with similar words of encouragement. Even more plausible is the reaction of individuals forced into arenas of brutal interpersonal competition over forms of cultural capital that, because they are generated as constantly shifting styles, fashions and means of expressing identity in the arcane and distant realm of global consumer capitalism before they are deposited in the locale, are not entirely *understood* or *appreciated*. Our data suggested constantly that this is a world of brutal struggle over these dimly understood cultural forms, where everyone else is an 'arsehole', a 'cunt', a 'poser', a 'smart-arse' or a 'worky-ticket' out to 'take the piss' in the sense of posing a potential threat to the traditional *doxic* order and the physical integrity and dignity of the self. For the most part this is about achingly ordinary people preparing themselves for the inevitable violence and the possible domination and humiliation that exist somewhere 'out there' as routine hazards in competitive-individualist societies. Here the connection between the real and the perceptual appears to be quite strong, because of course the potential of violence and humiliation *does* abound in today's ultra-competitive and unstable culture (see also Hall, 2002), so we could pose the question that any generative or reproductive effects on cultural mores, the individual psyche or the *habitus* might be purely incidental and unintended:

> Me Dad was just normal really, from what I can remember. He worked in the shipyards and when he got laid off he did a bit of jobbing about all over ... He died about three years ago [of cancer]. He used to smoke like a chimney ... [He never really told me anything] about fighting, just like, don't be a mug, don't get pushed about, and that type of thing ... I think he was the type of person who didn't take any shit and he just wanted me to be able to look after myself, because if you don't there's people round here that'll just walk all over you, just take the piss.

Ray is a little circumspect about describing specific incidents of violence where he was the instigator. Again, on the surface of it Ray might be employing 'techniques of neutralization' that exonerate the self and avoid the issue of personal responsibility. Taylor (1999) was indeed correct to criticize Katz's (1988) negligence of this concept, and it seems quite plausible that what Katz described as an innate 'seductive' attraction to violence and other forms of criminality, and general transgression of norms, may be better explained as one amongst the many common techniques of neutralization (see Matza, 1964) concocted to cover up the abdication of personal responsibility and the concomitant failure to resist sub-cultural pressure. However, both explanations are based upon a rather simplistic conception of the existential battle between the authentic will and its inauthentic impostors, which, as well as over-simplifying the constitution and dynamics of the internal psyche, neglects the whole theoretical area based upon external realities, practices and *habitus*-formation, which we will explore later. Again, although Ray is more often a perpetrator, his explanations, like those of the victims, suggest a painful awareness of the *very real* and potentially dangerous, humiliating threats posed by others in a climate where very little guidance, predictability or protection is provided by norms, codes or legitimate state agencies, and individuals' restraining inhibitions can often be significantly attenuated by a combination of intoxication and the general heady atmosphere:

> It just happens. I wouldn't say I go out to work myself [cause trouble] or anything, it just happens. Mostly it's not my fault. People act like arseholes all over, so really you can't be blamed. I'm not saying I've never hit people, but like every time there's a reason or something, or something's happened, so it's not like me being a bully or anything, because 9 times out of 10 you've going to get people working themselves wherever you go. I don't care who you are, there's people out there who's just got no respect for anyone and they just get used to pissing all over people and people not doing anything ... Someone acts the arsehole with me, they better be able to back it up, that's the way I see it.

It is the absence of understandable and reliable moral and behavioural codes in Ray's immediate environment that seem to trigger his disgust, his fear and his violent reaction, which, in a brutal way, is almost an act of restitution, an attempt to restore an ethico-practical order that satisfies his sense of social justice and appeases his fear of potential personal injury and humiliation. Rather perversely, his allegiance to his mate could be read as a mark of civilization, the ability to imagine his mate's fear and humiliation and how this might reflect upon Ray's sense of self, but, in the absence of the agents of a legitimate moral authority to which he could appeal without losing face, his own way of restoring his preferred moral order simply adds to the general climate of violence, exacerbating and reproducing the problem that he himself views so fatalistically:

> Well, one time someone's tried to take a bag of coke off me mate in the bogs [meaning toilets], so I smacked him ... he [his mate] just pointed him out, and I've just gone up and knocked him out ... See, he got what he deserved, because he's playing the big shot, so I just walked up and hit him ... I just get angry with people like that, if he'd never done it then none of it would've happened. He's just taking the piss, thinking he can walk all over people, and that just fucks me right off, so I'm thinking, you fucking

arsehole, who the fuck do you think you are? And just getting wound right up about it, and then it's like you've got to hurt him because he's a dick and deserves all he gets … It just gets me angry. You can just feel it building, and I hate bullies so he's the one to blame …

As Ray spoke these words his anger rose once again, at once a kind of retrospective emotional justification for his actions and the reassertion that those who transgress the increasingly vague boundaries of the moral and cultural order that he continues to imagine into existence will be swiftly and unsympathetically dealt with. Although violence in the night-time economy can be clearly associated with the palpable lack of a police presence or any of the other re-branded 'risk-management' agencies of neo-liberal governance (see Hobbs et al, 2003; Hobbs et al, 2005), the suspension of daytime moral regulation and its corresponding set of behavioural norms tells us quite a lot about the way many young people negotiate the multiplicity of incidents that may lead to violence. Ray seems to be driven to perform brutally restorative actions, to repair that which has been broken, and which exists in such a state of disrepair for the duration of the foray into the night-time economy. Intoxication and the relaxation of restrictive codes can allow the rapid degeneration of actual behaviour, but this also tends to relax restrictions on the actions that can be performed by more moralistic, proactive and less fearful individuals to restore a still quite widely accepted but outdated moral order:

I hit this bloke in a taxi queue once. He was just trying to be a clever cunt in front of their lass. He's brought it on himself, pissed out his head, slagging everyone off, making jokes … He shouldn't be acting like a fucking smart arse and he wouldn't have got hurt. Just that type of thing, mostly same thing or there's been some bother with one of the lads. That's how it happens … [That time] I suppose you could just feel the anger building, and he's keeping talking and his voice is just really pissing me off, and I'm just saying to myself over and over, shut the fuck up, you cunt! But you bite your lip, and he's saying this and saying that and he takes the piss out of this lad standing behind me, and this lad just stands there, and then you start thinking, why the fuck should I bite my lip? He's the one who should be biting his lip, not me, so I says, shut the fuck up, or something, and he shuts up a bit but he's kind of making a joke out of it, and I turned around to tell him again, and he's pulling faces behind me, so I smacked him. His girlfriend never said anything, just kind of tried to help him up, and there's a few people in the queue saying different things, but I wasn't really listening because I was still boiling. I just got in the next taxi and fucked off.

It's just people with bad manners. Just have a drink and enjoy your night, you know? Most fighting that happens is because people get cocky in drink and think they can act the big man. A lot of the time you get these arseholes who wouldn't say a word during the day, mouthing off and trying to push people around. Just arseholes, they get too much down them and think they've got to prove themselves to their mates or something, I don't know … It makes you think, something like that, how many people just stand there and take it? There's people I know who hate bother and maybes would just let a cunt like that take the piss, just to avoid the bother. There must be loads of people who just let these arseholes go on like cunts, and that's why they keep doing it. They think they can get away with it maybes. But the thing is, nobody can work themselves all the time and get away with it, because sooner or later someone's going to stand up.

To us, Ray's expression of his moral indignation and his restorative urges seems too heartfelt to be merely a technique of neutralization, and far too morally driven and coordinated to be nothing more than an unstructured, unconscious attraction to violence. The foundation of Ray's behaviour – closely related to *habitus* and self-identity – is a normative, cohesive and structured understanding of how specific types of people should and should not behave in certain situations with others. However, layered on top of this is the same quest for ritualized excitement and peer-group affirmation expressed by many of the victims, combined with the almost humble admission of fear and possible loss in the face of a powerful 'opponent'. Ray does not have to 'win' or achieve a position of dominance to earn the respect of his peers, he just has to face up to the monster and come through the experience without undue humiliation (see also Jackson-Jacobs, 2005). Again, bravery and fortitude carry the most value of all the forms of cultural capital specific to this group of young men in this environment, and in a post-productive culture where fame is reliant on spectacular acts and has become, as Bauman (1995, 2001) suggests, 'compulsory' in the absence of more traditional, localized and diverse means of achieving respect, the possibility of being 'talked about' has become significantly more important than it has been in the past:

When its happening you get like butterflies, because the idea's in your head, there's going to be bother. And then you're like nervous and excited at the same time. Have a look around, see if there's a squad of them, see if there's a bouncer or something. Then as it gets closer your guts go weird, sometimes I go all shaky. Then that's it. Either it starts or you think fuck it, there's off [you punch first] ... Once you're into it it's good, I mean you're still all hyped up, but your head's clearer and you just get on with it ... After's the best, because you can have a laugh about it with the lads and everyone's saying, did you see this, and did you see that, and just having a laugh really. People tell you well done, and talk about the punch and that ... everyone loves fights, and they just go on and on about it.

I like the way it makes you feel ... Like before, when you get nervous. That feeling in your guts, the excitement, all that ... I mean, if you catch them right you're OK, but I've broken my hands loads of times and it fucking hurts ... The noise, like when you hit them, that's when you can tell you've hurt them.

Whilst the excitement elicited by violence is clearly present in Ray's description, taking part in this partially ritualized violence with fortitude and dignity appears to be more important than denying personal fear or inflicting serious physical harm on the 'opponent'. Again, Ray expresses a concern that the violence remains within a codified boundary set by the ubiquitous 'not taking any shit' rule, and he makes a rather 'fuzzy distinction' (see Bourdieu, 1984, 1990; Robbins, 2000) between the violence that is necessary to reproduce his masculine order and that which should be repressed because it poses a threat to the general moral-behavioural order that should be maintained to protect everyday 'young lads' and 'young couples' who have no wish to enter the demarcated world of the self-styled nocturnal urban warrior:

> I'm not saying I don't get nervous, because it's only right you get nervous, because I've seen people seriously hurt. You can properly hurt someone with just the one punch … It's like being a bit scared, but doing it anyway makes it better because you didn't bottle out or run off or anything, and that's how you get the respect … Fighting's a horrible thing though. It just spoils a night out. I go out to enjoy myself, and when you see these kind of people, you just think, fucking hell, you know, because you can't be bothered. There's them type of people who just go out to cause trouble. That's what a night out is to them … it makes you think because there's a lot of bullies who must just murder all these young lads and young couples who just come out for a good night.

Ray is a self-appointed urban knight, and this metaphor can be employed unromantically – and therefore entirely appropriately – if one stresses the morally driven thuggery of medieval knights rather than their alleged nobility (Runciman, 1954). Throughout the telling of his story, Ray makes an obvious distinction between those who he regards as unrestrained 'arseholes' or 'cunts' who indulge in inappropriate behaviour and those who, like himself, are out to either enjoy themselves or engage in violence in appropriately codified ways. The 'arseholes' are represented as the bullying, 'piss-taking' drunks who pick on the weak and attempt to upset the erstwhile harmony that, to brutal idealists such as Ray, might otherwise reign in after-dark leisure environments. These brash transgressors are to blame for the unpredictable and immoral violence that has an increasing presence in the night-time economy; it is they who purposefully set out to disrespect and intimidate all who they encounter, directly and indirectly provoking violence with their every deed and utterance. The 'arseholes' and 'cunts' are beginning to replace the meek consumers far too rapidly for Ray, who sees himself as a sort of knightly protector of the latter and the nemesis of the former. That said, Ray's understanding of events and his allocation of blame clearly cannot be taken at face value. It's not hard to imagine Ray's victims categorizing him as the same violent, predatory 'arsehole' that he regards as such a blight upon contemporary night-time leisure. Indeed, the difficulty we have experienced here is to work out if these new, predatory and disreputable purveyors of unpredictable violence are figments of Ray's imagination – even an impure demon constructed by Ray himself so that he can distinguish his own violence as a moral defence of the sacred, an imaginary problem to which Ray and his restorative violence are imaginary solutions – or if they are the harbingers of a new era in which the codes that govern violence are rapidly evaporating.

Ray has other reasons for his ambivalent love-hate relationship with violence. He has been arrested a number of times, and recently faced a jail term for inflicting grievous bodily harm upon an adversary outside a local pizza shop:

> I got community hours, but I was lucky. But mostly it's been bad luck because like the last four times I've had a fight I've been arrested and when you get a record it just starts getting serious. I keep telling myself to just stay out of trouble, but sometimes you can't. It's not your fault, it's just unlucky. The last time I said, that's it, I'm never going down the town again, but I caved in after a couple of weeks cos I was bored out me head stuck in the house on a Saturday night ... I mean, I know if something happened I couldn't just walk off and leave it because I'd just feel like a complete waste of space, just some fucking idiot. I'd probably go to jail rather than let someone take the piss.

Robert

Robert's attitude to violence is far less restrained and structured by moral and behavioural codes. On the face of it, he seems to be driven by Katz's (1988) notion that young men are clearly attracted to violence as a means of satisfying a universal urge for thrills and excitement in an otherwise mundane and repressive world. However, his constant referral to prolonged exposure to various forms of identity and *habitus* formation yet again suggests that Katz's model needs to be reconsidered. Young men like Paul and Harry who we discussed in Chapter 6, socialized in relatively non-violent environments or environments where violence is heavily codified and sublimated and regarded as a phenomenon for intellectual reflection, often appear not to relate excitement with interpersonal violence. Katz's thesis box-presses the concept of 'seduction' into an existential attraction to the excitement of transgressing the norm, yet our respondents are excited simply by conforming to an alternative norm that happens to transgress a set of institutionalized norms, to which they demonstrate only a partial and contingent allegiance. This normative conflict seems to indicate the mutation and cultural continuity of vestigial class differences rather than an existential struggle for personal liberation. Indeed, some of the data below seem to confirm the idea that a strong psychosomatic attraction to violence is not pre-existent but constructed during the experience of being socialized in a general *doxic* climate where real violence is routinely encountered yet shorn of traditional ritual codes and mythological meanings, and reflected constantly in young people's choices of mass-mediated imagery (Hall et al., 2005):

I've just always been into that kind of thing [violence]. When I was a boy I used to sit in front of the Rocky films all day, just everything about it [violence] is just interesting to me ... Ever since I was a kid I've loved boxing and just watching people fight, then I tried different martial arts for a bit, but really if I'm honest it's just regular fighting that interests me the most. Just the excitement of it, everything, just the way it happens, the buzz you get, there's nothing like it.

I used to see fights around ours [the estate upon which he grew up] all the time when I was young. I remember seeing our boy [his older brother] in a few, and then there was always a one on one to watch with the lads from around ours and other squads from all over the town. You'd see them in The Wolf and Rabbit [the local pub on his estate] on a Friday night sometimes. We'd hang about outside and wait for it to kick off.

Robert remembers that in his earlier days, when his initiation was incomplete, his feelings towards violence were more ambivalent, that violence elicited feelings of fear as well as fascination and that perpetrators of violent acts did not represent his own personal interpretation of the norm:

When I was young watching fights and that was like, amazing. There's a kind of excitement that's hard to explain, something that draws you to it. When I was young it would be a bit weird watching these older lads because it's a bit dodgy and you don't know what's going to happen. People would be going nuts and that.

The conventional idea that the peer group assumes a more important role in the reproduction of cultural practices as the young person grows older seems to be confirmed in Robert's case. However, as we noticed earlier, the principle seems to be based upon the ability to react defensively, without losing face, to both threats and acts of violence that have become normalized and expected. In the case of violence, the belief is not established chiefly by the guarantees of others who share it, as de Certeau (1985) famously argued, but rather by an impenetrable cycle of experientially based expectation and fear:

I think the more you see it the more you do it. At school there'd always be daft fights and that, and we'd have gang fights with [other schools]. It's just part of growing up. You learn how to handle yourself. I mean, to be honest, I never had any time for those people at school who couldn't stand up for themselves. It makes me think, what's going on in your head? The lads I hung about with mostly at school was older lads, and they kind of bring you up a bit and you meet all the lads. Now when we're all out there's some proper hard cunts there, the older lads and some our age.

Robert's conviction that willing engagement with violence is all part of 'growing up' and accruing 'self-respect' quite obviously contradicts the civilized normative conceptions of maturity and valuable human characteristics, especially the pacified characteristics that are now valued as functions in the domesticated consumer/service economy. However, it continues to affirm the 'tough' characteristics that were functional in the military/industrial era and encouraged in codified forms amongst working class males (see Hall and Winlow, 2003). However, it's more interesting to note that his palpable fear of the 'evil' others who might hurt him if he fails to resist runs alongside a partially repressed attraction to his more 'easy-going' friends. In the hands of the romantic existentialist this could signify the existence of an autonomous rational ego and a conscience that can, if they escape the attentions of significant others, construct themselves in a hermetically sealed psychological cocoon. However, it seems more likely that he has been caught in the confusing hiatus between a number of conflicting normative systems, but the imperative not to be 'soft' and not to be seen to be 'soft' is currently dominant. This is not an existentialist struggle between the authentic self and the corrupt world, but a struggle between a number of competing and intersecting codes in which a new logic of practice is beginning to emerge:

> My first fight at school I had to have because me brother was watching. So I just went daft and just started swinging, trying to show off a bit probably. I had loads of fights at school ... It's all about standing up for yourself, especially at school because they're always trying to work out who's the hardest and that ... Most of the lads wanted to be seen as tough I suppose, but I think I was more bothered about being the hardest, and so you've got to prove it over and over. It's just all part of growing up ... I suppose it's about just not being soft mostly because people can be evil if you let them fuck with you. If you stand up for yourself people know and they leave you alone ... You've got to get people to show a bit respect, that's all. Like now, I don't go around hitting people for no good reason. You've got to set me off, say something or do something, or else I'm no bother to nobody really ... when there is trouble I do like it though. I'm not so bothered about all that hardest stuff, you kind of grow out of it. It's just the excitement and being with the lads and that. It's about respect. Self-respect, that's all ... You don't want to look like a dick in front of the lads, but mostly it's about yourself ... I think about it a lot. Like why does it bother me when there's loads of lads I know who are just, you know, kind of easy going blokes? When I've had a bit of chew [conflict], it goes over and over in me head until I know I have to do something about it.

Once again, this constant internal dialogue, informed by powerful external stimuli, creates boundaries around what Robert is willing to take, and determines how he should respond to a persistently threatening social world. Robert's constant ruminations on perceived slights and actual threats indicate not simply a concern with status and cultural esteem, but also an active role in the construction of self. Even when he is clear of the ever-attentive cultural audience, he continues to interpret testing situations as dangerous not simply in a practical manner, but also to his psychic well being. The cultural command that he must respond, even if the chances of success are minimal and resistance appears counterproductive, seems to be very deeply internalized in the durable *habitus*:

> I know you want details but I don't really know what to tell you because, see, it's not really talked about is it? People just think that that's the way it is. It's just soft is bad and hard is good mostly ... You do get the respect off the lads when you know how to look after yourself. You can definitely tell they start treating you a bit different, so you get the benefits of it in a lot of ways. But mostly it's about what you think of yourself than what the lads think. I'm not bothered about proving myself to the lads anymore, although I know I did when I was younger. Now, if there's any trouble, or if someone winds me up or whatever, I'm not bothered about any of that ... It's about respecting yourself because you don't want people taking advantage ... Letting someone get away with something wouldn't be natural because that's who I am.
>
> Worst thing I did was nearly kill someone. Stamped on his head. I went too far. It worried me a bit ... at the time, when it was happening, you just get caught up in it and you're fucking furious and you want to hurt him. Later when you've calmed down a bit you realize you went too far ... I knocked this young kid out once. Fifteen or sixteen maybe. He's only small. He was setting his lip up in this pub, and I told him, but he kept on winding me up and winding me up so I just lost me rag and floored him ... I felt bad really cos he was only a kid, but he should've packed in when I said ... Some of the lads went a bit quiet on me because he was someone's brother or something but I could tell they knew that he shouldn't have done what he did.

Robert's concern to maintain his hard-won status amongst the peer group, and his self-image of a tough man who will not be taken advantage of, comes across clearly in his vague justifications for violence. Here, being able to cope with people 'taking the piss' is an obvious aspect of his masculine *habitus*, but the line between light-hearted banter and direct challenge is indistinct both to the group and the individual. Robert clearly constructed the boundary in a very different place to his eventual victim, now lying prostrate on the floor. But for Robert, the failure to adequately decode the profusion of signs renders the victim culpable for the eventual assault. Robert's rather perverse Kantian presumption is that the victim should have known better; should have looked at Robert, assessed his demeanour and simply known; looked at the growing discomfort of the audience and known; assessed Roberts face, his shoulders, his hands, sensed the impending doom and retreated, and, of course, responded to Robert's direct order to cease. Robert's point may not be entirely without foundation. An embedded awareness of cultural signifiers should have been all Robert's quarry needed to desist and depart. Even those external to this *habitus*, were they in such a position, should be able to decode the signs after this prolonged preamble (the interviewer was left with the sense that a direct threat from this man would lead many to leave the country). Although there's no direct evidence, it may be that the eventual victim is playing upon his relative youth, or testing the boundaries of jocularity that are such an important facet of these masculine cultures; he may be attempting to place the onus on Robert's ability take a joke, and it's likely that at some subtle level the victim is attempting to boost his fledgling masculine renown. Yet all this is based in a normative demand that it is the victim's personal responsibility to know and practice the cultural rules, and that transgression warrants punishment. In this case, the *habitus* expects another to be fine tuned onto the same wavelength, to be able to read the signs in a given situation and respond according to the cultural rules of the specific social order in which the *habitus* was forged. This is not a mentality that is accustomed to dealing with difference.

Robert seems to be aware of some aspects of traditional modernist codes that still remain in place and govern the public use of violence. More importantly, transgression can still invoke feelings of guilt, which shows that the modernist version of the super-ego has not been entirely dismantled and replaced by ego-calculation (see Wouters, 1999). However, when pressed, the determination not to be overpowered or humiliated in public takes over. The following incident, where a young woman attempts to assault him, represents a reactive transgression of a code that appears more fragile today than it ever has been. For Robert, the negotiation between upholding traditional protocols in relation to male/female disputes and maintaining the robust, no-nonsense persona that is so central to his self-identity is a tough one. Robert clearly feels the expectation and exhilaration of the audience and thus the pressure to react 'correctly', but the correct response in this environment at this point in history is far from straightforward. Ultimately it appears that the young woman's transgression of her traditional feminine code is an incitement that justifies the transgression of his sense of traditional masculine codes:

Probably what everyone else thinks is the worst is I knocked a lass out. I can't remember what started it. It's probably someone's felt her arse or something, but anyway she starts shouting and bawling, getting right up in my face ... It's a bad spot to be in because you don't know what to do right? I wasn't me that touched her arse. So everyone's laughing and that. But she's right up in my face, and she's screaming and bits of spit are hitting me and I'm thinking, this isn't funny anymore and I can feel me mood changing. I've telt her to pack in, telt her it wasn't me, so I tell her, you know, fuck off, like, whatever ... She goes back to the bar, puts her drink down and tries to smack me. She just starts swinging. The first one caught me a bit around the ear, but she's only small so she can't really reach to get a good one on me. I mean I've told her to pack in, but she's just gone nuts. So I'm trying to push her away, and then I've just lost my rag and given her a clip. I mean I didn't, like, pull back and give her a proper smack just like a really soft jab ... She's gone over and then the bouncers come. You feel a bit bad after but really there's nothing else I could do I don't think ... It's her fault: first off, she should be able to take a fucking joke; she should be a bit clued up and not blame me – I was just standing there. Then, she should have left it when I told her. She was right out of order going on like that. It pisses me off thinking back cos she's started wacking me, and she must be thinking, he wouldn't dare hit me back. Like it's all right for her to just be hitting people and they won't hit her back. If she had anything about her at all she would've walked away. And now see what happens, right? I feel like a twat for hitting her, she obviously isn't too happy and it's a bad situation all around. But that's what happens ...

[When it was happening] I don't know what I was feeling really. You just lose your temper ... It was a joke at first and I was having a bit of a laugh with it. But then she tries to hit me and you just think this isn't funny anymore. It's like you can feel your mood change in a couple of seconds or whatever. I had to do something; she's taking the piss. I mean I still feel a bit bad about it but really there's was nowt else for it.

Robert's assessment of contemporary night-time leisure hardly corresponds with that of his peers. At twenty-seven years old, his jaded, pessimistic view of the here and now and the rose-tinted view of the past could be associated more easily with a much older man:

Nowadays the town's full of gangs of lads, about five or ten or maybe more of them. And they're out. What have they come out for? They maybes want to get laid or whatever, they want to get pissed, but when you've got that many people about and they're all pissed up, then you're going to get all sorts of people acting up. Why do they want to act up? It's mostly the drink but you get a lot of lads out who want to show off a bit. Even people I know, who've got no right to be working themselves, they get a bit edgy when they've had a pint. A lot of the time it's not even their mates they're showing off too, because it [trouble] can happen anywhere. It's more like they've got something to prove; they've got to prove what a big man they are. It's this kind of thing that causes a lot of trouble down the town and it's them type of lads who I've had bother with mostly. Just pissheads, don't know what they're doing, and you get a lot of bullies looking to pick on some kid just because he wants to play the big man.

Robert's changing attitudes seem to confirm Matza's (1964, 1969) celebrated observation that most young people will grow out of crime, but of course this attempt to establish a naturalistic universal law must be tempered in the light of the current changes in attitudes to and the availability of employment (see Chapter 2). Despite this, early transitions into work and other traditional institutions still appear to have mild 'civilizing' effects on young men who were caught up in violent cultural forms, although, on the other hand, evidence of long-term desensitization was common throughout our research:

I've got regular work now so I can't be doing with court appearances and all that so mostly you try to keep out of it. I still go over the match but mostly I leave the away games alone. I'm not as bothered about fighting as I was because I know I can do it if I have to ... I'm not bothered about getting hurt or any of that because once it's happened it's happened a thousand times you know? I'm not after a reputation or any of that. I go to the gym and try to keep in shape so I can still do it, but really the fighting in the town is just pissed up kids, and you grow out of it ... I did my share and I probably hurt a few people, but then I've had kickings as well so it evens out ... I broke knuckles, mostly on my left hand here, got me nosed bust about four or five times, and then just little things like split lips and black eyes ...

I think mostly what I kept getting into trouble for when I was a young'un I was just going out and being young really, because you grow out of it a bit ... I had a bit of a point to prove I suppose and I did start fights just because I wanted some excitement really. You want to prove yourself and be the tough guy.

Robert's grudging acceptance that a good deal of his youthful violence was a result of concerns with being the 'tough guy' represent an important self-depre-cating admission, given that he uses this apparent character flaw in others to explain much of his own reactive violence. For Robert, the maintenance of the masculine self-image is either a passing concern during youth that will ultimately be resolved by the eventual transition to real adulthood, or a durable and insur-mountable fault in the inherently fragile masculine identities of the 'arseholes' that appear to be such a crucial constitutive part of the night-time leisure scene.

Tim

Tim retains an attitude to violence that appears almost infantile. To him the cartoon-like absurdity of intoxicated young men fighting is high comedy, but underlying this is strong evidence that the ubiquitous cultural command not to appear 'soft' to the self and others drives and justifies his violence more than any-thing else. Tim is one of the respondents who stressed a general 'liking' of vio-lence, an attraction that seems to be based on the adrenalin rush that it causes, but this is shaped and tempered by his 'mood', which in turn seems to be influenced by external factors such as the condition of his relationships with girlfriends. The attraction of the adrenalin rush is also balanced in an almost rationally calculated manner with the presence of friends to 'back him up' and thus minimize the chances of losing, the feeling of power and invincibility invoked by being a member of a large crowd (see Chapter 6), a conscious awareness of the possible consequences of causing excessive damage to a victim and the fragile vestige of the super-ego applying emotional inhibitions to the deployment of extreme vio-lence:

This one time, there's me, Eric, Andy, and James, and we're walking down to the [taxi] rank. We're off our nuts right ... we'd had pills mostly and a couple of lines of coke and that, so we're bouncing all over the place. And as we turn the corner there's this big ruck, like a riot or something, maybe about 10 lads getting stuck into each other. And we're just standing there, and this lad goes, do you want some? Or something like that. And we're like, eh? What's he going on about, and Eric's laughing and this lad just comes up and starts wading in to Eric. I mean, Eric is a bit of a tough cunt. He's not the biggest, but he can have a right go. So it just all kicks off with these lads, and we're fighting for about 10 minutes, no coppers, no nothing, right? I can remember every bit of that fight. It was probably the best fight I've been in because it was just a right laugh, you know? Everything that was said, the lot. These lads were taking it dead serious, but it was just a laugh to us. It's no point telling you really what happened cos you had to be there, you know? It's just one of them things I'll never forget ... we ended up flattening them, about five or six of them, and we're giving them a bit of a kicking and it probably doesn't sound it to you, but it's just the funniest things I've ever seen. Honest. Laughed about it for weeks.

About a year ago I split up with our lass, and I went a bit mad for a bit. I was just in a bad mood and when you have a drink, you just sometimes get right on top and work yourself a bit ... One lad I flattened in a pizza shop ... Just coz he was getting on me nerves really ... He was drunk and just acting up with a couple of his mates and it just right pissed me off the way he was going on, you know? I got thrown out of a few night-clubs for fighting ... It's nothing, it's just, I don't know, someone stares at you or pushes you about or just generally works themselves ... I wouldn't just get stuck in to them, but mostly I'd work myself a little and see if they wanted a go. If they did then I'd just fucking whack them.

It's difficult to explain. With me, I've always got back up, so I know most of the time that whatever happens, I'll be OK, unless it's like gangsters or something and then we'd back off. With people backing you up it's like there's less to worry about so you know if someone pisses you off you can't back down ... Mostly when I'm drunk I get in a good mood and nothing bothers me, but sometimes I just turn into a bit of an arsehole and starting acting myself a bit. But everyone's like that really. I've had people working themselves with me for no reason. It's just the way it is, and if you like a fight then you're going to find one down the town because it's just jammed with people who's pissed out their heads.

When I broke up with her, I'd just get nasty. When I was pissed, I'd just be looking to start something with whoever was about. It's just like you're angry and you want a fight, or you want to hurt someone. Like it'll make you feel better if you hurt someone you know? Because it does doesn't it, if you catch someone with a perfect punch, and you see them go spark out, it's just, it's just a good feeling ... It sounds weird but I think a lot of lads just like fighting. A lot of lads like it, but a lot don't get involved if they can help it, but they still like it ... Maybe it's something you grow out of a bit, as you get older, because I was more bothered about proving myself to the lads when I was a bit younger. There's still times when I want to have a fight though and there's no one about, so then it's not like I'm trying to prove myself, it's something else.

Just the adrenalin and that. The build up and then the punches and trying to kill them. Your heart beating really fast, and just the challenge of it really. That's the main thing [I like about fighting] ... It doesn't really make you feel more of a man exactly. It's more like proving yourself to yourself if you know what I mean ... Prove you're not soft, that you won't let people walk all over you, that kind of thing. I'm not really sure how to describe it.

We used to get in gang fights quite a bit. Not gangs, but it's like one of the lads starts a fight or something and then everyone jumps in … Part of it's you want to make sure your mate's all right, or you just want to get whoever's trying to flatten your mate. But a lot of the time when we were young it's like you didn't want to be left out, so everyone was jumping in whenever there was any trouble … I remember we kicked the shit out of this lad walking home one time. It was one of them where there'd been a bit of an argument in a pizza shop, not much, and we've all kind of gone outside and it's just gone from there. Eric I think was having a go about football or something, and there's four of us and two of them. It just keeps up, just having a go about football, but as we're going up onto Castle Road you can just start to tell it's getting more serious … I just think it's, there's no cameras or anything, not many people about, so it kind of puts it in your head that it could end up in bother here. We're walking up Castle Road and Eric just loses his loaf and starts getting in to him. It was nasty because it was like we were all boiling. This one lad put up a bit of a fight but the other one was just getting kicked to pieces. Eric's like properly kicking this lad in the head … We did go a bit over the top there … I was a bit worried, because we've just left them in the road and legged it, and so you're thinking, the next day, he's dead isn't he? That kind of thing.

Most of the time it's just a bit like that, but it happens quicker because if there's trouble right in the city the coppers are there or there's bouncers or whatever. I seen fights go on for ages though before the coppers turn up. Like there's something said, and then one of the lads says something and then they're getting the shit kicked out of them … The lads I go out with are mostly top-class lads. I wouldn't say we're like, super hard or nothing, but there's maybe five that I know are going to stand with me if I have any trouble … Most of us have had a beating ourselves, but when you're out in a big group there's not that many in this town that can touch us.

However, despite this complex and rather ambiguous set of possible motivations and justifications, Tim falls into line with the other respondents in the 'perpetrators' category and stops short of admitting fear. Even those who saw themselves as perennial victims would not admit the presence of fear in its raw form. The maintenance of a domineering image by constantly winning seems almost irrelevant, and the main motivation seems to be the ability to show fortitude, conquer fear and avoid humiliation; to stand fast and 'take it':

The type of lad I am is just, I'm not the type who's going to stand there and take shit from anyone really. I'm not the hardest bloke in the world, but it's just automatic if someone has a go at me. There's loads of people around here who could batter me, but I'm not bothered by it. I've had kickings before, it doesn't bother me. I'm not bothered by it. I'd rather stand and get a kicking than run off, because that's just not me.

Al

Al shows a fatalistic attitude to violence similar to that demonstrated by the majority of the 'victims'. Again, the avoidance of suffering either excessive damage or humiliation when faced with totally unavoidable violent confrontations is central to his thinking:

Al: What you've got to understand is that just because you have a fight doesn't make you a bad person. People like what'll read this book know fuck all about violence. People give it, violence is wrong and all that stuff, but why is it wrong? What makes it wrong? Because some posh cunt thinks it's wrong that's all. They think it's dirty and horrible and they don't want it next to them, but they know nothing about it. I'm not saying violence is great, because anyone who knows about it is going to tell you it isn't. It can be fucking horrible, believe me ... What I'm saying is that there's a time and a place for violence. It's not always wrong. Sometimes it's just necessary and there's nothing you can do about it. A lot of the time violence is a fucking horrible thing. When you get close up to it, you know, it's scary sometimes, and if you loose it fucking hurts. Other times, it's just the right thing to do.

People say it's wrong, but what are you supposed to do if someone just comes up to you and punches you in the face? And it happens all the time for no reason. What do you do? Is it wrong to have a go back? Maybe you're furious, you want to kill this cunt, is it wrong to give him a kicking if he's done something like that? For some people, something like that happens, they'll just lie there or run off screaming or something, but some people are going to be the opposite ... For me it's all about standing up for yourself ... To me sometimes you need to fight and there's times when it's just the right thing to do.

Al: Yeah, there's loads of times I've thrown the first punch. Loads. But so what? That doesn't mean it's my fault or anything does it? ... People test you all the time and they'll see how far they can push, pushing and pushing until you either think, that's it I've had enough, or you pussy out and walk off. But that's not me and it's not really any of the lads I call mates. What kind of man are you if you let people push you about? I've seen people bottle trouble loads of times and it makes you think, how do they live with it? Don't they understand?

Q: Understand what?

Al: Just that it doesn't help anything. They might get out of a beating, but really, what would you think of yourself if you let people just steamroller all over you? It's just got to boil your piss hasn't it? Me it would just send me around the bend. I'd be, ohhh! Arghh! Just going over it and over it because I couldn't get it out my head. And when you get like that, it just gets worse and worse until you do something about it. At least with me anyway. Me, it would get worse and worse.

Q: What would it feel like if you walked away?

Al: Hard to say. Depends on what happened. If someone's clearly pushing me, then if I walked away, like I say it would play on my mind ... It just would ... Just because

I'm not the type of lad who could do that. Walk away and then forget it. I'd be thinking, people think I'm a fucking idiot, don't they? Like you become a joke, people taking the piss and that, and I couldn't live with it, it would pray on my mind. I knocked someone out just last Saturday … They caused it. Just being mouthy with me when I'm drunk. I was going to leave it but then he set his lip up to my mate so I just smacked him … It was on the way home, just on Manchester Road … It started waiting for Herbie at the cashpoint. He's trying to flag down a taxi and he's just acting like a cunt in front of his two mates. Asks for a slice of my pizza. That's what happened … Just seeing him act like a cunt put me in a mood because you've always got to be wary because there's that many arseholes down the town. So you just kind of automatically go on edge, because you can see what's coming. He wants to be centre of attention and show off in front of his mates, and he's giving it this, and giving it that, and then he asks for a slice of pizza.

Q: Explain how he's working himself, asking for a slice of pizza.

Al: He just is and everyone knows it. You don't just go up to someone at three in the morning, give ez a slice of pizza. What do you think's going to happen? Would you do it, just go up to someone like that? Why not? Coz it's a fucking arsehole thing to do. Anyone does it is just working themselves [meaning trying to cause trouble]. If he had any sense he should've just taken his act down the street … he should've been able to tell that I wasn't about to take it … Just tell by looking at me. I'm not having a laugh with him, he doesn't know me. You want to act like a clown, do it to someone else.

I just told him to fuck off and pushed him. He said sorry and that but he's still hanging about, but I can see his face change a bit, which means either he's got the message or he's going to kick off. He started talking to this lass and his mate's trying to flag a taxi, then he asks Herbie for a slice or pizza, and he's saying, your mate's a tight cunt and wouldn't give me any and stuff like that, then one of his mates walks over. Then I just hit him.

Q: Why then?

Al: Because with his mate coming over you don't want one of them throwing the first punch. You wait, before you know it one of them's thrown a daft one and you're on the floor getting kicked about. I had a think about cameras, but there's none I don't think down there … You just size it up really. There's three of them but they're pissed. They could do some damage if they caught you, so you've just got to pick you punches and take your chances. There's none of that, you know, go on then! And all that shouting and stuff. Just wait for a chance … like wait for him to look away so you can get a good dig in … There's no rules. You don't wait for a bell or anything. Just get in to it and that's it … He just went over, then kind of rolled on his side and covered his head and we legged it.

To Al and the other respondents, dealing with violence is not simply a matter of choice, agency or personal morality. The inevitability of violent encounters is an immutable part of an historical *doxa* that has been operating for a long time as a practical and emotional logic way below the level of autonomous agency, hegemony, negotiated meaning, ritual enactment or iterative practice. This is an objective phenomenon that has been naturalized in the culture and individual psyches of the young men quoted above, and must be negotiated without showing the fear or suffering the humiliation that would endanger the group and its individual members or bring them into disrepute and make them an easy target for more violence. To Al, male interpersonal violence is such a common and natural aspect of his *doxa* that simply labelling it 'wrong', in the way that the domesticated and protected middle classes often do, is as useful to its reduction or transformation as doing the same to a hurricane or an earthquake.

If any single explanation can draw the evidential and interpretive strands of the victims and perpetrators together, it is that their stoical, fatalistic and reactionary attitude to violence is a deeply entrenched and highly reproductive form of 'survivalism' that infuses the localized culture and the *habitus* of its male members. This has for a long time been common in extremely hostile social and natural environments, traditional military units and groups engaged in heavy and dangerous forms of productive work. The nature of this complex drive seems to be ultimately defensive, based on the refusal to suffer excessive physical damage and humiliation and the practical logic of maintaining a violent reputation as a deterrent to others in what is perceived as an immutably violent environment, and as a means of establishing some semblance of status and control. Here lies the extreme difficulty of reducing violence in an environment where it has become naturalized as a core component of the *doxa*: accepting and displaying a pacified and civilized personal constitution is too risky, so the fact that perpetrating acts of violence is in the last instance a question of moral understanding and personal choice and responsibility is largely avoided because it carries with it the unacceptable risks of inviting further and more intense forms of humiliation and physical injury. Individuals who resist this *doxa* tend to do so by keeping their heads down so low that they risk crushing their own personalities, withdrawing into defensive subgroups or escaping entirely across the class-barrier into another world, which of course, as Wilson (1987, 1996) argues, leaves the 'old world' to degenerate even more rapidly. Violence is reproduced as a practice and a psycho-cultural norm by a gridlocked double bind, a stand-off that resembles the basic relations of the Cold War. The romantic humanist strategy of cultivating the internal 'resistance' and 'dissent' of emergent progressive forces does not seem to be the answer, and unravelling this tangled cultural knot seems to be a virtually impossible task without the initial intervention of some sort of third party to prevent violence by means of authoritative regulation, which is the subject of the next chapter.

–8–

Policemen's Stories

While central and local government make piecemeal changes to licensing and regulation in an attempt to assuage public disquiet about high levels of violent crime in and around after-dark drinking strips (see Hobbs et al., 2005), little of any consequence is being done to improve the control of what should be a central concern of crime control policy (Hobbs et al., 2003). As the State yields yet further ground to the market and appeals to the better nature of the business community to 'responsibilitize' itself by organizing its own regulation and policing, the underlying market-driven reality seems to plot its own course unhindered by political agency. As we have seen in Chapters 6 and 7, generations of lived experience in the night-time economy's climate of normalized violence have established in the minds of most young people the expectation of encountering violence, thus contributing to the anxiety that now permeates a fragmented and increasingly distrustful society (see Taylor, 1999; Bauman, 2001, 2004) and the palpable absence of traditional state policing compounds this problem further.

The task of controlling the denizens of the night has been, for the most part, handed to the market and private policing, usually in the muscular form of bouncers. These privately employed regulators are recruited from traditional forms of working-class 'hard masculinity' (Winlow et al., 2003), and their occupational cultures and working practices are driven by market imperatives rather than rational evaluations of effective ways to ensure public safety. Their job is to protect the property of club and pub owners, ensuring that their premises maintain a reputation for providing the 'safe hedonism' that attracts mainstream consumers (see Monaghan, 2004; Sanders, 2005).

Bouncers are under no obligation to ensure public safety in the broader night-time urban environment, and the methods they employ to prevent violence appear to do little to reduce the climate of fear and risk; in fact, in many ways, they are an integral element in its constitution and reproduction. A relatively small number of police officers have been delegated the task of maintaining public order in a night-time economy in which recorded violent incidents outnumber those of the day-time economy by three to one. Further research, of course, indicates that the number of unrecorded violent incidents is significantly higher (Lister et al., 2001; Shepherd, 1990).

The extracts below highlight the multifarious problems faced by this small band of police officers. Most of those we interviewed were rather stoical about working evenings at the weekend and dealing with persistent drunkenness and violence. They often dealt with the worst excesses of the contemporary leisure industry, regularly witnessing violence, fending off violence and abuse directed at them, pacifying aggressive young men and women, nursing near comatose drunks and arresting young people in various phases of combat. For these officers, the connection between alcohol, violence and most of the other problems encountered in the night-time economy was crystal-clear and in no need of obfuscation by academics. They were unanimous in suggesting that a reduction in alcohol consumption would result in a reduction in this sort of behaviour. However, some interviewees showed symptoms of a mild case of conservative declinism, believing that problems of the night-time economy were more deeply rooted in a general social malaise that these young people represented. To these officers, such high levels of intoxication were nothing new and they related the scale of crime and disorder that they witness today to a decline in respect, discipline and morality. The majority, however, were reluctant to offer broader explanations, tending to suppress their recorded comments and simply describe practical policing issues.

When asked to consider how society and its political institutions might address the general disorder of the night-time economy, our police interviewees were perplexed. These were practical men dealing with real crime problems, and uncovering root causes was not part of their remit. They tended to see their role as cleaning up the detritus left by young night-time revellers, who drank too much and cared too little. They approached the problem in a rather jaded fashion, and they did it unquestioningly; it was a dirty job but someone had to do it. Meeting these police officers, and reflecting at length on the transcripts, suggested that most of them were indeed resigned to the mundane yet occasionally dangerous task of having to deal with the aftermath of excessive drinking. However, they were also keenly aware that violence and disorder were indeed serious problems, worthy of their best efforts and far greater consideration by the 'top brass'. If solutions do exist, they are to be found in the traditional principle of preventative policing, but some appeared rather contemptuous of the state's current attempts to apply it. Most felt that 'adequate management' of the night-time economy would make their job easier and increase general public safety, but what actually constituted 'adequate management' was unclear. There were vague comments about making the drinks industry act responsibly and there appeared to be a broad consensus about the necessity of putting more police officers on duty to cover the rush of revellers into the city centre on weekends, but all of our interviewees stopped short of criticizing current policing strategy and government policy. Unlike our interviews with young people, there were relatively few unguarded moments and no cathartic venting of frustration and dissatisfaction by these policing professionals.

The British political classes, who eventually agreed to fund state policing by taxation in the early nineteenth century, did not expect the police to solve the complex problems of crime causation. Instead, the police have evolved as a utilitarian form of crime control; prevention by the low-level deterrence they create by maintaining a 'visible presence' on the streets. Those officers we spoke to seemed to approve of this approach, regarding it quite automatically as the best solution to most common types of public disorder. They were unanimously keen to raise awareness of the scale of alcohol-related disorder yet they were either unaware or unenthusiastic about most of the potential solutions currently under debate. However, the current updating of the licensing laws received some cautious approval. Allowing bars to stay open for longer might reduce the build-up of large numbers of inebriated people at specific times, therefore possibly preventing the occurrence of 'flashpoints' of violence, but on the other hand it might ultimately lead to more drunkenness and the dispersal of a problem population, making its management even more difficult (see Hadfield, 2002). The strategy of taxing specific venues – or licensed premises generally – to provide additional police cover received some lukewarm approval but generally they seemed sceptical that such a scheme could be managed adequately. The response to the policy initiatives brought up in the interviews was often a resigned and rather doubtful facial expression. 'Maybe, possibly, this might do some good' was the stock response. None of our interviewees were wholly committed to proposed initiatives aimed at reducing violence and disorder, and, generally speaking, they appeared to believe that the only meaningful way of addressing violence in the night-time economy was a significant increase in the number of officers on patrol.

Below is an edited selection of the data we gathered from police officers with recent experience of policing the night-time economy. All live and work in the north of England and are drawn from a variety of forces. All names and area descriptions have been changed.

Bill

Bill is in his late thirties and works mostly around Scarville, a small town in the north of England. On Bill's patch a lack of resources means that specific officers cannot be designated to police the night-time economy. Bill and his colleagues have to respond to the usual range of Friday and Saturday night emergency calls, so keeping the area's growing drinking strip under control is just one task amongst many.

> We'll have to go from say, a fight in the main street over to a domestic dispute or a burglary, or whatever else is happening, but we're mindful of [the town centre] and what can happen … [Saturday is] usually the busiest night of the week, and on a busy night

you can be flying from one call to another ... I think the common denominator, on a Saturday night, is alcohol ... A lot of the violence we get is close to Main Street and around the main pubs, but then you can be called out on all sorts of jobs, and in a lot of cases at least, you're kind of going to find that [alcohol has] played a part... It's just part of the job and I think it's accepted ... It's not exciting or anything like that, not most of the time. You're there to do a job. I'm not going to come out and say you don't get times when you get a little anxious, because there's been times when, and this isn't unusual, when it's touch and go. People will react when they've had a drink and you get that aggression a lot.

It's like most jobs, I suppose. You just kind of get used to it. I mean, there's always surprises ... once you get out on the street and things can change around really quick, but most of the time it's just water off a duck's back ... You're dealing with petty disorder, drunkenness and occasionally a few serious incidents ... There has been a number of serious incidents, even in a place like ours... violence really. Some serious assaults ... [This] part of the job [policing the night-time economy] has it's ups and downs, but I think most would prefer to be doing day shift and just getting on with everyday policing rather than dealing with the things you see on a Saturday night.

Bill appears to be suggesting that dealing with the weekly round of disorder and violence can become rather mundane. Prolonged exposure to the general climate and the forms of behaviour that come to the fore when the everyday rules of social comportment recede, have dulled Bill's moral indignation towards those he encounters while at work in the night-time economy. Drunkenness, rudeness and violence are clearly the norm, and Bill is a relatively old hand at this type of policing.

Bill's small corner of the world does not experience the scale of disorder experienced in the larger cities but, on the other hand, there are fewer officers on duty to deal with the violence and disorder that does regularly occur. Scarville has experienced a range of social problems since the area was forcibly de-industrialized. Drugs, which were a minor police consideration in the mid 1980s, are now a 'serious problem', and Scarville and its surrounding areas exhibit a number of social and economic problems often associated with 'permanent recession' (see Lea, 2002; Hall et al., 2005). Young people with adequate economic resources continue to seek the bright lights of the nearby big cities but there has also been a resurgence of the local drinking strip, as the old pubs and clubs have attempted to cash in on the national obsession of youthful night-life, stocking bottled lagers as well as the usual ales, and employing DJs rather than relying on the outdated jukebox. However, it lacks diversity and the intensity of hedonistic experience on offer in the nearby cities, and perhaps as a consequence there's a more direct focus on extreme intoxication. Those who stay local and spend the night in Scarville often cannot afford the trip into the city, and some are less inclined to seek out specific forms of dance music or consumerized festivities that carry a particular cultural cache. Others regard themselves as veterans who have experienced the big city carnival and are now content with the local drinking strip, where they know all the regulars and from which they can simply walk home without the hassles and expense of waiting and paying for taxis.

Scarville might not embody the glamorous image of Britain's thriving night-time economy but weekend drinking continues to produce a range of serious assaults, disturbances and a general climate of disorder. Being rather cut off from the nearby big cities and surrounded by a number of villages and small towns, Scarville's night-time economy has a slightly different dynamic from many we encountered. The culture is based on hard drinking rather than conspicuous and stylish hedonism, and the atmosphere is rather dour, populated by figures of robust masculinity and talk ranging from football and sex to impending socio-economic doom. The age range of drinkers is quite diverse. Groups of men and women from outlying areas regularly come into Scarville for a Friday or Saturday night out in the popular bars that are compressed into a small number of adjoining streets. In a town of this type, extended friendship and family networks reproduce a set of distinct parochial histories, cultural meanings and logics of practice that remain hidden from the passing drinker. Here, traditional working-class forms of excess are not heavily sublimated by flashing lights, smoke machines, the hypnotic thud of house music or the symbols of consumer fashion. Such niceties are unnecessary, and a visceral, foreboding and rather masculine air permeates the proceedings, with a constant and barely disguised undercurrent of potential danger that is distinct from the big-city drinking experience on offer some ten miles along the road.

Bill acknowledges the persistent threat of violence and real aggression that he frequently encounters, but he appears to play down the impact of the turmoil of the night-time economy upon him personally and his attitude to the job. The key concern for police officers regularly tasked with policing the night-time economy is 'losing control of the street' to the 'sheer numbers' of people who populate after-dark drinking strips. The inadequacy of police cover relates directly to what Bill considers to be the most potent threat of all: potential inability to protect the public:

I think the key problem is the sheer number of people on the street. Obviously drunkenness is an issue, and through that you get a range of anti-social behaviour, but the key thing is controlling the street, and often times we haven't got the resources to cover it … The sheer number of people always leads to confrontation when you consider the level of drunkenness that seems to be standard these days. It's really a cause for concern because you see so many people who are paralytic and just don't know what's going on around them. When you're in that state you run the risk of seriously damaging yourself, and it can lead to all kinds of other safety concerns … From a purely public safety standpoint, it's obvious that something needs to be done about the levels of intoxication we see … Changing the licensing laws is I think the first step, because we do see a lot of incidents that are directly related to people gathering out on the street in numbers and at particular times. Whether or not allowing pubs to stay open longer is sending out the right message I'm not sure, but from a policing standpoint preventing the build-up of people at around eleven and twelve is I'd say a step in the right direction ... [I don't think] having people out on the streets at different times [would be] detrimental, because what we're talking about is manageable groups. I can see the argument, but the sooner we can get people safely off home the better. When you get that build up, that's when things can go wrong.

We do some high profile and get out onto the streets, and you've got back up who'll respond to a blue light, but a great deal of it is left up to the shift that come on at seven ... On a weekend, you can expect to be kept very busy ... our primary job is really keeping control. We're trying to keep a lid on things and most of the time we're trying to prevent violence, and we basically try to create a safe environment for the public.

A lot of the time, you realize, the street can become more crowded than during the day, and this creates a range of policing concerns, because when you add alcohol into the mix there, there's always the chance that things will flare up. In terms of crime prevention, well, we're occupied dealing with incidents, getting to them quickly. We can't be there all the time, simply to step in. The area we've got is just too big and we've got such massive numbers ... You can get quiet periods early on but there's still things to keep you busy, and then after ten there's the rush ... On patrol we tend to cover the main areas ... We'll go around the clubs between eleven and twelve, that kind of thing.

Bill was keen to highlight the scale of drunkenness that he and his fellow officers encounter each weekend. At various points during the conversation he appeared keen to reiterate just how excessively drunk many night-time revellers actually become. Drunkenness appeared to be the norm, and the results of extreme intoxication were often strewn around the streets of the drinking strip:

We'll pick up people if they're drunk and incapable. At the moment we try to get them home, because putting drunks in cells, things can get very crowded ... There's the occasional incident where we'll take them straight to hospital. There's been times where you find someone lying in the road, and it's not immediately clear if they've been attacked or if they've [just] passed out ... But what we tend to focus on is getting to disturbances quickly and trying to nip things in the bud before they escalate.

What you'll find is that when you move in to make an arrest, it often causes a knock-on effect. People get just drawn towards the scene. You might have friends of the party you're arresting, a girlfriend. The general equilibrium of the street can change so quickly that you run the real risk of losing control. You can see a chain reaction along the street as brawls start and you're simply trying to keep order until you can get support to the scene ... [There's times when] your priority really is to prevent people getting hurt, and you're hoping that a van is going to pull up, whatever, and that's going to allow you to move in and make arrests.

While Bill acknowledges that he is in no way a specialist, he regularly occupies a particularly useful vantagepoint from which he can observe the unfolding disorder of after-dark leisure. Drunkenness and violence are core elements of a Saturday night shift, and the rather obvious answer to these problems is grounded in the hard won pragmatism often related to the occupational culture of the British police (Manning, 1977):

I'd say the majority of our arrests are a direct result of drunkenness ... Oh, I think you get used to it [being around drunken people]. You can see it on their faces ... It [alcohol] undoubtedly creates difficulties for us, but the way things seem to be going there's not much anyone can do about it ... [If it was up to me] I'd put pressure on licensee's to serve drink responsibly. These happy hours, you can see the problems they create, and I think there should be an effort to make them aware of the problems ... [Whether the licensee should pay for additional police cover is] a tricky one. I know it's been suggested but I'm not sure how it would be managed. Any additional policing, any additional funding, obviously needs to be looked at very carefully, because it might be a cliché, but we need the extra manpower, right across the board ... [Changes to existing licensing] might have some effect but ultimately isn't going to stop drunkenness and violence ... [Private policing] is unavoidable isn't it, but understandably the public want police officers out there. When their son or daughter heads out for a night on the town they want to be sure that they're going to be safe, and I agree entirely with that ... Other things? I'm not sure because I can see both sides. As a policeman you want to clamp down on the cause of the problem, but they [licensees] are entitled to make a living and there's clearly a lot of people who want those types of services.

While it's clear that we should not expect a single police officer to come up with the definitive policy solution to such a pressing social problem, Bill's responses here indicate that he has little faith in the current crop of policy suggestions relating to the future regulation of Britain's night-time economy. Bill is not one to ruminate on the broader and deeper socio-economic and cultural issues that underpin the problems he confronts every day. The job has made him a pragmatist:

[With bouncers] well, to be honest, there's often a bit of doubt there. We've had to deal with a lot of incidents where bouncers have been implicated in some way, and until recently, you could see a lot of men who were known to us in one way or another working the doors ... I think [the licensing and training has] been a godsend really. It has cleaned things up substantially. I certainly wouldn't suggest that bouncers are always perfect, but in terms of how things used to be, there's definitely been a step forward. We as a force have made efforts to get to know door staff across [the region], and I think this has been beneficial to all concerned ... A club in the city, I won't say the name, they'll now get in touch with us, and hand over people they've found with drugs, things like that, and it makes our jobs so much easier, having a cooperative relationship with door staff ... We've worked hard to simply get a dialogue going. [The radio system, linking door staff to the police] has also been a lot of help. They pass on information about bits and pieces, and of course they can get in touch should they need assistance if there's a disturbance of any sort ... We still have bouncers who pose us problems. I'm not going to say things are ideal, but it's a lot better these days, and really it's one less thing to worry about ... We couldn't do it [control licensed premises as well as the street]. No, we're a long way short of that. As long as we can keep the door staff controlled, and monitor the [security] firms involved, then in terms of public safety, it might seem strange to say it, I think we do need them, and in fact I'd be happy if more places employed them.

Bill appears to believe that the licensing and training of door staff will expel the bad apples from the occupation, helping to make the night-time economy a safer place. His intuitive response appears to vindicate the state's attempt to convince the population that the privatized regulation of the night-time economy is an unproblematic development. However, recent media coverage of violence and disorder in the night-time economy has raised public concern. Although the popular media is usually cast as the villain in sociological analyses, sensationalizing reality to sell its commodities and support authoritarian governance, in this case it seems to have hit a nerve. Britain's market-dependent state has responded to public concern with a high-profile, low-content agenda geared towards the vindication of the business community's efforts to exploit profit-maximizing opportunities. Licensing and training for door supervisors is perhaps the most obvious example of the state attempting to convince the voting public that this highly profitable economic zone is not lawless and dangerous, which, paradoxically, is exactly the 'underground image' that the night-time economy has covertly cultivated amongst its consumers. The government's plan for the future is based on an idealized image of the cosmopolitan centres of European high culture, with a diversity of cool and urbane consumers taking advantage of a self-regulating twenty-four hour economy. However, the mutually observable reality of the robust, visceral and parochial cultures in an anxious, Americanized post-Thatcher Britain is of course very different. The current perception of night-time disorder as a serious problem has elicited from the state a concerted effort to convince consumers and the voting public that the problem is not too deeply rooted in British culture's interaction with the post-industrial consumer economy, and thus minor policy adjustments and licensing initiatives will provide solutions. However, most of these actual 'initiatives' are based upon eighteenth-century utilitarian notions of deterrence, the most recent of which is the criminalization of intoxicated consumers. This has simply drawn attention away from the criminogenic nature of market-driven night-time leisure towards individual pathologies and their deterrence, a regressive way of thinking that British political culture once appeared to have superseded with more advanced ideas.

The stereotypical image of muscle-bound, steroid-crazed, hyper-violent bouncers also needed to be counteracted in order to maintain belief in the safety of the night-time economy and secure public support for its continued development. However, a body of social scientific evidence suggests that licensing and training represent little more than a form of window-dressing, fashioned to distract the public from the state's declining ability to regulate interpersonal violence (see Lister et al., 2001; Hobbs et al., 2005). Given the staggering amount of investment pouring into the night-time economy (Hobbs et al., 2003) – a proportion of which ends up in the coffers of the state – a serious attempt to regulate this burgeoning locus of commercial enterprise and its intoxicated inhabitants appears to be quite distant. The daunting truth is that the coalface task of regulating consumer behaviour is now carried out by a twenty-first century version of the 'private policing' that was such a resounding failure in the eighteenth century (see Johnston, 1992). Squads of occasionally spectacularly muscular bouncers, operating in accordance with the mores of a hyper-masculine occupational culture and concerned exclusively with maintaining the profitability of entrepreneurs' business activities, can hardly be dubbed 'civil' or 'progressive', and remind us of just how many aspects of so-called 'post-modernity' are revivals of some of the worst aspects of early modernity. Government attempts to sanitize and validate the door security industry have further aided the social acceptance of the state's gradual relinquishment of its control of a socio-economic sector that contributes more than any other to the high levels of interpersonal violence exhibited in British crime statistics since the 1980s. As Hobbs et al. (2003, 2005) have noted, private policing in the night-time economy involves the complex interaction of commercial imperatives and a powerful masculinist occupational culture, and, as public interests clash with these commercial imperatives, the mixture of private and public policing in the night-time economy suggests not the extension of the 'police family' but rather the development of a 'dysfunctional police family' (Crawford and Lister, 2003). As the control of night-time leisure – the final frontier of publicly regulated mass culture – is inexorably yielded to commercial enterprise, the total marketization of cultural life looms closer.

As our interviewees confirm, the state is acutely aware of the rather volatile and precarious form of hedonism cultivated by the night-time economy, yet serious attempts to tackle the complex underlying economic, cultural and psychosocial conditions that precipitate alcohol-related violence appear a world away. The British state is now fully committed to furthering the interests of capital, and it no longer possesses the will to extricate itself from the yoke it fashioned for itself during its quite deliberate capitulation to global market forces during the Thatcher era (MacInnes, 1987; Evans, 2004). A visit to Britain's burgeoning night-time economy should display this fact clearly, and as these interview data appear to confirm, the state seems to be pursuing this course at the expense of public safety. Bill continues:

[There are] other things we have to deal with, although our focus has to be public safety, and so we end up dealing with the standard drunkenness and violence mostly ... We've made attempts to combat the drug culture in the local clubs, but this is a long, hard process and you aren't about to see results over night. We know what goes on. We know where it goes on, and some times we know who's doing it. We've made arrests, but, you know, it's something that we have to address ... We've have had people clearly under the influence of drugs, and that is something that causes us concern because the last thing we want is kids overdosing in clubs. But it's a big issue that needs to be tackled in a more broad-ranging manner, because of course we haven't got the resources to start making headway with that kind of thing ... We've not had that kind of gangsterism associated with door security in Northernville. When I say we haven't had it, well, there's probably that element, but we haven't seen it spilling over into violence or anything like that. I'm probably not the person to ask about that part of it. We've had crime, probably linked to drugs and what not, and we've seen some serious incidents in the past, but not as much lately.

[The worst thing I've seen is] difficult to say. There's a lot of times, you'll see a young girl or a young lad assaulted, through no fault of their own, but in terms of scale we've had serious, large scale disturbances a number of times ... We had a football-related disturbance, where there'd been a fight in a bar that spilled out onto the street; we've had what are effectively gang fights that have taken quite a bit of time to get under control, and of course we've had serious injuries, glassings, and just sustained attacks where someone's been kicked on the floor.

Jerry

Jerry is thirty-four and works mostly in the small town of Castleville. Castleville poses problems similar to those experienced by Bill in Scarville. Castleville has not experienced the same degree of economic decline and social problems that have befallen Scarville, and its local bars and clubs attract a more diverse weekend population:

We'll pick people up if we think they're either a threat to themselves or a threat to the general public, although in most cases we'll do what we can to quell the situation and move them on without making the arrest ... of course, you've got fights that break out, where we'll make an arrest and try to get numbers to the incident as quickly as possible.

Well, you tend to get confrontations for a number of reasons, but basically the common denominator is drink. You'll see young men who've been ejected from bars, and they want to take on bouncers, or simply remonstrate with those involved, and it goes from there. When you're drunk the slightest thing can lead to violence, so petty little things can eventually cause what turns out to be quite a serious disturbance. You get a kind of crowd mentality where people feel they have to be involved, and that is the real danger ... Pizza shops and taxi ranks are the stereotype. We tend not to get problems at taxi ranks because we've got a lot of camera coverage in that area, but outside bars we see quite a few problems developing, but these things can start anywhere. An argument or whatever starts, they move on down the street, and then it becomes violent ... The main streets, where you get a lot of people moving backwards and forwards between pubs, is usually where we see the majority of problems.

I like a drink and I can see why people want to go out and have a few drinks, and I'm not really one of those that believes it's wrong or anything like that. It's just an aspect of the job, and we're there to make sure that people are safe first of all, and then to ensure that if anyone steps over the line that they're arrested and charged.

I think since it's been in the papers and been on TV that people have begun to take an interest, but the things that have been proposed, I'm not sure what the effect would be. It's not for me to say ... Licensing, staggering opening times, that kind of thing, might be of some use I suppose, but it was reported that they're not going to change much, because licensees don't actually want to stay open longer ... The tax stuff I haven't paid much attention to.

The main thing would be just to get more coverage, either foot patrols or just get more people in through the night, who could respond when necessary ... I think the cameras have had a slight calming influence because anyone with any sense is going to act accordingly, knowing they're being watched ... [but] they're not the be all and end all. You've got to get them all working first off, then there's issues about who's actually watching the footage and are things being picked up, and even then you've got the issue of can we get officers to the incident quickly, because on a busy Saturday night, you can be kept busy all night, and if a call comes in there's no guarantee you're in a position to take it.

Although the growth of CCTV coverage in urban areas is often seen as a positive development, Jerry suggests that the pressure exerted upon police officers prevents them being used properly. Personnel shortages mean that arriving at incidents quickly enough to make arrests still remains a problem, but the cameras' constant revelation of a stream of violent incidents adds a psychological element that increases the overall pressure:

I've had very little to do with door staff actually. I've had a couple of cases where it's clear that people have been assaulted and haven't wanted to give evidence ... I think in an isolated number of cases, there's still people working who should really not be doing that job. There's a stereotype that they're all these violent bullies; that's clearly not the case, but the vetting of door staff certainly hasn't solved the problem entirely ... It can be a little frustrating. They throw people out onto the street, and then it's kind of our business, but if you ask them what's happened, or ask them for a statement, there's a tendency for them to be a little non-committal sometimes ... I think slowly but surely things are changing though. We are seeing an increase in door staff who are clearly moving away from this rough stereotype and do recognize the need to build a relationship with officers who're on the street ... Oh, I think, without them things would be a thousand times worse. I've been in pubs myself when I've seen door staff act responsibly, and they definitely help to prevent incidents, especially violent incidents, from occurring … even if bouncers are simply ejecting troublemakers out on to the street, it's easier to deal with and we can respond. Without that, without their presence there, a fight could be raging for some time before we became aware of it, so I think, with … private security, there's a positive there … Now, when they do their training, there's a much greater focus on policing rather than simply throwing people out, and that's what we need to move towards … Well, there's probably elements of organized crime around here, but I'm occupied with the rest of it really … We've become more aware of drug use in recent years, and we do what we can to keep that kind of thing under control … Well, it's a problem as much as it's a problem anywhere. We haven't been spared that kind of thing, and we're minutes away from Easternville which, of course, has serious drug problems so we're not blind to it.

[The worst thing I've seen is] after this one incident, we get there, and someone's has tried to bite the young fella's nose off. Seriously. Really, very nasty indeed. There are things like that, where people are getting quite seriously hurt, that happen fairly regularly … To a certain extent you become a bit immune to it, but as a police officer the major concern is simply losing control and not being in a position to adequately police the streets. There has been times where we've been stretched so thin that I've not been in a position to do my job, and that's when it becomes a major problem.

In a very similar vein to Bill, Jerry's major concern is the possibility of 'losing control'. With so many people out on the streets – for whom, of course, the privately employed bouncers have no responsibility – confrontation is highly likely and incidents can spiral out of control. Even when officers are in attendance in small numbers, they are often unable to move in and make arrests or protect people who are being attacked. Despite technological advances such as CCTV cameras, personalized radio communications and mobile phones, police officers often face overwhelming numbers of inebriated, non-compliant people creating situations of disorder that are virtually unmanageable. In these situations police officers can do little other than restrain the most violent two or three individuals whilst waiting for the general melee to eventually 'fizzle out' of its own accord. In the general melee others can receive quite serious injuries literally under the nose of police officers, and this appears to represent the most frustrating part of the job. Despite their best efforts, the police are not always in a position to enforce the law and protect people from violence.

Dean

Dean is in his early forties and works in one of north-east England's major cities. He faces similar problems to both Bill and Jerry, but the scale of night-time revelry and disorder in Northville is significantly greater. Tens of thousands of young people flock to the city's assortment of bars and clubs, spending huge amounts of money (see Hobbs et al., 2003), attracting a diverse number of satellite industries, and causing regular large-scale disorder. Many are locals who know their way around, others are weekend visitors from outlying areas, and others still are tourist drinkers attracted by the city's reputation as a centre of Bacchanalian excess. As night closes in, the darkness symbolizes the loosening of daytime authority and regulation (Turner, 1969), and one can sense the trepidation and excitement generated by the weekly adventures into this frontier economy.

At night the city is structured by three broadly defined drinking strips, but to the uninitiated the arrangement of bars and clubs might well appear haphazard, as if randomly scattered by Smith's invisible hand throughout the centre of the city. Unlike Scarville, and on a very different scale to Castleville, the visitor cannot help but be struck by the magnitude and sheer dynamism of Northville's thriving night-time economy. A Saturday night there epitomizes the normalization of disorder and a peculiarly aggressive form of hedonism and excess (Gofton, 1990; Tomsen, 1997), and a large part of the attraction of the politically sanitized forms of 'transgression' that thrive there are firmly connected to the violence and drunkenness that clutter Dean's working night. As we discussed earlier, these forms of transgression might be better explained by the emergence of domesticated, pseudo-hedonistic normative code rather than a genuine opportunity to enact the urge to 'transgress'. By seven o'clock the streets of the city centre are crowded with people and by ten o'clock they are packed. Around midnight a mixture of drunk, frustrated and financially indisposed young people form huge taxi queues as they try to arrange the final journey home. Others head off to one of the many nightclubs, the most popular of which are surrounded by thick lines of young people trying to make it inside for one last throw of the dice, to prolong the hedonistic promise and delay the disappointment that accompanies the inevitable come down.

The pizza shops and kebab houses are jammed with ravenous 'beer-hungry' young men suddenly overcome with the urge to fill swollen stomachs with a quick fix of carbohydrates and saturated fat. Most bars have cleared out their interior walls and furniture to accommodate more of what the industry names 'mass volume vertical drinkers' (with the heart-warming humanistic touch for which it is famous). The crowds are now akin to those that stood on football terraces in the 1970s, and people push to the bar, keen to swap their hard-earned money for overpriced bottled alcohol. Conga lines of people snake their way to the toilet, to the bar and to the exit through the mass of bodies that are becoming gradually less concerned with style and symbolism as the night wears on. As time passes, the crowds increase as people make their way to the key venues along the drinking strip. The subtle strut and ostentatious posing of the early bar route slowly becomes a drunken sway as this inebriated pageant staggers forward to the next

bar. The subtle sensibilities and rigorously enforced codes of daylight comportment have been stripped to the bare bones, and occasionally abandoned altogether,
and now that the 'time and space' that constitutes Northville's night-time economy
has been clearly zoned in opposition to the daily grind (see Giddens 1984: 119),
young people dive headlong into it like children into a heated swimming pool. As
the clubs close down, more queues of young people, occasionally rather disap-
pointed and even embittered by the failure of manufactured hedonism to deliver its
promises, form at taxi-ranks, and by four o'clock all but a few have finally succeeded in hailing a taxi or embarking upon the perilous, meandering stumble
homewards. A few stragglers linger in doorways and outside clubs waiting for
taxis, the occasional police van passes, and the streets are strewn with discarded
food wrappers, cans and bottles, cigarette packets and flyers for clubs and bars.
The music has stopped and there's a palpable air of melancholy as the haze of
drunkenness subsides and the predestined hangover draws closer. The majority of
those who descend upon Northville pass relatively peacefully through the night-
time experience, but every weekend brings violence and disorder and it's the job
of police officers like Dean to deal with it:

> I think until recently people just didn't know what it was like in a city centre like ours.
> There was kind of the perception that it was just a few drunks and nothing much to
> worry about, but if you go into the city centre, about two o'clock Sunday morning then
> you can't help but see the extent of the problem, because you've got literally thousands
> and thousands of mostly young kids, and they're mostly drunk out of their minds. I
> don't want to stereotype, but the level of drunkenness is amazing really. And it's
> because they're all that drunk, you're going to get all kinds of things happening that
> call for the police to get involved.
>
> It's not just weekends as well now, because on Thursday's they've got cheap drinks
> night and you get a lot of problems as a direct result of that ... About six months ago
> the central area of the city was completely quiet after six or seven o'clock. Now you've
> got a massive increase in people, drunk, out on the street, and simply keeping pace with
> it becomes a problem, because it's not just the centre we've got to police. We've got
> patrols and some extra coverage at a weekend, but on a Thursday night things can get
> very busy indeed ... [On Thursdays] you get a broad mix. You get your regular drinkers,
> up to about thirty, and you get a lot of students making the most of the cheap drinks,
> and there's also been times when you get groups of people who really aren't regulars
> in the city centre who come in purposely to get drunk ... [On Thursday's], there's
> around four or five nightclubs open and they're running drinks promotions. And of
> course, beforehand, you've really got, what would you say, up to twenty bars that are
> also offering cheap alcohol ... We've been in consultation with licensees for some time
> now to make them aware of policing issues and simply to try to create a relationship to
> deal with a range of issues that we come up against, and we've put a stop to the 'pay at
> the door and drink for free' promotions, which we could see had a direct impact ... out
> on the street ... What they'd do is charge people, maybe ten pounds, but once they're

in they can drink as much as they like without paying. Clearly that kind of thing is just shortsighted. The state they'd [the customers] get in was unbelievable really, and then it's just a matter of time until there's serious violence or someone gets very seriously ill … You'd see real serious levels of drunkenness, and in the clubs there'd be confrontations and outside, in pizza shops all around the place you'd see an increase in disorder and violence … [Now] the problem is perhaps less pronounced, but we're still forced to deal with problems created by these type of promotions … I think, clearly, alcohol needs to be sold and marketed in a far more responsible manner, but the fact that you've got a variety of groups, some from quite far afield, out on the streets on a mid-week night, with generally low levels of policing is something that needs attention quite quickly … When you've got alcohol at, what would it be, about half its usual price, then there's always going to be people who will drink excessively … Yes, I'd say the vast majority of violence is the result of alcohol. You simply don't see that kind of behaviour unless people have been drinking.

The majority of our problems occur at a weekend … it seems to me that this culture of drinking is really on a massive scale now … You see young girls, no more than eighteen years old, who can't stand up, can't speak, all through this idea that getting completely out of your head is the thing to do. You see them, God knows what they're doing to themselves … I mean, there's drinking, but we've had incidents, and this isn't just me, where young girls are actually fighting, I wouldn't say as much as the men, but in my years I'd say there's been an increase in young girls drinking and getting involved in violence and what not as a result of it … it's something we've had to keep pace with, because the young girls can be quite violent.

It's the men of course who are what we deal with week in week out. It's mostly them who are drinking the spirits and going around in big groups and all the rest of it, and there's almost nothing you can do about it … What happens, there'll be a spark, something will happen, and then instead of thinking they get involved in disturbances which would never happen if there's no alcohol … Our job, I suppose, is to minimize the danger to the public, the people who want to go out and enjoy themselves without getting drawn into these kinds of disputes. If there's a danger, we get there quickly and make sure things don't escalate, if we've got an assault, we'll do what we can to find those responsible, aside from that, I suppose, we're there to try and reassure the public and simply get people to behave in the proper manner.

I think there's probably an element of truth to it [the suggestion that violence is under-reported]. We do see people with injuries, and there's times when they simply don't want to talk to a police officer … [when you get an assault] on licensed premises, we're keen to talk to door staff … We have had incidents with door staff where there's been the suggestion that they've assaulted people, but even when there's no suggestion they're involved, simply getting people who've witnessed whatever's gone on to come forward can be quite difficult. There's no real set rule. Even out on the street when we can get to an incident quickly, trying to get people to give evidence can be hard, and you often tend to arrive at the tail end of it, so in most cases working out who's done what can be nigh on impossible … you just scoop them up, and try to make the best of the situation.

It's not all we do. You can run into all sorts of things in a city like ours, because we are beginning to see the city being used by different people ... We've had racist incidents, football related violence, we've had drug dealing of course, a rape recently, prostitutes are increasingly coming in to the city ... if you're interested in the night-time economy, then these things need to be considered.

I don't think I can think of an incident that really stands out as the worst, because it's all part of the job. There's been terrible injuries. A girl got beaten up by her boyfriend recently, who was know to us, and was really quite badly hurt ... We just found her in the street ... we had some CCTV evidence, but ultimately it lead to naught ... we see a lot of facial injuries, but I think there's less injuries as a result of glassings than there used to be, but I might be wrong. You see people who've been badly beaten up, kicked and what have you, and of course, that kind of thing is a regular occurrence ... I used to put it on a par with the [football] match, with the numbers of people, but now things are way harder to deal with. In terms of actual assaults, injuries, there's no comparison.

My son has started going out, and I suppose that all of this is a bit current with me ... there's a bit of anxiety about what he's up to, and that I'm sure that's the way a lot of people feel. But what you do about it, I've no idea. You can't really stop them [young people] and I for one wouldn't really want to ... The tendency at the moment is to look at licensing ... there's probably some truth in it ... [that] people won't be drinking so quickly or it'll result in less people spilling out on to the street at particular times ... My attitude is that there need to be a concerted effort to maintain control of it [the night time economy], so whatever that can be done with that in mind I think is a step in the right direction.

Conclusion

As a crisis of public expenditure looms forever closer and the dominance of neo-liberalism becomes embedded in the British economy and its accompanying cultures (Bauman, 1998), the 'impossible mandate' we hand to our over-stretched and under-funded police force becomes painfully obvious (see Manning, 1977). With so few officers actually on duty to deal with public disorder in the night-time economy, the expectation that the police can somehow regulate the effects of the relentless pursuit of the economic interests that are now shared by the market-bound state and the business-community seems to be quite misguided. Consistent throughout our interviews with police officers working on the front line was the perception that they simply do not have the resources to make a significant impact on the crime and disorder that occurs in the night-time economy. The police have been effectively hamstrung by the inability of the state to challenge the dominance that the neo-liberal market economy exerts over the specific times, spaces and leisure pursuits in which youth cultures constitute and reproduce themselves. For all the talk in the 1990s about 'cool Britannia', the devolution of culture and burgeoning opportunities for creative self-expression (see for example, Epstein, 1998; Gibbins and Reimer, 1999), the individuals who inhabit mainstream youth cultures seem to seek the manufactured hedonism offered by expensive bars and clubs whenever they have the time and money to do so, and a general climate of disorder and violence, that neither the state nor the forces of civil society seem capable of regulating, is becoming one of the primary sites for the sociogenesis and psychogenesis of the relationships, cultural codes and individual sensibilities and *habitus* of future generations.

–9–

Conclusion

One of the principal motivations behind this book was the wish to make a small contribution to the revival of a critical approach to sociology and criminology. Social science appears to have been partially neutralized and increasingly immobilized in the centre of a triangle of powerful romantic forces. At one corner stands conservative declinism seeking to restore some mythological Golden Age of order and virtue, and at the other two the defensive optimism of the liberal-humanist left, which politicizes street-crime and violence as a signifier of potential resistance to the dominant order, and the overt utopianism of neo-liberalism that sees the market mechanism as a panacea for all our social problems and the key to the good life. Critique hung on in some schools of thought such as Left Realism and feminism, but during the brief insurgency of post-modernism it became devolved as the traditional class power-struggle was imagined to be fragmenting into elementary dyads of oppression and resistance that were connected to single-issue 'gesture politics' (see Žižek, 2000). Only the politics of gender and race could still lay claim to be addressing 'big' social issues, but their inherently tight focus and their tendency towards liberal reformism and culturalism weakened their grasp on the totality of relations in advanced capitalist societies. As we have argued at further length in the past (Hall, 1997, 1999; Hall and Winlow, 2003) the existence of inexhaustible sources of cultural autonomy and resistance – whether reactionary or progressive – is the common assumption shared by these influential discourses. We do not suggest that autonomy and resistance will be impossible to bring about in the future, but we do suspect that, in their current conditions, youth cultures are showing very few signs of anything that could not be postulated as a form of incorporation into the logical requirements of consumer capitalism.

We cannot possibly claim that the findings of our small sample are generalizable, but they did corroborate past work and suggest the need for some further social scientific research from a position external to the metaphysical triangle we have described above. Rather than resistance, virtue and the buds of new sociability, we found a deep immersion in the consumer economy, its practices and its values. In service work, higher education and the burgeoning after-dark leisure economy we found that, beneath the surface of fun and fashion, life was being lived against a background static of social division, atomization, instrumentalism, hostile interpersonal competition and anxiety. Human energies were being applied to the struggle to maintain temporary and fragile friendships amidst the atomizing forces of the competitive individualist ethic that has now – in a flow too powerful to manage with the traditional techniques of judicious repression and sublimation – leaked through the broken barrier that once separated business from life. High levels of anxiety and insecurity now permeate all aspects of the lives of the young people in our sample.

When we framed our study in the context of historical process, we found that, from the late 1970s onwards, youth cultures have been emerging in an epochal shift from exploitative stability to anxious instability. Our study confirmed the standard observation that the erosion of productive work, class-based community and collective politics has interrupted – probably permanently – traditional modes of socialization into specific class and gender roles (Faludi, 1999; Beynon, 2002). However, it also tended to confirm the less well received claim that classical capitalism's methods of grooming young men for exploitative physical labour in heavy industry and military expansion has constituted a very durable form of tough masculinity – one that in many former working-class locales still reproduces its *habitus* despite the profundity of recent social change. Despite the presence of this form of life, together with others that would have been rather unpalatable to today's progressive liberals, shared experiences and parallel biographies in traditional working-class communities encouraged enduring friendships and quite high levels of political resistance to exploitation, and, commonly, to the system itself. This appears all the more significant as it provides a stark contrast to the extreme atomization and anxiety that characterize the more fragile and ephemeral relationships forming between many young people today as they attempt to climb upwards through blurred social boundaries to hazy occupational destinations.

In the midst of the rapid expansion of consumerism and the accompanying mirages of freedom, self-determination and resistance that appear on its landscape, our interviewees' work and leisure lives demonstrated beyond doubt that old-fashioned exploitation still exists at the heart of capitalist social relations, despite the attempt to bury this plain word under a heap of spectacularly complex post-modern euphemisms (see Bourdieu and Wacquant, 2000). After the demise of class-based cultures and politics in Britain, which made their last stand in the miner's strike of 1984, the anxiety stimulated by the increased possibility of constant unemployment throughout the life course, compounded by the even more terrifying prospect of symbolic insignificance in the 'democratized' culture of conspicuous consumption, has been felt particularly hard by the young males who inhabit the remains of once thriving working-class areas (Hall and Winlow, 2005). Here, exploitation and economic insecurity were once compensated by collective solidarity and social stability, and positions of micro-status in work and leisure could be achieved without expensive immersion in conspicuous consumption and frenetic alterations of identities, beliefs and personal images. Our young interviewees' experiences of work, education, friendship and leisure constantly brought home the banal but largely underestimated fact that they were struggling through various dimensions of an entirely different context for achieving status, reward and security. Despite the deepening and widening of structural inequality and the intensification of exploitation in unstable re-casualized labour markets (Westergaard, 1995; Taylor, 1999), the young working-class people we interviewed demonstrated no conception of, or orientation to, the traditional oppositional strategies of solidarity and organized collective resistance. Rather, this brief exploration of our respondents' feelings felt like tiptoeing through a minefield; the pressure created in each individual by atomized interpersonal competition and the other anxiety-inducing aspects of advanced capitalist life seemed likely to explode into some spectacular emotional response. Perhaps, in that case, there were many moments when our interviewers did not press matters too hard.

In the 1980s, neo-liberal ideology, although not nearly so influential in Europe, swept through the Anglo-American world like a cyclone. Its basic claim is that free markets unhindered by state interference and traditional politics will lead anyone who follows their logical demands into a more liberated and prosperous life. In Britain and the United States, this was followed with religious zeal under the Thatcher and Reagan regimes, whose political economies immediately abandoned Keynesian demand management. Huge swathes of traditional manufacturing industry were moved abroad where labour costs and taxation were lower. This was bolstered by the revived classical liberal principle of choice and self-determination, which for a short time seemed plausible as business, consumption and lifestyle opportunities proliferated. However, in the early twenty-first century, after over thirty years of the political application of this ideology, we found a much bleaker reality: cynical instrumentalism in the institutions of work, education and relationships and very little evidence of deep and lasting friendships across the life course. Indeed, many of the friendships we did find were themselves permeated by instrumentalism and competitiveness in tension with the permanently unrequited urge for communality with others. The insecurity and anxiety caused by economic and social disruption now had to be born by the individual in an atomized society. The upshot was the profound disruption of 'figurations', the traditional networks of social interdependencies that Max Weber saw constructing themselves in early modern Europe's nascent capitalist economy (see Swedberg, 1998), and Norbert Elias (1994) claimed were essential to modernity's 'civilizing process'. These figurations set the context for the sociogenesis and psychogenesis of the sorts of sensibilities and *habitus* that are required for reasonably convivial ways of life.

In the educational field, the basic upshot of the massive expansion of higher and further education is that, apart from a minority of successful entrepreneurs, service professionals and technocrats, the current labour market cannot match graduates with appropriate jobs. As the majority of them stop a long way short of the glittering prizes that are supposed to follow a life of diligent study and deferral of gratification, they often sink back into the casual labour market. However, mentally, many remain convinced that these jobs are mere stepping-stones on the path to greater things, and these high expectations continue to grind against a contradictory reality with considerable friction. Over the years many come to accept the bleak fact that much of their lives will be given over to the daily grind of a minor bureaucratic role, partially compensated by the fleeting narcotic effects of serial consumption. To make matters perhaps even worse, this post-industrial update of the traditional daily grind lacks the traditional compensations of relative security, communality and the beautiful, dangerous dream of collective revenge and justice. Instead, young people lead an atomized and anxious existence attempting to navigate through the rocks of graduate unemployment, consumer debt and tense personal relations.

Accreditation has now expanded into every nook and cranny of economic existence. Employability, an arcane combination of academic qualifications, personal qualities, work experience and estimations of potential 'market performance' have replaced the concepts of apprenticeship and tenured employment. This suite of nebulous qualities must be matched to the demands laid down by the global labour market, in which Britain has had little choice but to focus chiefly on high-tech information processing, personal services and business enterprise to maintain pay levels. Low-skilled jobs are now forced to compete with Third-World wage levels, and thus the drop from the skilled profession to the unskilled lumpenproletarian position appears terrifyingly steep, more so if one considers the casualization of the professions, which also shifts most qualified people within clear sight of the precipice. Neo-liberal market principles, which, amongst other things, were supposed to strengthen the work ethic and encourage a more responsible and determined attitude to the acquisition of work, have in many ways had the opposite effect. Long-term planning has become very difficult, adolescence has been extended and young people seem extremely apprehensive about committing themselves to specific occupations and relationships. Regular soaking in the hedonism of the leisure economy distracts many young people from making firm decisions. Most regard education as simply a means to an end but, in a volatile labour market, the end itself was, even as a broad occupational category, often unclear. Smooth transitions into adulthood have virtually disappeared.

Neo-liberalism has fulfilled its egalitarian promise in a rather perverse way, distributing anxiety across most of the social body and democratizing the opportunity to acquire large debts serviced by all manner of extremely unstable livelihoods. Despite the problems that seem to permeate each stage and each dimension of the life-course, the free market's accompanying ideological paradigm shows few signs of crumbling under a critical gaze. Divisions and inequalities widen and anxieties deepen, yet the dream is stronger, the great illusion is more powerful than ever. To employ the term 'proletarianization' as a description of the process of allowing market forces to erode the middle class career and replace it with anxiety-inducing short term contracts and constant market-performance measurements, as Gray (1998) and Lea (2002) do, is useful but perhaps a little one dimensional. Our research suggests that, for young people at least, the casualization of most employment combined with the atomization of class identity, collective politics and communal solidarity could be construed as the lumpenproletarianization of socio-economic life. However, the overall effect on the young person's life has been compounded further because interpersonal competition and the threat of symbolic insignificance in the realm of conspicuous consumption have promoted an intensified embourgoisement of cultural life. With this concept we could be a little nearer to explaining the anxious instrumentalism we found in our research, because the insecurity faced by Engel's demoralized lumpenproletarianized male worker, combined with something near to the status anxiety and neuroses suffered by Freud's bourgeois women, could perhaps provide the beginnings of an explanation of today's peculiarly intense form of anxiety. For everyday young people who lack personal contacts in high places, the only real way out is by means of personal entrepreneurship and instrumental single-mindedness in the marketplace. This is the crucible where the values, identities and *habitus* of the next few generations will be forged.

For most of the young people we interviewed, education was simply another site of atomized instrumental competition over the acquisition of the symbolic and cultural capital necessary for favourable selection in the labour market and upgraded participation in social life, which is now loosely and fluidly structured by various modes of conspicuous consumption known as 'lifestyles'. Not once in our interviews was it expressed as an opportunity to stretch the intellect and widen social experience. In an increasingly commercialized university sector, the move backwards to acting as a mere talent-spotting machine for business and public administration has diminished its social role, amplifying anxiety and competitive instrumentalism amongst individuals in the staff and student bodies. This market-driven form of individualism is also spilling over from work and education into commercialized leisure and friendships, a realm that was once offered respite from it all. It seems that the dimensions of life that once were to varying degrees separated from the market economy in the early stages of British capitalism – family, community, friendship, education, state, culture, leisure – are now merging with its normative codes.

Our research indicated that many young people are likely to conform to the current trend and delay marriage, maintaining a hedonistic and self-interested bachelor/ette lifestyle as long as possible. In many cases this seemed to be influenced by a heightened awareness of the restraints and sacrifices involved, which now seemed to contrast more starkly than ever with the seemingly unlimited gratifications of singledom in the consumer leisure scene. The young women we interviewed appeared increasingly pragmatic in their approach to family and career, preferring to maintain an uncommitted finger-buffet lifestyle in the consumer-leisure nexus. The lack of trust from both sexes regarding sexual fidelity and commitment was quite striking. The general expectation was that if a partner does not let you down in sexual matters, other aspects of life might strain the couple's ability to remain committed to each other; job and geographical mobility seemed to be the most commonly anticipated problems. Many young women appear to regard high earnings and engagement in hedonism and conspicuous consumption as the principal outcome of the feminist struggle for equality and personal opportunities. If commitment can be made, the wedding was viewed principally as another opportunity for a 'consumer experience' in which the lifestyle can be publicly displayed. Divorce, if not inevitable, was probable.

This new life seemed to cast a shadow of insecurity and anxiety over all social relations, but the solidarity necessary to ward it off was simulated rather than real. The theatrical simulation of traditional forms of communality and politics takes many forms based on myriad interests and tastes, but in our study long courtships with over-dramatized altercations, and the formation of what Maffesoli (1995) has misnamed 'tribal' groups that distinguish themselves using various style codes in the leisure economy, were the most common and spectacular. Rather than signifying a 'decline of individualism', as Maffesoli suggests, these forms of artificial *communitas* are inextricably linked to consumer lifestyles, and, as such, they are driven by the temporary alliances that grow in the midst of hostile interpersonal competition, a manifestation of neo-capitalism's currently preferred form of individualism. Young people's 'cultural innovation' – that throughout the heady 'rock-'n'roll era' captured the imagination of incautious romantics as an expression of almost everything on a spectrum from existential freedom to imminent revolution – has now simply revealed itself more clearly for what it always was; a series of fake revolts, an incorporated and domesticated dynamic force created by and harnessed to consumer capitalism. This concatenation of simulacra masks the intense lifestyle competition in the consumer economy at the same time as giving it a fluid dynamic structure and propagating the illusion that, no matter how cynical the world becomes, there are always possibilities of a life rich in the beautiful joys and tribulations of the affective community. However, our interviewees spoke of no such comfort zones. They seemed to be swept along by a riptide in which agitated, atomized individuals were fighting relentless interpersonal battles for prosperity and distinction for the main functional purpose of generating human energy to drive forward the consumer economy. The end result is a new mode of fluid, culturally driven class division with the possibility of solidarity and resistance removed, where the threat of dropping into total insignificance – always a distinct possibility if any symbolic game is played badly – is born almost entirely by the individual. The appearance of an intensified cult of celebrity in the mass media

seems to echo the actual feelings that we found bubbling up in our young interviewees: the threat of total social insignificance hangs over everyday life, and,
amidst the terminal illness of *communitas* and its politics, the fracturing of the
familial legacy and the wrenching of culture out of practical community (Hall,
2000) and linear history (Canetti, 1987) into a history unfolding to create simulations of previous forms (Baudrillard, 1993), fleeting opportunities for personal
worth must be fought for in the simulated realities of the here and now by the lone
individual.

Recently, by an act of political will, working people in the West were shunted
quite abruptly from servicing the demands of capitalist manufacturing industry to
servicing the demands of the consumer economy, and we now live in a market
society rather than a society with a market economy. In the midst of this, commercialized leisure became one of the principal economic replacements for the
loss of manufacturing in Britain, and our research threw up constant reminders
that both mainstream and 'alternative' youth cultures – much more than the cultures of older generations – were in an advanced stage of losing the ability for
autonomous and creative generation of meaning, identity and *habitus*.
Consumerism's expansionary logic requires the constant proliferation and incorporation of lifestyle desires, which need to be orientated towards the symbolic
value of commodities in order to produce faster rates of circulation. The novel
styles of youth's putative *avant garde,* as far as we could see, have been thoroughly
overblown and misrepresented as signs of resistance by contemporary cultural theorists (see Hall and Winlow, 2004), and the likely reality is that these novelties are
quite systematically cultivated by the consumer machine to maintain the once
linear but now circular and regenerative momentum of the fashion-based industries. In our sample, resistance and alternative political thought were more atomized and marginalized than they ever were amongst the adult working-class
populations of classical capitalism. The traditional leisure pursuits that once ran
alongside work, family and community as a potential site for the relatively
autonomous forging of the *habitus* have now been entirely commercialized. There
is no real carnival and no real inversion of power – rather the constant and rather
tedious derogation and affirmation of fleeting isomorphic styles in loose cultural
hierarchies, *simulacra* in constant circular motion.

In our research, night-time leisure seemed to be nothing more than the cynical
marketing of spectacular hedonism aimed at persuading young people to consume
and accept their vicarious existences in themed, simulated realities. It was a
mythologically maintained normative end in itself, serviced by work and education, and one of its principal socio-economic purposes is the commercialization of
competitive social interaction amongst young people, the economic harnessing of
mimesis. All commodity markets thrive on status competition, and this is no excep-
tion. Competition in an atomized and unregulated zone breeds insecurity and the

construction of closed defensive groups (Eagleton, 2000) and, here, social lives, which once demonstrated the potential of the broad solidarity amongst essential differences that civilized life demands, appeared to exist in a condition of agitated fragmentation. Most of our male and some of our female interviewees felt that the night-time economy's 'edge' is grounded in a general background static of hostility that bubbles under and constantly threatens to erupt into verbal altercations and violence. Of course, the same forces of competitive individualism permeate daytime life in the Anglo-American world, but in an after-dark zone minimally regulated by the state, where human inhibitions are weakened by chemical intoxication, the inflation of the calculating hedonistic ego and the attenuation of the super-ego (see Wouters, 1999), and the expectation of encountering violence, a higher level of violent incidents is not too difficult to predict.

The heightened psychological insecurity that most of our respondents seemed to feel could be construed as a product of the 'competitive conformity' of the night-time fashion scene, in which the disorientating pressure of the paradoxical double-bind – in this case the contradictory command to fit in and stick out at the same time – finds fertile ground for strong growth. The interaction of mass conformity and individuality is no great mystery, a simple affair not unlike the binding of opposite forces in an unstable atom, and its dynamic force can be very easily unlocked and commercially harnessed by the organized manufacture and promotion of diverse and competing styles amongst insecure individuals who possess no real alternative sources of identity. With today's global markets, flexible manufacturing methods and mass communication systems, this is a very simple and highly lucrative enterprise that can now rely on an endless supply of expectant but anxious young people. The cultural glorification of *bricolage* allows the individual to regard conformity as something that others are trapped in and the self has avoided, yet at the heart of conformity is this dynamic individualist illusion itself. The interpersonal competition that fuels the dynamic sets the context in which friendships are now enacted, and this represents a profound break with the past. Work, education and leisure are no longer essentially communal affairs, and although our data suggest that more friendships are made in education and leisure than at work, today they have an increased tendency to flounder. Some life-long friendships survive, especially those forged at school, but most tended to be unavoidably instrumental, where the fashionable seek other fashionable individuals to maximize their status and increase the value of their hedonistic 'lifestyle returns'. Those who fail to provide some worthwhile utility, who fail to 'pull their weight' as fashionable hedonistic consumers, can be quickly jettisoned, risking isolation or at least drifting perilously close to the consumer underclass.

The night-time economy, as our police officers confirmed, is a zone minimally regulated by the state, where frequent incidents of alcohol-triggered violence teeter on the verge of unmanageability. However, violence was not perceived by many of our young consumers as a dangerous and unpalatable phenomenon to be avoided at all costs. It was a known risk keenly felt by most of our interviewees, but to many it was not only a risk worth taking because of the attraction of the potential hedonistic benefits but some felt it added to the attraction by making the hedonistic experience more exciting and 'edgy', in direct contrast to the mundanity of work, education and daytime relationships in the service economy. Neo-liberal ideology has now firmly equated what only a few decades ago would have been regarded as quite extreme and risqué hedonistic experiences with the spoils of the 'transgressive' struggle towards individual liberty and pleasure. However, the conformist counter-force was constantly indicated in our research by the competitive way that the manufactured signifiers of these rights are acquired and displayed by young individuals. The night-time economy is the site of suffocating conformity and endless games of one-upmanship over image, 'coolness', sexual success, drinking prowess and triumph or endurance in violent encounters. The desire to be fleetingly accepted and to acquire a measure of esteem on the night-time economy's fluid terrain unavoidably produced significant levels of anxiety, and despite extreme conformity, nothing much could be taken for granted. In this cauldron of competitive distinction, new class divisions, based on engagement with the simulated realities of consumer culture, are beginning to emerge.

Interviewees who stayed sober often found the night-time economy utterly mundane and tacky, which suggests that alcohol and drugs alter the perception of the individual to a state where they can be recruited into the liminal illusion (Turner, 1969). As the illusion enters their consciousness, the need for alcohol is increased, for without it the bubble will burst and the hedonistic rewards that have been promised will elude them. Their senses must be stimulated so that they can collude in the illusion by adding symbolic and emotional depth to the tacky surface glitz of the night-time economy. Alcohol allows the individual to imagine the relaxation of norms and enhances the perception of pleasure, so it is the perfect drug for recruiting individuals as rashly profligate consumers. It is also the perennial *post hoc* justification, the chemical scapegoat that excuses the self after the event, a broad-spectrum excuse that can justify all behaviours across the spectrum that stretches from extreme activity to extreme passivity. The loosening of ego and super-ego controls is bound to produce a degree of disorder, which is itself part of the attraction if it can be regulated, but the fact that it spills over into regular incidents of violence in such an anxious and competitive environment is not surprising. The fact that the *habitus* of these young individuals has been forged in a general climate of insecurity in their daytime lifeworld makes the violence more likely because, as Wouters (1999) argued, this emergent 'new nature' of the individual in neo-liberal society relies more on the calculative control of the ego than the emotional control of the super-ego and, when ego-control is impaired in a condition of intoxication, the currently less effective unconscious inhibiting mechanism of the super-ego – the conscience – struggles to restrain the individual from participating in violence.

Some of our interviewees had avoided all but the most minor incidents of violence, but many had witnessed or participated in quite extreme incidents. Even those who purportedly regarded violence as distasteful also found it memorable, and many recounted their experiences with enthusiasm. Some women also found it quite entertaining but their views of it tended not to be quite so reverent or mythological as those of the males. For a brief moment, the suffocating conformity of life in the consumer economy, the mundane sitting at check-outs or desks in call-centres, dozing in lectures about urban planning or staring at television screens, erupts into a spectacular visceral conflict, a genuine transgression where the interpersonal style-competition is forgotten and most eyes become riveted on the spectacle like a crowd in a schoolyard. The organized witnessing of normally forbidden activities as a commercial enterprise has a long history. The violence that once signified the superiority of Roman gods and emperors in Vespasian's Coliseum had been sublimated and organized into rule-bound games and commercialized by sports entrepreneurs in nineteenth-century Britain (Holt, 1989), and then broadcast by mass media in the post-war years of the twentieth century. However, in the simulated reality of consumerism's hyper-sublimated peacetime the sight of real, raw violence unbound by rules and conventions has been denied, and the eruption of spectacular violence in the night-time economy is, for most people, the only opportunity to see this primal activity. There is no commercial conspiracy at work here, it is simply a natural attraction, like the brief appearance of a real tiger on a simulated safari trip, which is more likely to occur regularly in an environment where minor infractions of the rules are tacitly encouraged.

Many violent incidents tend to be unreported and unrecorded (Lister et al., 2001), and many of our interviewees suggested that stranger violence seems to be as common as violence between people who know each other, which conflicts with the trend based on reported violence. The possibility of stranger violence tends to elicit more anxiety than the possibility of occasional altercations between friends, and the male victim's experience of it was often passed off amongst peers as a glorious status-enhancing war wound. At a deeper level, however, it tended to agitate and justify the feeling of a hostile and vicious world full of potentially violent individuals, greatly compounding this vague but powerful anxiety, and also identifying other young men as the physical manifestations of it, the objects of fear. This was not a mass-media construction or a paranoid delusion but the reflexive appraisal of life as it is, based on bitter experience. It fed into mistrust, cynicism, misanthropy and the wary interpersonal distancing and atomization that the cult of competitive individualism requires, and contemporary masculinities were being constructed in the midst of a pressing need for physical and psychological defence against potential hazards rather than the reproduction of patriarchal domination. Fortitude in the face of inevitable violence – especially against the 'specialist warriors' represented by bouncers and reputable local hard men – was highly valued amongst the victims, who showed both enthusiastic and fatalistic attitudes towards violent encounters.

The genuine excitement expressed by many of our interviewees suggested that they were actively seeking the return of a reality in which meaningful rituals could take place, because a ritual within a simulation is meaningless and therefore impossible. If the victims felt pulled into the ritualistic display of fortitude, many of the more regular perpetrators tended to feel pushed into violent encounters by an internal hankering after a traditionally rugged and visceral existence, an atavistic cultural form in today's world of automation, symbol processing and service work. There was surprisingly little evidence of seeking status and reward or maintaining patriarchal entitlements, which means that some of the orthodox profeminist analyses of male violence (see Messerschmidt, 1993) are difficult to apply to this environment. Instead, permeating the psychological world of the perpetrators was a fatalistic acceptance of who they are – their own durable *habitus* (see Horne and Hall, 1995; Winlow, 2001) – and a strong need to preserve physical integrity, dignity and modest reputations whilst negotiating inevitable violent encounters. This duplicates the general misanthropy and fatalism of the victim group, but the difference is that these individuals have been brought up not to accept any form of humiliation or affront to their dignity. The perpetrators seemed to regard the world as increasingly nihilistic and hostile, and faith in norms, codes or legitimate state agencies was minimal. The only faith was in an atavistic moral code that needed to be reproduced by the individual, who must set himself against the corrupt world to defend this code against threats; the archetypal 'reluctant hero' so beloved of the producers of American literature and cinema (Slotkin, 2000).

Adherence to traditional masculine codes cultivated frequent feelings of moral disgust towards those who refused to show respect for others, and the idealized relations of respect were surprisingly egalitarian, with hierarchies forming only as a consequence of displays of disrespect. Thus, their ire was targeted on bullies and 'smart-arses', and driven by a moral duty reflected in self-identity, a subterranean categorical imperative, to put things right, to conserve this traditional culture of respect and maintain a robust masculine self-image. When the order was disturbed by outbursts of brazen individualism and effrontery, they sought to temporarily level the social playing-field by administering the occasional dose of salutary violence, 'teaching a lesson' in a very real way as an antidote to the way that identity is asserted in a simulated social world that is energized by a constant struggle to *symbolically* out-compete and humiliate the other. This might be construed as an attempt to restore an old communal moral order, to slap down the spectacular individualist who tries to act 'clever' in public, to become a moral policeman, a Dirty

Harry or a Judge Dredd on the streets of a superseded order that exists only in the cultural memory of *habitus* and normative practice. It signifies the nostalgic need to take action in a world shorn of humility and respect, where outwardly smug and cocky (but inwardly anxious) individualists play a risky game of displaying their brash individualism in spectacular but often rather clumsy ways under the disinhibiting influence of alcohol or drugs. The *habitus* of those about to perpetrate violence forbade conspicuous attention seeking, and fairly innocent displays of 'cockiness' could often stir the ire of those who continued to cling to outmoded forms of enclassed masculinity and sociability.

Many positioned themselves as brutal idealists trying to prevent the rise of the spectacularly assertive individual who is struggling out of the enforced modesty of industrial modernity's old communal cultures. But this only happened amongst a small circle of like-minded friends and acquaintances who shared this atavistic *habitus*. In the wider culture it acts as a means of social differentiation, in this case a serious demotion in the eyes of the 'higher order' of radically fashionable passive consumers. It is a few steps along the historical road from Paul Willis's (1977) 'lads', who rebelled themselves into conformity, but in this case they are rebelling themselves into relative insignificance by staging a moral rebellion against the ostentatious competitive individualism of a consumer order that, unlike industrial capitalism, no longer provides roles for the culturally demoted. This insignificance can only act to intensify frustration and add more irrational factors into the concatenation that precipitates violence. This form of aggression was not simply about envy, or thuggery, or maintaining dominance, but more closely associated with the moral task of preventing others from becoming dominant in ways that were difficult to compete with. It was not aimed specifically at those who were regarded in masculine culture as 'subordinate', as Connell (1995) and others suggested, but rather it seemed to represent some antiquated egalitarian morality that has been reduced to frustration and misanthropy because of the ubiquity of the irrepressible and spectacular individual asserting himself in a competitive individualist culture. Constant failure to satisfy the demands of the *habitus* and perform the task of reproducing the masculine codes of the past resulted in more explosive frustration, which could erupt almost any time when an overt representative of assertive individualism was encountered. Students, for example, are often the targets of the anger of these anxious, economically obsolete moral enforcers (see Davies, 1997). Above all, violence is a form of behaviour that strips away the hollow facades of consumer culture and allows men such as these to communicate with the core of themselves in a deeply meaningful manner. In an increasingly confused and disorientated social world characterized by cavernous anxiety and the rather desperate search for meaning and identity, violence continues to provide an emotive script for marginalized masculine forms out of sync with the new demands of sociability.

Other perpetrators seemed to be responding to threat. They were defensive realists who accepted that the ability to exercise violence is a valuable personal quality justified by the presence of the hostile other and the need to retain dignity. The need to maintain a moral order was slightly less pronounced, but nevertheless the victim was expected to know the rules of respect, so the same culture is being referenced. Most of our interviewees were still capable of feeling guilt if they themselves transgressed the traditional codes, perhaps by misjudgement or due to the influence of drugs or alcohol. The super-ego is still integral, although the ego seems to take over as they grow tired of the 'aggravation' and grow into older and grumpy personalities who just accept that they are destined to inhabit a hostile, confusing and immoral world full of 'arseholes'. Even though some interviewees showed no sign of intimate attachment to old egalitarian codes and seemed to be driven by an almost infantile, adrenalin-driven fetish for violence, the need to show fortitude and avoid humiliation was still paramount, so we might suspect that vital aspects of the broader masculine codes still retain some influence. Whether it was attached to a moral crusade or not, this seems to be the commonality, and it is not the product of free inter-subjective negotiations over meaning, but an historical product of *habitus*-creating practices and codes from the industrial-modern past. What seemed undoubtedly common to all, however, was the need occasionally to witness or experience raw reality as a site for the performance of ritual and the testing of fortitude.

In the urban spaces of Britain's former industrial cities, the night-time economy is the principal site for the formation and reproduction of youthful consumer identities, and to extricate oneself from this *simulacrum*, this marketing strategy masquerading as a culture, is to risk a form of social exclusion that is quite daunting to today's insecure young people. Here, our data suggests that anxiety and interpersonal hostility are now important shared experiences and perceptions amongst young people, present in most spheres of daytime activity but felt in more intense and spectacular forms in the night-time economy. However, they are not temporary reactions to some external enemy or objective problem but are generated constantly and internally by the competitive interactions of the inhabitants themselves, where the very presence of other stylish and competitive young people is becoming a Kierkegaardian threat to the integrity of the individual, especially if that individual feels he or she is slipping too near to the terrifying precipice at the edge of consumerism's social reticulation. In this climate of weakly sublimated hostility and alcohol-fuelled hedonism, eruptions of serious interpersonal violence are now common, and youth cultures, identities and *habitus* are now being generated and reproduced amongst young males and increasing numbers of young females around various emergent practices through which life in this environment can be confronted and managed. The night-time economy is now the primary site for interpersonal violence in Britain (Winlow et al., 2003), and not only has this violence increased markedly since the mid 1980s (ibid), but young people are becoming accustomed to its presence as a normal aspect of a *doxa* in which potentially durable forms of cultural practice, identity and *habitus* are being forged. As young people become accustomed to violence as a norm, and begin to expect to encounter it, a suspicious, anxious and hostile climate with its own practical logic evolves, and these sentiments, along with the dispositions needed to react in defence of the body and avoid humiliation in the eyes of others, establish themselves amongst the core dynamic properties of the durable *habitus*.

As this book draws to a close, the reader could be forgiven for thinking that we have offered an essentially pessimistic view of contemporary youth identities, and that we have taken a polemical position in order to reinforce a theoretical critique of the contemporary capitalist economy. Certainly, the aim was to draw the reader's attention towards the continued inequities of life under consumer capitalism and the real problems created by its ethic of compulsory individualism, yet our position is of course not without justification. The words we have used as epistemological bases for our depiction of this tumultuous, increasingly fractious and anxious social world are the words of those young people who are currently struggling to plot a course through it. Some may succeed; the university sector is still, after all, the primary means of acquiring the skills demanded by high-paying professions. But the truth of the matter is that many will fail. Ray, for example, clinging desperately to an increasingly obsolete masculinist work culture, runs the risk of a rapid descent into the socially excluded micro-community that he is desperately trying to avoid. Robert is already beginning to explore the pleasures and pains of illegal business. Emma appears destined to live with her parents for the foreseeable future, continuing to work in shops at a little over minimum wage. Branching out on her own or with her boyfriend is impossible, because the minute she leaves the parental home the cruel reality of her economic position will envelope her. Joanne might indeed slay the competition in the graduate labour market and secure that most prized of things, a real job, but failure will mean a continual fight to stay socially connected and cope with the drudgery of low-level service work. Many of our other respondents face similar defining moments in the not too distant future, and we wish them the very best of luck.

The suggestion that 'the kids are all right', that they are free-willed, resistant and innovative is – just like the suggestion that the lower reaches of the former working classes continue to be driven by the ineradicable spirit of rugged nobility, rebellion, liberty and communal sentiments – currently perpetuating rather than counteracting the serious multifaceted problems that they face. There is much about contemporary society to criticize, and if we forget that we also forget the history and purpose of sociological enquiry. There is much that social science can do to create a critical distance between itself, conservative declinism, neo-liberalism's compulsory optimism and post-modernism's endlessly proliferating and increasingly purposeless analyses of allegedly 'transgressive' micro-exotica. What we hope we have revealed is not baseless pessimism but a realism that is currently being shunned, a realism that confronts squarely the distinct probability that, as the logic of the market seeps into every facet of human life, the continuation of the reasonable degree of conviviality in interpersonal relationships that modernity had achieved cannot be guaranteed.

Bibliography

A

Adeney, M. and Lloyd, J. (1988), *The Miners' Strike 1984–5,* London: Routledge & Kegan Paul.

Adorno, T. (2002), *The Culture Industry*, London: Routledge.

Ahmed, K. (2002), 'Easy Exams Make Pupils Unfit for Jobs, Say Bosses', *Guardian,* 20 July.

Althusser, L. (1971), 'Ideology and Ideological State Apparatuses: Notes Towards an Investigation', in *Lenin and Philosophy and Other Essays*, trans. Ben Brewster, New York: Monthly Review Press.

Amin, A. (ed.) (1994), *Post-Fordism: A Reader,* Oxford: Blackwell.

Angell, I. (2000), *The New Barbarian Manifesto*, London: Kogan Page.

Armstrong, G. (1998), *Football Hooligans: Knowing the Score*, Oxford: Berg.

B

Bailey, P. (1987), *Leisure and Class in Victorian England,* London: Routledge & Kegan Paul.

Bain, P., Watson, A., Mulvey, G., Taylor, P. and Gall, G. (2002), 'Taylorism, Targets and the Pursuit of Quantity and Quality by Call Centre Management', *New Technology, Work and Employment*, 17: 3.

Bakhtin, M. ([1965]1984) *Rabelais and His World,* trans. Hélène Iswolsky, Bloomington: Midland-Indiana University Press.

Ball, S., Maguire, M. and Macrae, S. (2000), *Choice, Pathways and Transitions Post-16: New Youth, New Economies in the Global City,* London: Routledge.

Banks, M., Bates, I. Breakwell, G., Bynner, J. Emler, N., Jamison, L. and Roberts, K. (eds) (1992), *Careers and Identities*, Milton Keynes: Open University Press.

Baudrillard, J. (1983), *In the Shadow of the Silent Majorities,* New York: Semiotexte.

Baudrillard, J. (1993), *The Transparency of Evil: Essays on Extreme Phenomena*, London: Verso.

Bauman, Z. (1991), *Modernity and Ambivalence*, Cambridge: Polity.

Bauman, Z. (1992), *Intimations of Postmodernity*, London: Routledge.

Bauman, Z. (1995), *Life in Fragments*, Oxford: Blackwell.

Bauman, Z. (1996), 'From Pilgrim to Tourist – or a Short History of Identity', in S. Hall and P. du Gay (eds), *Question of Cultural Identity*, London: Sage.

Bauman, Z. (1998), *Globalization: The Human Consequences*, Cambridge: Polity.

Bauman, Z. (1999), *Work, Consumerism and the New Poor*, Buckingham: Open University Press.

Bauman, Z. (2001), *The Individualised Society*, Oxford: Blackwell.

Bauman, Z. (2003), *Liquid Love*, Cambridge: Polity.

Bauman, Z. (2004), *Wasted Lives: Modernity and its Outcasts*, Cambridge: Polity.

Beaumont, P. (1987), *The Decline of Trade Union Organisation*, London: Croom Helm.

Beck, U. (1992), *Risk Society: Towards a New Modernity*, London: Sage.

Beck, U. and Beck-Gernsheim, E. (1995), *The Normal Chaos of Love*, Cambridge: Polity Press.

Beck, U. (2000), *The Brave New World of Work*, Cambridge: Polity.

Beck, U. and Beck-Gernsheim, E. (2002), *Individualization*, London: Sage.

Bedell, G. (2005), 'When Words Fail Them', *Observer,* 20 February.

Belcham, J. (1990), *Industrialization and the Working Class: The English Experience, 1750-1900*, Aldershot: Scholar.

Belt, V., Richardson, R. and Webster, J. (2002), 'Women, Social Skill and Interactive Service Work in Telephone Call Centres', *New Technology, Work and Employment*, 17: 1.

Bendix, R. and Lipset, S. (1967), *Class Status and Power*, London: Routledge & Kegan Paul.

Bennett, A. (2000), *Popular Music and Youth Culture: Music, Identity and Place*, Basingstoke: Macmillan.

Bennett, A. (2001), *Cultures of Popular Music*, Basingstoke: Open University Press.

Benney, M. (1978), 'The Legacy of Mining', in M. Bulmer (ed.), *Mining and Social Change*, London: Croom Helm.

Beynon, H. (1984), *Working for Ford*, London: Penguin.

Beynon, J. (2002), *Masculinities and Culture*, Buckingham: Open University Press.

Blackshaw, T. (2003), *Leisure Life: Myth, Modernity and Masculinity*, London: Routledge.

Blackwell, T. and Seabrook, J. (1985), *A World Still to Win*, London: Faber & Faber.

Blanden, J., Gregg, P., and Machin, S. (2005), *Intergenerational Mobility in Europe and North America: A Report Supported by the Sutton Trust*, London: Centre for Economic Performance, LSE.

Blauner, R. (1964), *Alienation and Freedom*, Chicago: University of Chicago Press.

Bogdanor, V. and Skidelsky, R. (1970), *Age of Affluence,* London: Macmillan.

Bok, D. (2003), *Universities in the Marketplace: The Commericalization of Higher Education*, London: Princeton University Press.

Boni, F. (2002), 'Framing Media Masculinities: Men's Lifestyle Magazines and the Biopolitics of the Male Body', *European Journal of Communication*, 17 (December): 465–78.

Botton, A. de (2005), *Status Anxiety*, London: Penguin.

Bourdieu, P. (1977), *Outline of a Theory of Practice*, Cambridge: Cambridge University Press.

Bourdieu, P. (1984), *Distinction: A Social Critique of the Judgement of Taste*, London: Routledge & Kegan Paul.

Bourdieu, P. (1990), *The Logic of Practice*, Cambridge: Polity.

Bourdieu, P. (1998), *Acts of Resistance – Against the New Myths of Our Time*, Cambridge: Polity Press.

Bourdieu, P. and Passeron, J. (1977), *Reproduction in Education, Society and Culture*, London: Sage.

Bourdieu, P. and Wacquant, L. (2000), 'New Liberal Speak: Notes on the New Planetary Vulgate', *Radical Philosophy*, 105: 2–5.

Bourke, J. (1994), *Working Class Cultures in Britain 1890-1960: Gender, Class and Ethnicity*, London: Routledge.

Box, S. (1983), *Power, Crime and Mystification*, London: Routledge.

Box, S. (1987), *Recession, Crime and Punishment*, London: Macmillan.

Brake, M. (1980), *The Sociology of Youth Culture and Youth Subcultures*, London: Routledge & Kegan Paul.

Branaghan, T. (2005), 'Lib Dems Warn of Consumer Debt Crippling the Economy, *Guardian*, 17 February.

Braverman, H. (1974), *Labour and Monopoly Capitalism*, New York: Monthly Review Press.

Bridges, W. (1995), *Jobshift: How to Prosper in a World without Jobs*, London: Nicholas Brealey.

Brint, S. (2001), 'Professionals and the "Knowledge Economy": Rethinking the Theory of Postindustrial Society', *Current Sociology*, 49(4): 101–32.

Brohm, J.M. (1978), *Sport: A Prison of Measured Time*, London: Interlinks.

Brown, P. (1995), 'Cultural Capital and Social Exclusion: Some Observations on Recent Trends in Education, Employment and the Labour Market', *Work, Employment and Society*, 9 (March): 29–51.

Brown, P. (2000), The Globalisation of Positional Competition? *Sociology*, 34 (November): 633–53.

Brown, P. and Hesketh, A. (2004), *The Mismanagement of Talent: Employability and Jobs in the Knowledge Economy*, Oxford: Oxford University Press.

Brownell, K. (2004), *Food Fight*, New York: Higher Education.

Budd, T. (2003), *Alcohol-related Assault: Findings from the British Crime Survey*, London: Home Office.

Bulmer, M. (1975), Sociological Models of the Mining Community, *Sociological*

Review, 23(1): 61–92.

Bulmer, M. (1978a), 'Social Structure and Social Change in the Twentieth Century', in M. Bulmer (ed.), *Mining and Social Change*, London: Croom Helm.

Bulmer, M. (1978b), 'The Decline of Mining: A Case Study in Spennymoor', in M. Bulmer (ed.), *Mining and Social Change,* London: Croom Helm.

Byrne, D. (1989), *Beyond the Inner City*, Milton Keynes: Open University Press.

Byrne, D. (1999), *Social Exclusion*, Buckingham: Open University Press.

C

Calcutt, A. (1998), *Arrested Development: Popular Culture and the Erosion of Adulthood*, London: Cassell.

Callinicos, A. and Simons, M. (1985), *The Great Strike*, London: Socialist Worker.

Callois, R. (1959), *Man and the Sacred*, Glencoe: Free Press.

Campbell, B. (1993), *Goliath: Britain's Dangerous Places.* London: Methuen.

Campbell, J. (2004), *Iron Lady,* Vol. 2, London: Pimlico.

Canetti, E. ([1960] 1987), *Crowds and Power,* Harmondsworth: Peregrine.

Cappelli, P. (1997), *Change at Work*, Oxford: Oxford University Press.

Carr, E.H. (1990), *What is History?* London: Penguin.

Chambliss, W. (1975), 'Towards a Political Economy of Crime', in *Theory and Society*, 2: 149–70.

Chaney, D. (1993), *The Fictions of Collective Life*, London: Routledge.

Charlesworth, S.J. (2000), *A Phenomenology of Working Class Experience*, Cambridge: Cambridge University Press.

Chatterton, P. and Hollands, R. (2001), *Changing Our 'Toon': Youth, Nightlife and Urban Change in Newcastle,* Newcastle: University of Newcastle.

Chatterton, P. and Hollands, R. (2003), *Urban Nightscapes: Youth Cultures, Pleasure Spaces and Corporate Power*, London: Routledge.

Chomsky, N. (1999), *Profit Over People*, London: Seven Stories Press.

Chomsky, N. (2003), *Hegemony or Survival*, New York: Metropolitan Books.

Cieslik, M. and Pollock, B. (eds) (2002), *Young People in Risk Society: The Restructuring of Youth Identities and Transitions in Late Modernity*, Aldershot: Ashgate.

Clark, J. and Critcher, C. (1985), *The Devil Makes Work: Leisure in Capitalist Britain*, London: Macmillan.

Clinard, M. and Yeager, P. (1980), *Corporate Crime*, New York: Free Press.

Cohen, A. (1955), *Delinquent Boys*, Chicago: University of Chicago Press.

Cohen, P. (1972), *Subcultural Conflict and Working Class Community,* Working Papers in Cultural Studies, No. 2: 5–52, Birmingham: CCCS, University of Birmingham.

Cohen, P. and Robins, D. (1978), *Knuckle Sandwich: Growing up in the Working Class City,* Harmondsworth: Penguin.

Cohen, S. and Taylor, L. (1976), *Escape Attempts,* Harmondsworth: Penguin.

Coles, B. (1995), *Youth and Social Policy: Youth Citizenship and Young Careers,* London: UCL Press.

Connell, R.W. (1995), *Masculinities,* Oxford: Blackwell.

Corrigan, P. (1979), *Schooling the Smash Street Kids,* London: Macmillan.

Crawford, A. and Lister, S. (2003), *Plural Policing: Policing beyond the Police in England.* Paper presented to the Law Commission of Canada, In Search of Security Conference, Montreal, February.

Crewe, L., Gregson, N. and Brooks, K. (2003), 'The Discursivities of Difference: Retro Retailers and the Ambiguities of "the Alternative"', *Journal of Consumer Culture,* 3 (March): 61–82.

Croall, H. (1992), *White Collar Crime,* Buckingham: Open University Press.

Crouch, C. (1986), 'The Future Prospects for Trade Unions in Western Europe', *Political Quarterly,* 57(1): 5–17.

Currie, E. (1997), 'Market, Crime and Community: Towards a Mid-range Theory of Post-industrial Violence', *Theoretical Criminology,* 1(2): 147–72.

Currie, E. (2004), *The Road to Whatever,* New York: Metropolitan.

Curtis, P. (2002), 'NATFE Warns of University Redundancies', *Guardian,* 15 March.

D

Davies, N. (1997), *Dark Heart: The Shocking Truth about Hidden Britain,* London: Vintage.

Davis, M. (1990), *City of Quartz,* London: Vintage.

Davis, M. (1998), *Ecology of Fear,* London: Picador.

Day, K., Gough, B. and McFadden, M. (2003), 'Women who Drink and Fight: A Discourse Analysis of Working Class Women's Talk', *Feminist Psychology,* 13 (May): 141–58.

Debord, G. (1998), *The Society of the Spectacle,* New York: Zone.

De Certeau, M. (1984), 'What We Do We Believe', in M. Blonsky (ed.), *On Signs: A Semiotics Reader,* Oxford: Basil Blackwell.

De Certeau, M. (2002), *The Practice of Everyday Life,* California: University of California Press.

Deery, S., Iverson, R. and Walsh, J. (2002), 'Work Relationships in Telephone Call Centres: Understanding Emotional Exhaustion and Employee Withdrawal', *Journal of Management Studies,* 39: 4.

Deller, J. (2002), *The English Civil War, Part II: Personal Accounts of the 1984–5 Miners' Strike,* London: Artangel.

Delves, A. (1981), 'Popular Recreation and Social Conflict in Derby 1880-1850', in E. Yeo and S. Yeo (eds), *Popular Culture and Class Conflict 1590-1914,* Brighton: Harvester.

Dennis, H., Henriques, F. and Slaughter, C. (1969), *Coal is Our Life: An Analysis of a Yorkshire Mining Community*, London: Tavistock Publications.

Dennis, N. (1993), *Rising Crime and the Dismembered Family*, London: IEA.

Donaldson, M. (1991), *Time of Our Lives: Labour and Love in the Working Class*, Sydney: Allen & Unwin.

Douglass, D. and Krieger, J. (1983), *A Miner's Life*, London: Routledge & Kegan Paul.

Duncan, M., Al-Nakeeb, Y., Nevill, A. and Jones, M. (2004), 'Body Image and Physical Activity in British Secondary School Children', *European Physical Education Review*, 10 (October): 243–60.

Dunning, E., Murphy, P. and Williams, J. (1988), *The Roots of Football Hooliganism: A Historical and Sociological Study*, London: Routledge & Kegan Paul.

E

Eagleton, T. (1991), *Ideology: An Introduction*, London: Verso.

Eagleton, T. (1996), *The Illusions of Postmodernism*, Oxford: Blackwell.

Eagleton, T. (2000), *The Idea of Culture*, Oxford: Blackwell.

Ehrenreich, B. (1997), *Blood Rites: Origins and History of the Passions of War*, London: Virago.

Elias, N. (1994), *The Civilizing Process*, Oxford: Blackwell.

Elias, N. and Dunning, E. (1986), *The Quest for Excitement: Sport and Leisure in the Civilising Process*, Oxford: Blackwell.

Epstein, J. (ed.) (1998), *Youth Culture: Identity in a Postmodern World*, Oxford: Blackwell.

Etzioni, A. (1994), *The Spirit of Community: Rights, Responsibilities and the Communitarian Agenda*, New York: Touchstone.

Evans, E. (2004), *Thatcher and Thatcherism*, London: Routledge.

Evans, J., Hudson, C. and Smith, P. (1985), 'Women and the Strike: It's a Whole Way of Life', in B. Fine and R. Millar (eds), *Policing the Miners Strike*, London: Lawrence & Wishart.

Ewan, B. and Ewan, C. (1982), *Channels of Desire*, New York: McGraw-Hill.

F

Faludi, S. (1999), *Stiffed: The Betrayal of Modern Man*, London: Chatto & Windus.

Ferrell, J. (1996), *Crimes of Style: Urban Graffitti in New York*, Cambridge, MA: MIT Press.

Ferrell, J. (2001), *Tearing Down the Streets: Adventures in Urban Anarchy*, New York: Palgrave.

Ferrell, J. and Sanders, C. (1995), 'Culture, Crime and Criminology', in J. Ferrell and C. Sanders (eds), *Cultural Criminology,* Boston: Northeastern University Press.

Fiske, J. (1987), *Television Culture,* London: Verso.

Fiske, J. (1991), *Understanding Popular Culture,* London: Routledge.

Fiske, J. (1993), *Power Plays, Power Works,* London: Verso.

Frank, L. and Engelke, P. (2001), 'The Built Environment and Human Activity Patterns: Exploring the Impacts of Urban Form on Public Health', *Journal of Planning Literature,* 16 (November): 202–18.

Frank, R. H. and Cook, P. J. (1996), *The Winner-Takes-All-Society,* London: Penguin.

Freeman, E. (2002), *The Wedding Complex: Forms of Belonging in Modern American Culture,* New York: Duke University Press.

Fukuyama, F. (1992), *The End of History and the Last Man,* New York: Free Press.

Fukuyama, F. (1999), *The Great Disruption: Human Nature and the Reconstitution of Social Order,* London: Profile.

Furlong, A. and Cartmel, F. (1997), *Young People and Social Change,* Buckingham: Open University Press.

G

Galenson, W. (1994), *Trade Union Growth and Decline: An International Study,* London: Greenwood Press.

Gallie, D. (1978), *In Search of the New Working Class,* Cambridge: Cambridge University Press.

Galilee, J. (2002), 'Class Consumption: Understanding Middle-Class Young Men and Their Fashion Choices', *Men and Masculinities,* 5 (July): 32–52.

Gans, H.J. (1995), *The War Against the Poor,* New York: Basic Books.

Gibbins, J. and Reimer, B. (1999), *The Politics of Postmodernity,* London: Sage.

Giddens, A. (1984), *The Constitution of Society,* Cambridge: Polity.

Giddens, A. (1992), *The Transformation of Intimacy,* Cambridge: Polity Press.

Gill, O. (1977), *Luke Street: Housing Policy, Conflict and the Creation of a Delinquent Area,* London: Macmillan Press.

Gilmore, D.D. (1990), *Manhood in the Making,* London: Yale University Press.

Gofton, L. (1990), 'On the Town: Drink and the "New Lawlessness"', *Youth and Policy,* 29 (April): 33–9.

Goldthorpe, J.H. (1980), *Social Mobility and Class Structure in Modern Britain,* Oxford: Clarendon Press.

Goldthorpe, J.H., Lockwood, D., Bechhoffer, F. and Platt, J. (1970), *The Affluent Worker,* Cambridge: Cambridge University Press.

Gorz, A. (1982), *Farewell to the Working Class,* London: Pluto Press.

Graham, G. (2002), *Universities: The Recovery of an Idea,* London: Imprint Academic.

Gramsci, A. (2000), *The Antonio Gramsci Reader*, edited by D. Forgas, New York: New York University Press.

Grant, J. (1992), *Blood Brothers: Division and Decline in Britain's Trade Unions*, London: Weidenfeld & Nicolson.

Gray, A. (1992), *Video Playtime: The Gendering of a Leisure Technology*, London: Routledge.

Gray, J. (1998), *False Dawn: The Delusions of Global Capitalism,* London: Granta.

Gurr, T. (1981), 'Historical Trends in Violent Crime: A Critical Review of the Evidence', in M. Tonry and N. Morris (eds), *Crime and Justice: An Annual Review of Research,* Vol. 4, Chicago: University of Chicago Press, pp. 295–353.

Gurr, T., Grabosky, P. and Hula, R. (1977), *The Politics of Crime and Conflict: A Comparative History of Four Cities*, Beverley Hills: Sage.

Guy, A., Green, E. and Banim, M. (2001), *Through the Wardrobe: Women's Relationship with their Clothes*, Oxford: Berg.

H

Hadfield, P. (2002), 'Open All Hours?' *Police Review*, (16 August): 21.

Hadfield, P. (2004), 'Invited to Binge? – A Response to Montgomery', *Town and Country Planning,* 75(7/8): 235.

Hadfield, P., Collins, J., Flynn, R. and Doyle, P. (2004), 'The Prevention of Public Disorder', in P. Kolvin and J. Phillips (eds), *Licensed Premises: Law and Practice*, London: Butterworths.

Hadfield, P., Lister, S., Hobbs, D. and Winlow, S. (2001), 'The "24 Hour City" – Condition Critical', *Town and Country Planning,* 70(11): 300-2.

Hall, Steve (1995), 'Grasping at Straws: the Idealisation of the Material in Liberal Conceptions of Youth Crime', *Youth and Policy,* 48: 49–63.

Hall, Steve (1997), 'Visceral Cultures and Criminal Practices', *Theoretical Criminology* 1(4): 453–78.

Hall, Steve (1999), 'Grasping at Straws: the Idealisation of the Material in Liberal Conceptions of Youth Crime', in N. South (ed.) *International Library of Criminology, Criminal Justice and Penology, Vol. 1: Youth Crime, Deviance and Delinquency.* Aldershot: Ashgate.

Hall, Steve (2000), 'Paths To Anelpis, 1: Dimorphic Violence and the Pseudo-Pacification Process', *Parallax,* 6(2): 36–53.

Hall, Steve (2001), 'Violence And the Nocturnal Economy', *Criminal Justice Matters*, 42: 10-11.

Hall, Steve (2002), 'Daubing the Drudges of Fury: Men, Violence and the Piety of the "Hegemonic Masculinity" Thesis', *Theoretical Criminology,* 6(1): 35–61.

Hall, Steve and Winlow, S. (2003), 'Rehabilitating Leviathan: Reflections on the state, economic management and violence reduction', *Theoretical Criminology*

7(2): 139–62.

Hall, Steve and Winlow, S. (2004), 'Barbarians at the Gate: Crime and Violence in the Breakdown of the Pseudo-Pacification Process', in J. Ferrell, K. Hayward, W. Morrison, and M. Presdee (eds), *Cultural Criminology Unleashed*, London: Cavendish.

Hall, Steve and Winlow, S. (2005), 'Anti-Nirvana: Crime, culture and Instrumentalism in the Age of Insecurity', *Crime, Media, Culture*, 1(1): 31–48.

Hall, Steve, Winlow, S. and Ancrum, C. (2005), 'Radgies, Gangstas and Mugs: Imaginary Masculine Identities and the Culture Industry in the Twilight of the Pseudo-pacification Process', *Social Justice*, 32(1): 100-12.

Hall, Stuart (1980), 'Encoding/Decoding', in S. Hall, D. Hobson, A. Lowe and P. Willis (eds), *Culture, Media, Language*, London: Hutchinson, pp. 128–38.

Hall, Stuart, Critcher, C., Jefferson, T., Clark, J. and Robert, B. (1978), *Policing the Crisis: Mugging, the State and Law and Order*, Basingstoke: Palgrave Macmillan.

Hall, Stuart and Jacques, M. (eds) (1983), *The Politics of Thatcherism*, London: Lawrence & Wishart.

Hallsworth, S. (2005), *Street Crime*, Collumpton: Willan.

Hayward, K.J. (2004), *City Limits: Crime, Consumer Culture and the Urban Experience*. London: Cavendish/Glasshouse Press.

Hebdige, R. (1979), *Subculture: The Meaning of Style*, New York: Methuen.

Hesse-Biber, S. (1997), *Am I Thin Enough Yet? Cult of Thinness and the Commercialisation of Identity*, Oxford: Oxford University Press.

Hobbs, D. (1988), *Doing the Business*, Oxford: Oxford University Press.

Hobbs, D. (1994), 'Mannish Boys: Danny, Chris, Crime, Masculinity and Business', in T. Newburn and E. Stanko (eds), *Just Boys Doing Business?* London: Routledge.

Hobbs, D. (1998), Going down the Glocal: the Local Context of Organised Crime', *The Howard Journal*, 37(4): 407–22.

Hobbs, D., Hadfield, P., Lister, S. and Winlow, S. (2002), 'Door Lore: The Art and Economics of Intimidation', *British Journal of Criminology*, 42(2): 352–70.

Hobbs, D., Hadfield, P., Lister, S. and Winlow, S. (2003), *Bouncers: Violence and Governance in the Night-time Economy*, Oxford: Oxford University Press.

Hobbs, D., Hadfield, P., Lister, S., Winlow, S. and Hall, Steve (2000), 'Receiving Shadows: Governance and Liminality in the Night-time Economy', *British Journal of Sociology*, 51(4): 701–17.

Hobbs. D. Winlow, S. Lister, S. and Hadfield, P. (2005), 'Violent Hypocrisy: Governance and the Night-time Economy', *European Journal of Criminology*, 2(2): 161–85.

Hobsbawm, E. (1994), *Age of Extremes: The Short Twentieth Century, 1914–1991*, London: Abacus.

Hollands, R. (2002), 'Divisions in the Dark? Youth Cultures, Transitions and Segmented Consumption Spaces in the Night-time Economy', *Journal of Youth Studies*, 5(2): 153–73.

Holt, R. (1989), *Sport and the British*, Oxford: Oxford University Press.

Homel, R. and Clark, J. (1994), 'The Prediction and Prevention of Violence in Pubs and Clubs', in R.V. Clarke (ed.), *Crime Prevention Studies*, Vol. 3, New York: Criminal Justice Press.

Homel, R., Tomsen, S. and Thommeny, J. (1991), 'The Problem of Violence in Licensed Premises: The Sydney Study', in T. Stockwell, E. Lang and P. Rydon (eds), *The Licensed Drinking Environment: Current Research in Australia and New Zealand*, Melbourne: National Centre for Research into the Prevention of Drug Abuse.

Homel, R., Tomsen, S. and Thommeny, J. (1992), 'Public Drinking and Violence: Not Just an Alcohol Problem', *Journal of Drug Issues*, 22(3): 679–97.

Horkheimer, M. and Adorno, T. (1972), *Dialectic of Enlightenment*, London: Allen Lane.

Horne, R. and Hall, Steve (1995), 'Anelpis: a preliminary expedition into a world without hope or potential', *Parallax*, 1(1): 81–92.

Hutton, W. (1995), *The State We're In*, London: Vintage.

Hutton, W. (2001), *The Revolution that Never Was: An Assessment of Keynesian Economics*, London: Vintage.

Hutton, W. (2005), 'Time to Let Brown Play his Ace', *Observer*, 13 March.

Hyman, R. and Price, R. (1983), *The New Working Class?* London: Macmillan.

J

Jackson-Jacobs, C. (2005), 'Taking a Beating: The Narrative of Fighting as the Underdog' in J. Ferrell, K. Hayward, W. Morrison and M. Presdee (eds), *Cultural Criminology Unleashed*, London: Glasshouse.

Jacobs Brumberg, J. (2000), *Fasting Girls: The History of Anorexia Nervosa*, New York: Vintage Books.

Jenks, C. (1996), *Childhood*, London: Routledge.

Johnston, L. (1992), *The Rebirth of Private Policing*, London: Routledge.

Jones, S. (2000), *Understanding Violent Crime*, Buckingham: Open University Press.

K

Katz, J. (1988), *The Seductions of Violence*, New York: Basic Books.

Kimmel, M. (1996), *Manhood in America*, New York: Free Press.

King, D. (ed.) (1991), *Culture, Globalisation and the World System*, New York: Macmillan.

Kirp, D. (2003), *Shakespeare, Einstein and the Bottom Line: The Marketing of*

Higher Education, London: Harvard University Press.

Knight P. T. and Yorke, M. (2003), *Assessment, Learning and Employability,* Buckingham: Open University Press.

L

Lasch, C. (1979), *The Culture of Narcissism,* London: Norton.

Lash, S. and Urry, J. (1987), *The End of Organised Capitalism,* Cambridge: Polity Press.

Lea, J. (2002), *Crime and Modernity,* London: Sage.

Lea, J. and Young, J. (1993), *What is to be Done about Law and Order?* London: Pluto.

Lefebvre, H. (2000), *The Product of Space,* translated by D. Nicolson-Smith, Oxford: Blackwell.

Levin, C. (1996), *Jean Baudrillard: A Study in Cultural Metaphysics,* Hemel Hempstead: Prentice Hall.

Lévi-Strauss, C. (1999), *Structural Anthropology,* London: Basic Books.

Lipietz, A. (1996), 'The Next Transformation', in M. Cangiani (ed.), *The Milano Papers: Essays in Societal Alternatives,* Montreal: Black Rose Books.

Lister, S. (2002), 'Violence as a Commercial Resource: Situating Bouncers and the Use of Force in Context', *Journal of Forensic Psychiatry,* 12(2): 245–9.

Lister, S., Hadfield, P., Hobbs D. and Winlow, S. (2001), 'Accounting for Bouncers: Occupational Licensing as a Mechanism for Regulation', *Criminal Justice,* 1(4): 363–84.

Lister, S., Hobbs, D., Hall, Steve and Winlow, S. (2000), 'Violence in the Night time Economy; Bouncers: The Reporting, Recording and Prosecution of Assaults', *Policing and Society,* 10: 383–402.

Lockwood, D. (1975), 'Sources of Variation in Working-Class Images of Society', in M. Bulmer (ed.), *Working-Class Images of Society,* London: Routledge & Kegan Paul.

Louw, E. (2001), *The Media and Cultural Production,* London: Sage.

M

MacAndrew, C. and Edgerton, R. (1969), *Drunken Comportment,* Chicago: Aldine.

MacDonald, R. (ed.) (1997), *Youth, the 'Underclass' and Social Exclusion,* London: Routledge.

MacInnes, J. (1987), *Thatcherism at Work,* Milton Keynes: Open University Press.

MacInnes, J. (1998), *The End of Masculinity,* Buckingham: Open University Press.

Mackay, H. (ed.) (1997), *Consumption and Everyday Life,* London: Sage.

Maffesoli, M. (1995), *The Time of the Tribes: The Decline of Individualism in Mass Society,* London: Sage.

Malbon, B. (1998), 'The Club, Clubbing: Consumption, Identity and the Spatial Practices of Every-Night Life', in T. Skelton and G. Valentine (eds), *Cool Places: Geographies of Youth Cultures*, London: Routledge.

Malbon, B. (1999), *Clubbing: Dance, Ecstasy and Vitality,* London: Routledge.

Mallet, S. (1975), *The New Working Class,* Nottingham: Spokesman Books.

Manning, P. (1977), *Police Work*, Cambridge, MA: MIT Press.

Mars, G. (1982), *Cheats at Work*, London: Unwin.

Mattelart, A. (1980), *Mass Media, Ideologies and the Revolutionary Movement,* Brighton: Harvester.

Matza, D. (1964), *Delinquency and Drift*, New York: Wiley.

Matza, D. (1969), *Becoming Deviant*, Englewood Cliffs, NJ: Prentice Hall.

Marshall, G. (1997), *Repositioning Class*, London: Sage.

McClelland, K. M. (1991), 'Masculinity and the Representative Artisan in Britain 1850-80', in M. Roper and J. Tosh (eds), *Manful Assertions: Masculinities in Britain Since 1800,* London: Routledge.

McDonald, M. (ed.) (1997a), *Gender, Drink and Drugs,* Oxford: Berg.

McDonald, M. (1997b), 'Drinking in the West of France', in M. McDonald (ed.), *Gender, Drink and Drugs,* Oxford: Berg.

Measham, F. (2004), 'The Decline of Ecstasy, the Rise of Binge-drinking and the Persistence of Pleasure', *Probation Journal*, 51 (December): 309–26.

Merton, R.K. (1938), 'Social Structure and Anomie', *American Sociological Review,* 3 (October): 672–82.

Messerschmidt, J. W. (1993), *Masculinities and Crime,* Lanham, MD: Rowman & Littlefield.

Mestrovic, S. (1997), *Postemotional Society*, London: Sage.

Metcalf, A. (2005), *Leisure and Recreation in a Victorian Mining Community,* London: Routledge.

Michaels, E., Handfield-Jones, H. and Axelrod, B. (2001), *The War for Talent,* Boston: Harvard University Press.

Miles, S. (1996), 'The Cultural Capital of Consumption: Understanding "Postmodern" Identities in a Cultural Context', *Culture and Psychology*, 2: 139–58.

Miles, S. (1998), *Consumerism as a Way of Life*, London: Sage.

Miles, S. (2000), *Youth Lifestyles in a Changing World*, London: Routledge.

Miles, S., Cliff, D. and Burr, V. (1998), '"Fitting In and Sticking Out": Consumption, Consumer Meanings and the Construction of Young people's Identities', *Journal of Youth Studies*, 1(1): 81–96.

Mills, N. (ed.) (1991), *Culture in the Age of Money: The Legacy of the 1980s in America*, New York: Ivan Dee.

Milne, S. (2004), *The Enemy Within: Thatcher's Secret War Against the Miners*, London: Verso Books.

Milner, A. (1999), *Class*, London: Sage.

Monaghan, L. (2001), Bodybuilding, Drugs and Risk, London: Routledge.

Monaghan, L. (2004), 'Door Work and Legal Risk: Observations from an Embodied Ethnography', *Social and Legal Studies*, 13 (December): 453–80.

Moorhouse, H.F. (1989), 'Models of Work, Models of Leisure', in C. Rojek (ed.), *Leisure for Leisure*, Basingstoke: Macmillan.

Morris, M. (1993), 'Things to Do with Shopping Centres', in S. During (ed.), *The Cultural Studies Reader*, London: Routledge.

Mouzelis, N. (1995), *Sociological Theory: What Went Wrong?* London: Routledge.

Mullins, P., Natalier, K., Smith, P., Smeaton, B. (1999), 'Cities and Consumption Spaces', *Urban Affairs Review*, 35 (September): 44–71.

Murray, C. (1996), *Charles Murray and The Underclass Debate*, London: IEA.

N

Nelson, A., Bromley, R. and Thomas, C. (2001), 'Identifying Micro-spatial and Temporal Patterns of Violent Crime and Disorder in a British City Centre', *Applied Geography*, 21: 249–74.

Nettleton, S. (1995), *The Sociology of Health and Illness*, Cambridge: Polity Press.

Newburn, T. and Stanko, E. (1994), 'When Men are Victims: the Failure of Victimology', in T. Newburn and E. Stanko (eds), *Just Boys Doing Business?* London: Routledge.

Newman, K. (1999), *No Shame in my Game*, New York: Vintage.

O

ONS (2000), *Social Trends 30,* London: Office for National Statistics.

ONS (2001), *Social Trends 31,* London: Office for National Statistics.

Otnes, C. and Pleck, E. (2003), *Cinderella Dreams: The Allure of the Lavish Wedding*, LA: University of California Press.

P

Pakulski, J. and Waters, M. (1996), *The Death of Class*, London: Sage.

Parker, H. (1974), *View from the Boys,* London: David & Charles.

Parton, S., Siltanen, S., Hosman, L. and Langenderfer, J. (2002), 'Employment Interview Outcomes and Speech Style Effects', in *Journal of Language and Social Psychology*, 21 (June): 144–61.

Patrick, J. (1973), *A Glasgow Gang Observed*, London: Eyre-Methuen.

Patterson, G. (1988), 'Victorian Working Life', in M. Milburn and S. Miller (eds), *Sunderland: River, Town and People,* Sunderland: Thomas Reed.

Pearce, F. and Tombs, S. (1989), 'Bhopal, Union Carbide and the Hubris of a Capitalist Technology', *Social Justice*, 16 (June): 116–45.

Pearce, F. and Tombs, S. (1993), 'US Capital versus the Third World: Union

Carbide and Bhopal', in F. Pearce and M. Woodiwiss (eds), *Global Crime Connections*, London: Macmillan.

Pearson, G. (1983), *Hooligan: A History of Respectable Fears*, London: Macmillan.

Phillipps, K. C. (1984), *Language and Class in Victorian England*, Oxford: Blackwell.

Polk, K. (1994), 'Masculinity, Honour and Confrontational Homicide', in T. Newburn and E. Stanko (eds), *Just Boys Doing Business*, London: Routledge.

Polk, K. (1999), 'Males and Honour Context Violence', *Homicide Studies*, 3 (February): 6–29.

Poulantzas, N. (1978), *Power, Socialism*, London: Verso.

Presdee, M. (2000), *Cultural Criminology and the Carnival of Crime*, London: Routledge.

Purcell, N. (1997), 'Women and Wine in Ancient Rome', in M. McDonald, (ed.), *Gender, Drink and Drugs*, Oxford: Berg.

R

Ray, L. and Sayer, A. (eds) (1999), *Culture and Economy After the Cultural Turn*, London: Sage.

Redhead, S. (ed.) (1993), *Rave Off: Politics and Deviance in Contemporary Youth Culture*, Aldershot: Averbury.

Redhead, S., Wynne, D. and O'Connor, J. (1997), *The Clubcultures Reader: Readings in Popular Cultural Studies*, Oxford: Blackwell.

Reiss, S. (1989), *City Games: The Evolution of American Urban Society and the Rise of Sports*, Illinois: University of Illinois.

Rentoul, J. (1987), *The Rich Get Richer: The Growth of Inequality in the 1980s*, London: HarperCollins.

Richards, A. (1996), *Miners on Strike: Class Solidarity and Divisions in Britain*, Oxford: Berg.

Riedel, M. (1993), *Stranger Violence: A Theoretical Inquiry*, New York: Garland Science.

Rifkin, J. (1995), *The End of Work: The Decline of the Global Labour Force and the Dawn of the Post-market Era*, New York: Tarcher/Putnam.

Ritzer, G. (1998), *The McDonaldization Thesis*, London: Sage.

Robbins, D. (2000), *Bourdieu and Culture*, London: Sage.

Roberts, I. (1993), *Craft, Class and Control*, Edinburgh: Edinburgh University Press.

Robins, D. and Cohen, P. (1978), *Knuckle Sandwich: Growing up in the Working Class City*, Harmondsworth: Penguin.

Rojek, C. (1985), *Capitalism and Leisure Theory*, London: Tavistock.

Rojek, C. (1989), 'Leisure and the "Ruins of the Bourgeois World"', in C. Rojek, (ed.), *Leisure for Leisure*, Basingstoke: Macmillan.

Rojek, C. (1993), *Ways of Escape*, London: Macmillan.

Room, R. and Collins, G. (eds) (1983), Alcohol and Disinhibition: Nature and Meaning of the Link, NIAAA Research Monograph, No. 12, Washington: US Government Printing Office.

Rose, J. (2002), *The Intellectual Life of the British Working Classes*, London: Yale Nota Bene.

Runciman, S. (1954), *History of the Crusades,* Vol. 3, Cambridge: Cambridge University Press.

S

Sanders, B. (2005), 'In the Club: Ecstasy Use and Supply in a London Nightclub', *Sociology*, 39: 241–58.

Saussure, F. de (1974), *Course in General Linguistics,* London: Fontana.

Scott, A. (ed.) (1997), *The Limits of Globalization*, London: Routledge.

Sewall, G. (ed.) (1997), *The Eighties: A Reader*, New York: Da Capo Press.

Shepherd, J. (1990), 'Violent Crime in Bristol: An Accident and Emergency Perspective', *British Journal of Criminology*, 30(3): 289–305.

Skidelsky, R. (2004), *John Maynard Keynes 1883–1946: Economist, Philosopher, Statesman*, London: Pan.

Slotkin, R. (2000), *Regeneration Through Violence,* Norman: University of Oklahoma Press.

Smithers, R. and Curtis, P. (2005), 'Cambridge Rejects 5,000 Straight-A Students', *Guardian,* 22 February.

Stanley, C. (1996), *Urban Excess and the Law*, London: Cavendish.

St. Croix, G.E. de. (1989), *The Class Struggle in the Ancient World,* Ithaca: Cornell University Press.

Stedman-Jones, G. (1971), *Outcast London,* Oxford: Oxford University Press.

Stevens, R. (2004), *University to Uni: The Politics of Higher Education in England since 1944*, London: Politico's Publishing.

Swedberg, R. (1998), *Max Weber and the Idea of Economic Sociology*, Princeton: Princeton University Press.

T

Taylor, I. (1999), *Crime in Context*, Cambridge: Polity.

Taylor, P. and Bain, P. (1999), 'An Assembly Line in the Head', *Industrial Relations Journal*, 30: 2.

Taylor, P., Baldry, C., Bain, P. and Ellis, V. (2003), 'A Unique Working Environment': Health, Sickness and Absence Management in UK Call Centres', in *Work, Employment and Society*, 17 (September): 435–58.

Taylor, P., Mulvey, G., Hyman, J. and Bain, P. (2002), 'Work organization, control and the experience of work in call centres', in *Work, Employment and Society*, Mar 2002; 16: 133–50.

Taylor, S. (1998), 'Emotional Labour and the New Workplace', in P. Thompson and C. Warhurst (eds), *Workplaces of the Future*, Basingstoke: Macmillan.

Thatcher, M. (1995), *The Downing Street Years*, London: HarperCollins.

Thompson, H.S. (2003), *Generation of Swine: Tales of Shame and Degradation in the '80s*, London: Simon & Schuster.

Thomsen, J.P.F. (1997), *British Politics and Trade Unions in the 1980s*, London: Dartmouth.

Tomlinson, J. (1991), *Cultural Imperialism: A Critical Introduction*, London: Pinter.

Tomsen, S. (1997), 'A Top Night: Social Protest, Masculinity and the Culture of Drinking Violence', *British Journal of Criminology*, 37(1): 90–102.

Tonnies, F. (2001), *Community and Civil Society*, Cambridge: Cambridge University Press.

Toynbee, P. (2003), *Hard Work: Life in Low Pay Britain*, London: Bloomsbury.

Toynbee, P. (2005), 'Howard's Handful of Men are Chopping Blair to Pieces', *Guardian*, 9 March.

Trompf, G.W. (1994), *Payback: The Logic of Retribution in Melanesian Religions*, Cambridge: Cambridge University Press.

Troy, G. (2005), *Morning in America: How Ronald Reagan Invented the 1980s*, Princeton: Princeton University Press.

Turner, R. (1993), *Regenerating the Coalfields: Politics and Policy in the 1980s and Early 1990s*, Aldershot: Avebury.

Turner, R. (2000), *Coal Was Our Life*, London: Perpetuity Press.

Turner, V. (1969), *The Ritual Process*, London: Routledge & Kegan Paul.

W

Wacquant, L. (2002), 'Scrutinizing the Street: Poverty, Morality and the Pitfalls of Urban Ethnography', *American Journal of Sociology*, 107(6): 1468–532.

Walby, S. (1986), *Patriarchy at Work*, Cambridge: Polity.

Wallace, C. (2004), *All Dressed in White: The Irresistible rise of the American Wedding*, New York: Penguin.

Weber, M. (1930), *The Protestant Ethic and the Spirit of Capitalism*, London: Unwin University Books.

Weber, M. (1948), *From Max Weber: Essays in Sociology*, H. Gerth and C. W. Mills (eds), London: Routledge & Kegan Paul.

Westergaard, J.H. (1995), *Who Gets What? The Hardening of Class Inequality in the Late Twentieth Century*, Cambridge: Polity Press.

Whitehead, S. (2002), *Men and Masculinities*, Cambridge: Polity.

Whyte, W.F. ([1943] 1993), *Street Corner Society: The Social Structure of an Italian Slum*, Chicago: University of Chicago Press.

Widdicombe, S. and Wooffitt, R. (1994), *The Language of Youth Subcultures*, Basingstoke: Harvester Wheatsheaf.

Williams, R. (1961), *Culture and Society, 1780–1950*, Harmondsworth: Penguin.

Williams, R. (1979), *Marxism and Literature*, Oxford: Oxford University Press.

Williamson, B. (1982), *Class, Culture and Community*, London: Routledge & Kegan Paul.

Williamson, D., White, M., Yorke-Crowe, E. and Stewart, T. (2004), 'Cognitive-Behavioural Theories of Eating Disorders', *Behaviour Modification*, (November): 711–33.

Willis, P. (1977), *Learning to Labour*, Farnsborough: Saxon House.

Willis, P. (1979), 'Shop-floor Culture, Masculinity and the Wage Form', in J. Clarke, C. Critcher, R. Johnson (eds), *Working Class Culture*, London: Hutchinson.

Wilson, W.J. (ed.) (1993), *The Ghetto Underclass: Social Science Perspectives*, London: Sage.

Wilson, W.J. (1987), *The Truly Disadvantaged*, Chicago: Chicago University Press.

Wilson, W.J. (1996), *When Work Disappears*, New York: Vintage.

Winlow, S. (2001), *Badfellas: Crime, Tradition and New Masculinities*, Oxford: Berg.

Winlow, S., Hobbs, D., Lister, S. and Hadfield, P. (2001), 'Get Ready to Duck: Bouncers and the Realities of Ethnographic Research on Violent Groups', *British Journal of Criminology, Special Issue: Methodological Dilemmas of Research*, 41(3): 536–48.

Winlow, S., Hobbs, D., Lister, S. and Hadfield, P. (2003), 'Bouncers and the Social Context of Violence: Masculinity, Class and Violence in the Night-time economy', in E. Stanko (ed.), *The Meanings of Violence*, London: Routledge.

Worpole, K. (1991), 'The Age of Leisure', in J. Corner and S. Harvey (eds), *Enterprise and Heritage: Crosscurrents of National Culture*, London: Routledge.

Wouters, C. (1999), 'On the Rise of Crime since the 1980s and the Sociogenesis of a "Third Nature"', *British Journal of Criminology*, 39(3): 416–32.

Y

Young, M. and Willmott, P. (1961), *Family and Kinship in East London*, Harmondsworth: Penguin.

Z

Zimring, F.E. and Hawkins, G. (1997), *Crime is Not the Problem: Lethal Violence in America*, Oxford: Oxford University.

Žižek, S. (2000), *The Ticklish Subject: The Absent Centre of Political Ontology*, London: Verso.

Name Index

Subject Index